MEMORIES FROM THE 1950S, AND THE PHOTO
THAT CHANGED MY LIFE

THE GIRL
IN THE
SPOTTY DRESS

PAT STEWART WITH VERONICA CLARK

JOHN BLAKE

Published by John Blake Publishing Ltd,
3 Bramber Court, 2 Bramber Road,
London W14 9PB, England

www.johnblakebooks.com

www.facebook.com/johnblakebooks 🔲
twitter.com/jblakebooks 🔲

This edition published in 2016

ISBN: 978 1 78418 996 9

British Library Cataloguing-in-Publication Data:

A catalogue record for this book is available from the British Library.

Design by www.envydesign.co.uk

Printed in Great Britain by CPI Group (UK) Ltd

1 3 5 7 9 10 8 6 4 2

Papers used by John Blake Publishing are natural, recyclable products made from
wood grown in sustainable forests. The manufacturing processes conform to the
environmental regulations of the country of origin.

Every attempt has been made to contact the relevant copyright-holders,
but some were unobtainable. We would be grateful if the
appropriate people could contact us.

THE GIRL
IN THE
SPOTTY DRESS

For my husband Johnny, and my children,
Peter, Stephen and Rachel

CONTENTS

CHAPTER 1

BONNY BABIES AND BARE-KNUCKLE FIGHTS

The deafening rumble outside sounded like thunder as it made its way along the street. I jumped out of bed, just as the noise reached a loud crescendo underneath my bedroom window.

'Night George,' a voice called.

'Night, Arthur,' Dad replied as I pressed my face hard against my bedroom window.

It was almost impossible to see him because it was dark outside. I wiped the palm of my hand against the pane of glass to try and get a better look, but it was no good because the other side had been smattered with coal dust that had drifted through the air from the nearby pit. I bobbed my face around until I found a clear patch, and that's when I saw them – what looked like a hundred miners winding their way along the street below. Their wooden clogs clattered against the cobbled stones, making the awful din.

I watched as the men proceeded up and along the street like a blackened snake, peeling away, one by one, into various terraced houses. Our home was one of them. I heard the back door slam and the sound of Dad's clogs as he kicked them off to toast his feet against the kitchen fire.

'Use t'tin bath,' Mam's voice called out.

Dad groaned. Even though we owned a proper bath, Mam always made him use the tin one. His skin was so filthy with coal dust that he'd always leave a black rim around the edge, which took hours to scrub clean. Dad wore something called banickers – a type of big cotton shorts. They were baggy at the bottom, which meant that, whenever he knelt down, the banickers would cover his kneepads. Dad was a ripper – one of the miners who removed rock from above the coal seam and set arches to raise the height of the road as the coalface progressed – so he was always kneeling down. His banickers had big square pockets on the side where he carried his metal snap (lunch) tin. But because he wore them all the time, the shorts would be filthy by the end of the week.

'They'd stand up in t'corner of room if I put 'em there.' Mam joked.

Instead, after a week down the pit, she'd scrub them in the same tin bath, using a wooden dolly peg and rubbing board. It was hard work, trying to loosen a week's worth of coal dust, but Mam was proud and she'd spend ages trying to get them as clean as she could.

My father worked ten hours a day at the pit. He'd leave around midday, returning home well after 10pm. It was tough work, but the miners were a tough breed.

I was born in the village of Featherstone, just two miles from Pontefract, in West Yorkshire. I lived with my mam and dad in a small two-up, two-down house. Unlike other families in the street, I was an only child. Not that it bothered me, because there were always the neighbours' children to play with. My parents were called George and Sarah Wilson. They were what would be considered by national standards 'working-class poor'. Despite this, Mam made sure that I never went without. Before marrying Dad, Mam had worked as a maid in service for a wealthy family. Of course, she'd left as soon as she'd married but, unlike other women, she continued to work so she could give me the kind of chances in life she'd only ever dreamed of.

'I don't want yer to end up poor like me and yer dad,' Mam insisted. 'Yer need to work hard, our Pat. If yer do, yer'll do well in life.'

I listened intently. I knew Mam wanted me to have a better life. Not that she was unhappy. My grandfather, George Davis, was the groundsman at Featherstone Rovers rugby club. The whole village was obsessed with rugby league so my grandfather was a well-respected man.

'Why's Granddad only got one eye?' I asked Mam one day as she made dinner over a fire in the kitchen.

She stared hard into the bubbling pot of stew and gave it a stir with a heavy wooden spoon.

'He used t'work down t'pit, like yer father, but he had to give it up when he lost his eye. He were involved in an accident down Mashems' pit. It were terrible, our Pat. He were never right after it. Yer granny were dead worried about him and how they'd cope,

3

but then he got a job looking after t'grounds at rugby club, so it all turned out alright in t'end.'

I often thought about Granddad and Grandma. My grandmother had been equally maimed at work, trapping her arm in a loom at a cotton mill. But she'd gone on to meet my granddad, marry and have children of her own. I always enjoyed it when Mam told me stories about Dad's past and his family, because he never liked talking about it or them.

'Tell me about Dad again?' I begged.

'What about 'im?' Mam said, looking up from the bubbling stew.

'Tell me about him fighting at the fairgrounds. Go on, please!'

She stifled a smile and began to explain.

'Before yer were born, all t'miners came out on National Strike. It were tough going 'cause, if they didn't work, they got nowt,' she said, straightening up to wipe her hands against her pinny. 'Any road, yer father decided only way he could make ends meet was to become a prize fighter working at t'fairground.'

'So who did he fight?' I asked, my eyes wide as I pictured Dad taking on all sorts of opponents.

'Well, he fought anyone who asked. That were his job, see. People paid to fight him.'

I held up my hands and pretended to box the air.

'Like this?' I said, mimicking him.

Mam chuckled to herself.

'Yes, just like that,' she said, smiling and patting me on the head.

'And did he win? Dad, I mean?'

4

'Sometimes. Not always.'

My face fell as I pictured his disappointment.

'But what happened when he lost?'

Mam picked up the spoon and began to stir the stew once more.

'Well, if he didn't win, he didn't get paid. Simple as that.'

'But what happened when he did win?'

'Well, that's when he got paid.'

I smiled.

'How much? How much did he get paid, Mam?'

She drew a hand across her fair hair and pulled a few loose strands away from her face.

'Oh, not much. Only pennies. But he were fast, yer father. He weren't particularly strong but he were fast on his feet, so he managed to avoid most of t'punches. Sometimes he'd get caught but not very often. He had to be quick because, if he were quick enough, t'other man would soon get worn out from punching nowt.'

'But did he ever get hurt? Dad, I mean?'

Mam held out her hand and traced a finger along her knuckles.

'Sometimes he'd split his hands open across there,' she said. 'And sometimes they'd catch him on his face but mostly he were all right. He put on a good show and that's what people wanted to see – a good show. Although it were fighting, it were also entertainment to folks who were watching. Yer see, yer dad were a showman too.'

My mind wandered as I imagined him stepping into a boxing ring to thunderous applause.

5

'And did he love it?'

'He made a living from it, so I guess so.'

I'd never known much about Dad's background or his family. There'd been a fall out long before I'd been born. Dad had hated his sister, Aunt Edith. Mam said she was a horrible woman. She'd explained that Edith had once tried to push her underneath a horse and cart before she'd married Dad.

'But why?' I asked, shocked that someone would want to hurt my lovely mam.

'Because yer father were t'eldest boy, so he brought in most wages. Edith took all t'boys wages so, when yer father said he were gonna marry me, Edith weren't 'appy.'

My mouth fell open.

'So she tried to kill you, to stop Dad from marrying you?' I gasped.

'Aye, but it didn't work 'cause, look,' she said, patting her hands against her chest. 'I'm still here.'

But I was still horrified.

'So what happened after that?'

Mam settled down in her chair and smiled as she recalled.

'Well, we didn't 'ave much money, me and yer father, so we rented a room in someone else's house. It's what you did back then.'

'But what about Aunt Edith? What happened to her?'

Mam waved her hand in the air.

'Oh, Edith were all right. She always is. Granny Wilson had four other sons, so she just took money off them instead. But yer dad never spoke to her ever again.'

Mam explained how Granny Wilson had been married twice. She had three children with her first husband and five more with her second. But after Granny Wilson's second husband had died, Edith decided to take control. She'd take the wages off her brothers for 'housekeeping' and hand them a pittance in return. She'd called it their 'pocket money'. But when Dad met my mam, Edith realised he'd marry and leave home, so she hatched an evil plan. Thankfully, the cart had missed, but Dad and Edith had an almighty row and he moved out. He married Mam, and I was born shortly afterwards on a cold November morning in 1933. However, Edith continued to wreak havoc in the family home.

'What else did she do?' I asked, fascinated by evil Edith and her wicked ways.

'Well, Edith, the boys and Granny Wilson lived in a little house right opposite Mashems' pit. Edith watched t'men call at t'shop before they went into work to buy snuff and Woodbine tobacco. So she decided to take out t'bottom window of t'house and turn it into a shop.'

'And the miners, did they come?'

'Oh yes,' Mam said with a laugh. 'They came in their hundreds. So she started selling cigarettes, tobacco, pots of tea and boiled sweets. They'd suck 'em down the pit, you see, to keep their mouths moist. She even started selling bacon sandwiches!'

She explained that, in order to keep costs down, frugal Edith even reared her own pigs, which she kept in an allotment in the back garden. Once bacon supplies had run low, she'd simply go and slaughter another pig.

7

'But smell were terrible.' Mam recalled. 'All t'neighbours complained but Edith didn't care. As long as she were making money, she were 'appy.'

'So she's still got the shop then?'

Mam nodded.

'She'll stop at nothing to make money, that one.'

My mother told me the story of Uncle Eric. He was Dad's youngest brother, who also happened to be a brilliant runner.

'He were short, yer Uncle Eric, but he were quick on his feet, so Edith entered him into races. There were a lot of money to be made taking part in racing competitions.'

She explained that Edith often entered poor Eric into races with boys much younger than he was.

'But that's cheating!' I cried.

Mam nodded. 'Yes but Edith didn't care, as long as he won first cash prize – then she were 'appy.'

I scratched my head.

'But didn't anyone notice that he was a bit older?'

Mam sat back in her rocking chair and chuckled away to herself.

'Well, that were funny bit. Edith would sit Eric down and shave all t'hair off his legs to make him look younger. She didn't want anyone asking questions,' she said, tapping a finger against the side of her nose.

'So what happened?'

'Well, Eric continued to race, but then he left school at thirteen. Edith had given him a window-cleaning round to run, so he became far too old to enter t'competitions. Everyone spotted him on his window-cleaning round, so she had to think of summat else.'

My eyes were on stalks as I listened.

'So, what did she do?'

'Well, that were it. She knew she'd been rumbled so, whenever she entered Eric into a race, she'd call him Robert.'

'Eh?' I said, scratching my head.

Mam leaned forward in her chair and began to explain.

'She called him Robert and told everyone he was Eric's younger brother. She'd changed all t'other brothers' names too, until everyone was so confused that no one knew who was called what!'

I went to bed later that evening dreaming of Uncle Eric with his shaved legs, bringing home the cash prize. My mother was right; Aunt Edith sounded horrible. I just prayed I'd never meet her.

A few days later, Dad and I were standing in the back garden, pulling up some root vegetables, when he tapped me on the top of my arm.

'Quick, Pat. Look! There she is.'

I shook the soil from my hands and looked up to see a strange-looking woman pushing a cart along the back lane. There was a heavy wooden ladder balanced precariously across the top of it next to a bucket and a pile of rags. She looked more like a man because she was dressed in dirty old black overalls and wore a black beret on her head.

'It's your Aunt Edith,' Dad whispered. 'And look what she's pushing.'

'But I thought Uncle Eric did the window-cleaning round. Mam said—'

Dad held up his hand to shush me.

'Aye, he did. But Eric left home to join t'RAF, so now the tight old goose has to do it herself. Serves her right,' he said with a sniff.

He wiped his nose with the back of his hand and went back to his vegetable plot.

Dad never spoke a word to Edith that day. She'd also pretended not to see us, even though I knew she had. They held a mutual dislike of one another, and it seemed nothing or no one could heal the rift.

Although money was tight, when I'd been a baby, Mam and Dad scrimped enough together to have some professional photographs taken of me at Maud's photographic studio in Pontefract. With my blonde hair set in Shirley Temple-style ringlets, my mother was determined I'd become a child model. She entered me in lots of bonny-baby competitions and, to her delight, with all her preening and dressing up, I bagged first prize. I became so successful that I landed a modelling contract, promoting a teething product called Bikipegs. They were large, finger-shaped biscuits, and soon we'd become overrun with them. Mam handed them out to the neighbours' children because I decided I didn't like the taste. She was thrilled when a photo of me holding a Bikipeg later appeared in *The Parents* magazine. Alongside the picture were the immortal words: 'Hasn't she got lovely teeth? But they didn't grow like that by chance. When she was teething, her mother gave her Bikipegs.'

Of course, she'd proudly showed the magazine to everyone she could think of. In Mam's eyes, I'd just broken into the world of show business. It was a premonition of what was to come.

After my brush with fame, my parents decided I was destined for greater things so, when I was three years old, Dad took me along to my first dance class. It was held inside a studio in the Crescent Cinema, in Pontefract. I guess we must have looked quite a sight – a big, burly ex-prize fighter holding the hand of a curly-haired child, skipping along at his side – but I was accepted. Of course, I was much too young to join in the class, so the teacher allowed me to stand at the back and copy the older girls. By the age of five I loved dance so much that I'd run to my classes. Mam realised I had a natural talent for it and enrolled me in a much better school. Unlike the other school, this one had a reputation for preparing pupils for the Royal Academy of Dance. It was the kind of place a girl like me from a mining village in Yorkshire could only dream of. I worked harder than everyone else to try to become the best dancer I could be. Although I'd specialised in ballet, I adored all types of dance.

Soon it was time to start school. Although I'd made lots of new friends, I resented it because it just seemed to get in the way of my dance lessons. Half the time I'd sit in class, looking at the wall, watching the hands of the big brown Bakelite clock. I'd wait until they'd signalled it was time to go home, or more importantly, time to go to my dance class.

'I know yer love yer dance, our Pat,' Mum chided as soon as I ran in through the back door to grab my ballet pumps, 'but yer also 'ave to work hard at school if you want to do well.'

'Yes, Mam.' I agreed, although I'd already decided I wanted to become a dancer.

Nothing else mattered and school – or anything else for that matter – would stop me from doing it. But then something happened that turned our world upside down. I was sat at home in the kitchen one morning when a voice came on the radio. Mam shushed my chatter as she and Dad sat there solemnly, listening to every word. The voice belonged to Neville Chamberlain.

This morning, the British Ambassador in Berlin handed the German government a final note stating that, unless we heard from them by eleven o'clock that they were prepared at once to withdraw their troops from Poland, a state of war would exist between us.

I have to tell you now that no such undertaking has been received and that, consequently, this country is at war with Germany.

As soon as I heard, I ran straight into Mam's arms and began to sob. It was just before my sixth birthday, but I was old enough to understand. Mam lifted me up onto her lap and began to rock me gently back on forth in her chair.

'Don't worry, our Pat,' she soothed. 'Everything will be all right. I promise.'

Although she'd tried her best to comfort me, inside I felt terrified because I knew something dreadful was about to happen. Within the hour, our house was full of neighbours and friends, all with one subject on their minds – war. The adults huddled together around the kitchen table, drinking endless cups of tea. Most had questioned how long the war with Germany would last.

'It'll be over before yer know it, George,' one neighbour remarked to Dad.

He shook his head grimly.

'No, I don't think it will. Reckon this war will go on for years.'

Mam gasped and covered her mouth, as the other women discussed which men, sons and brothers would be called up to fight.

I was worried about my father, terrified the nasty Germans would kill him. The thought rattled around inside my head until, by the end of the day, I felt exhausted with concern.

'What's the matter, our Pat?' Mam asked as she cleaned away the cups from the kitchen table.

'It's Dad. Will he be called up to fight?' I asked, my voice trembling.

Mam smiled, placed the cups back down on the table and held me tight against her. Then she knelt down and tenderly kissed the top of my head.

'Your father's a miner, our Pat. They won't call t'miners up because they need 'em to man t'pits.'

'Really?' I asked, looking up at her through tear-stained eyes.

Mam nodded.

'Yes, they'll need someone to dig out t'coal to help fight Germans, won't they?'

Even though my mother had promised me Dad would be

safe, I still understood what war meant and that people would die and suffer.

'Are you sure we're going to be all right?' I whispered, trying to blink away my tears.

Mam lifted her hand and gently stroked away some hair from my face.

'Everything will be fine. I won't let those nasty Germans hurt our Pat,' she said, smiling.

I'd wanted to believe her because I felt absolutely terrified of what the following months and years would bring. The only thing I could be certain of was that life would never be the same again, because the Second World War had just begun.

CHAPTER 2

SCHOOL SCRAPES

Despite my fear and the war, life carried on pretty much as it had before. Of course, wartime rations were introduced, making times feel even tougher. But my mother was determined. To make up the extra money needed to pay for my dance classes, Mam picked peas and pulled potatoes in the farmers' fields. Sometimes, particularly during the school holidays, she'd take me along with her.

'No, our Pat, you need to pull the pods open and run your finger along like this to split t'peas,' she said, demonstrating with her finger.

I pulled off a pod and ran a thumbnail along the seam until it'd magically popped open in my hand, exposing a bed of peas nestled on a silken bed.

'That's right, clever lass!' she encouraged.

I was supposed to help, but always I ended up eating far more peas than I ever collected. At the end of the day, when all the sacks were finally weighed in, Mam would be rewarded for her hard work with a few pennies. The amount of money she received depended upon the weight of the individual sack. Pea-picking was back-breaking work, but it had taught me a valuable lesson that, with enough determination, it was possible to achieve your dreams, no matter how big they might seem.

Mam bought and traded fabrics on the black market so she could make my stage costumes. The lady next door had had a baby and was given a weekly allowance of fresh orange juice. My mother, fearing I'd become weak and malnourished under wartime rations, bought the orange juice from her to give to me. It was only orange concentrate, but she was determined that I'd have the best things she could lay her hands on. When meat was scarce, Dad would nip out into the fields and set traps to catch wild rabbits. He'd return home with his 'spoils' and Mam would cook them up into a delicious stew, bulking the dish out with vegetables so it would feed the three of us for days.

Even though the war raged on, I continued to dance. The years passed by slowly. When I was nine, I transferred to another dance school in Leeds. I'd travel there by bus twice a week. Mam would meet me at the school gates so that we could make the journey together.

I was usually hungry after a full day at school and, as soon as we sat down on the bus, I'd tuck into sandwiches that Mam would always bring along for me. Although the bombs continued to drop all around us, I didn't want to give up my dance classes. Earsplitting warning sirens would pierce the air, alerting everyone to the imminent danger of enemy attack, but I refused to be intimidated and I continued to dance my way through the war. Nothing, it seemed, could stop me – not even Hitler's bombs.

Although I'd specialised in ballet, I also loved tap. I'd wear a top hat to sing and tap dance my way through a song called 'The Darktown Strutter's Ball' – a popular Dixieland jazz song. Our dance class would perform at RAF and army base camps to try and keep morale high during the wartime years. I also joined an amateur dramatics group that staged theatre productions for the troops. I loved listening to ENSA – the Entertainments National Service Association – on the radio and hoped that one day I'd become part of it. But for now, I was happy to do my bit to help the allied troops beat the Germans.

'As long as troops 'ave a song in their hearts, they'll be 'appy,' Mam insisted.

She continued to cut and stitch my dance costumes by candlelight until I had quite a collection. As I grew, Mam traded in the smaller costumes for ones that fitted me. Although I'd excelled at dance, I wasn't quite as keen or, indeed, enthused by my schoolwork. As if proof were needed, I failed my grammar school entrance exam at ten years old. Of course, Mam and Dad were disappointed, so I took it again, only to fail once more. Mam was determined I'd go to the local girls' grammar school, so she decided she'd give me a helping hand.

'I've paid for you to have extra lessons in t'summer holidays,' she announced one day as we walked home from school.

My face fell.

'But it's the summer holidays!'

But Mam didn't care – she was having none of it.

'Tough! You'll just have to work harder and make sure you pass this time.'

While my friends were out skipping and sunning themselves in the local parks of Featherstone, I was stuck inside a classroom trying to pass a test I'd already failed twice. Maybe it was the thought of having to take it again and again but, somehow, I passed a third and final time. Thankfully for Mam and her pocket, I'd managed to scrape through by the skin of my teeth.

I started at the girls' grammar school the following September. Although I loved my posh new school uniform, I hated all the extra work that went with it. Almost overnight, there was no time for anything but study. With my head full of dance and my heart set on a life on the stage, I had little time for anything else. Instead, I'd sit in the lessons, my pencil poised in my hand, dreaming of dancing in grand theatres. I could only imagine what wonderful places they must be because I'd never actually been inside one. We were far too poor to afford the tickets for them, or even the cinema.

'Patricia Wilson, are you listening?' the teacher barked from the front of the class one day, snapping me back into the moment.

'Er, yes, Miss,' I lied, looking down at the textbook in my hands, desperately trying to find the right place. But the truth was I hadn't been listening, and both she and I knew it.

All too soon my first school open evening had arrived. My mother was desperate to come along to ensure all her hard work had paid off.

'You don't have to come,' I said, trying to convince her otherwise.

Mam was busy folding some washing in the corner of the room. As soon as I spoke, she put down the sheet, straightened up and rested the palms of her hands against the small of her back.

'Of course I'm coming. Why wouldn't I?'

My heart beat furiously as panic set in.

'It's just that most of the other parents said they weren't going to bother,' I lied, trying to avoid eye contact.

'Well, they might not bother but I will,' she insisted, turning her attention back to the pile of washing.

I realised then that I was doomed.

The evening soon arrived, but Dad didn't come along with us. He always left 'school things' up to Mam. He not only trusted her, he felt completely out of his depth when it came to matters of education. As a lad, Dad had left school barely able to read. But, as I grew and progressed through school, he became determined to learn how to read, and write too, so he enrolled at a nearby technical college. Dad had wanted to become a pit deputy but first he had to pass his papers. With the extra lessons and Mam behind him, he not only passed the exam, but he got the job and a much better wage.

So Mam pulled her only overcoat from a peg behind the door and we set off towards the school. Her coat was black, so it was suitable for all occasions – funerals or weddings. With no money to spare, a black coat made sound financial sense.

'Come on, our Pat,' she said, giving me a nudge towards the classroom door as we entered the school. 'Don't dilly-dally now. Teacher's waiting for us.'

My mouth felt dry, and my heart was beating ten to the dozen as I pushed open the door. I looked over at the open window and, for a split second, considered jumping out of it and running off down the road. But I knew it was pointless. My mother would know within minutes that I'd spent the past year doing very little work. Suddenly, a panic gripped me.

'What if she stops me going to my dance lessons? What then?' I thought, as my heart sank to my knees.

Thankfully, my teacher, Miss New, was a better person than me.

'Good afternoon, Mrs Wilson,' she said, standing up and taking my mother's gloved hand in hers.

'Afternoon,' Mam replied with a smile as we both sat down opposite the teacher.

Miss New glanced down at a big, brown marking book that was resting on the desk in front of her. I sat there with my tongue thick inside my mouth, too scared to speak, waiting for my whole world to come tumbling down.

'Yes, Patricia Wilson,' she remarked, tracing her finger down a list of names.

Miss New lifted her head and looked me directly in the eye. I felt myself squirm. The edge of the wooden chair bit hard against the back of my legs as I held my breath.

'Mrs Wilson, I'm delighted to tell you that we've decided to put Patricia up into next year. We plan to do this even though her exam results were, well, erm, not so good.'

The teacher's eyes were still boring into me, but I didn't dare look at her. I bowed my head, waiting for the rest of it. Grabbing the edge of the chair for courage, I waited for her damning verdict but, instead, there was a moment's silence. What she said next almost knocked me clean off my chair.

'Patricia is a very capable girl,' she said, leaning back in her chair. 'She also has a very competitive edge so I think, if she puts her mind to something, she could do very well indeed.'

The anxious breath I'd been holding inside came rushing out as a breath of relief. I'd just escaped a punishment worse than death! Although she knew I'd not performed brilliantly in my exams, my mother was absolutely none the wiser. Instead, she patted her hand fondly against my knee.

'Yes, Miss New. Her father and I, well, we're both very proud of our Pat,' she said with a smile.

As we left the classroom, I was still in a state of shock. Why had Miss New just saved my bacon? I'd been one of the laziest students in her class, so I was completely baffled as to why she'd decided not to let the cat out of the bag. But actually, Miss New was a very clever woman because, after that, I decided to repay the favour. Instead of daydreaming, I put all my efforts into excelling at school, working as hard as I possibly could. Looking back, the teacher knew me better than I knew myself because, from that day on, I applied myself. I wasn't clever, but I soon realised that, with enough hard work, I'd be able to achieve the same grades as my peers. When I finally took my school certificate a few years later, to Mam's delight, I passed it with flying colours.

'You're a clever lass, our Pat. I always knew yer had it in yer,' she trilled as soon as I shared the good news.

By now, I was excelling at school, as well as in my dance

lessons. I seemed to outgrow my old dance school and soon I was on the lookout for something bigger and better. I'd heard of another, more prestigious place, called Lilymans' Dance School, also based in Leeds. Lilymans was said to be the best school in Yorkshire, and I desperately wanted to go there. I knew they only accepted the best dancers, so I hoped that one day I'd be good enough to join.

A few years later, the war ended. I was still only twelve, but it felt as though my life had just begun because, for the first time, I was allowed some freedom. With the war over, Mam decided it was safe for me to travel alone to my dance classes. It'd also save her a fortune on bus fare.

One day I took advantage of my newfound freedom. I wandered through Leeds city centre looking for the Lilymans' Dance School. After a bit of a trek, I found it bang in the heart of City Square. However, because it was a Saturday, the school wasn't open. My heart sank as my hand pushed against the locked door. I tried again and again, but I kept missing the opening times. One Wednesday evening, I decided to give it one last try. To my delight, as I approached, I noticed that the door was slightly ajar. The telltale plink of piano keys carried through the air as I dared myself to step inside. My hand was still shaking as I pushed open the heavy wooden door, taking an extra deep breath for courage. As it swung open, a dozen girls' faces turned to look at me, but I was too busy standing in the doorway, taking it all in. I was rooted to the spot. It didn't look, or even feel, like any other dance school I'd ever been to before. Instead, it felt as though I'd just stepped inside a television studio.

'Yes, may I help you?' a voice called out from the back of the room.

It belonged to a grim-looking lady. She momentarily looked up from the piano, lifted a hand and beckoned me over. Dressed in a dour tweed skirt, thick brown tights and a brown cardigan, she looked a bit like a Sunday-school teacher. The dancers were standing at the bar in position, awaiting her instruction. They were dressed in a uniform of black leotards and pink ballet shoes, with matching Alice bands and nets in their hair.

'Keep your eyes forward, please, garls,' the woman scolded, tapping her hand sharply against the top of the piano. 'Stop looking at the young lady.'

The dancers did as they were told and the lady turned her attention back to me.

'May I help you?' she asked again, peering over the top of a pair of tortoiseshell-rimmed spectacles. She had streaky, short grey hair that made her look masculine and fierce.

'Er, er,' I stammered, trying to search for the right words.

I knew I could dance and that this school would be my passport to fame and fortune. Swallowing back my nerves, I stepped forwards and approached. The woman looked me up and down and waited for me to speak.

'Erm, I'd like to join your dance school,' I said, blurting out the words a little too quickly.

'Do you now?' she replied – more a question than an answer.

I thought she might ask me to audition on the spot. I was prepared to do it but she didn't ask. She must have realised how much nerve it had taken for me to walk across the room and approach her. After a slight pause, the teacher, who turned out to be Ms Lilyman herself, agreed to take me on.

'All right then, you may start next week,' she decided before turning back towards the other dancers.

'I said eyes front, garls!' she snapped.

The music started up and the dancers began to tiptoe in unison.

'Thank you!' I gasped. 'You won't regret it!'

I ran out of the building and back onto the street outside. I tried to catch my breath but I couldn't stop myself from smiling. I'd just been accepted into one of the best dance schools in Yorkshire! Then I remembered something and my stomach flipped with nerves – what on earth would Mam say?

I needn't have worried.

'I'm so proud of yer, our Pat,' she said, grabbing my face between both hands.

She pulled me forward and planted a wet kiss on my forehead.

'So you're not angry with me?' I asked.

'Angry? Why would I be? Yer used yer own initiative to get in there. I'm proud of yer, that's what I am.'

However, her face fell a little when I explained the fees would cost a little more.

Mam sighed and sat down heavily at the kitchen table as she worked out how and where she'd find the extra money.

'I'll just have to get another job,' she decided. 'But it'll be worth it when me and yer dad see you up on that stage.'

In the end, she took on extra waitressing to pay for my new lessons. After that, I attended Lilymans' four times a week.

With the war at an end, the following months felt full of joy and celebration. Peace must have filtered into the hearts of every man, woman and child because, a year later, in May 1946, I was asked if I wanted to meet up with Granny Wilson and the notorious Aunt Edith. Edith had approached Mam's youngest sister to tell her she was taking her daughter Lucy to London to watch the Victory Parade celebrations. Edith had planned to stay with Dad's half-sister, my Aunt Nellie, and wondered if I'd like to go with them.

'It's up to you,' Dad said as soon as he heard the news. He rose up from his chair and went over towards the fire to warm his hands. 'Just be careful. Yer know what our Edith's like.'

Although Mam had always hated Edith, she reasoned it would be a good opportunity for me to see London.

'If yer want to go, our Pat, then I reckon yer should.'

It was music to my ears.

Although I'd been wary of Aunt Edith, I decided that Mam was right. London was a place I'd always dreamed of going to visit. Even if it did mean travelling with Edith, it would be a small price to pay to see both the city and the parade.

'I think I'd like to go,' I replied. Mam glanced over warily at Dad.

'Like I say, it's up to you but, if yer do want to go, yer'll have to speak to Edith yersen and arrange it all, 'cause I've got nowt to say to her,' insisted Dad.

I was shaking in my shoes as I approached the back door of Edith's house but I took a deep breath, lifted a hand and tapped against it lightly. The back yard stank of pigs, just as Mam had

THE GIRL IN THE SPOTTY DRESS

said. Even though the animals lived in a sty in an allotment at the back of the house, mud had trailed in across the back step. I looked down at it and shook my head.

'Mam would go mad at that,' I thought as I waited for someone to answer.

Suddenly, the door creaked open and Aunt Edith stood there. Short, stocky and still wearing men's overalls, she beckoned me inside. But I couldn't take my eyes off her hair. It had been cropped short and she'd covered it with the same black beret I'd seen her wearing in the street.

'Come in, lass. Sit thee sen down,' she grunted in a broad Yorkshire accent. 'This is yer granny,' she said, gesturing a filthy hand over towards an elderly lady sitting in the corner by the window.

Edith's hands looked like shovels, with dirt pressed hard beneath her fingernails. In that moment, I made a mental note not to eat anything she gave me.

Granny Wilson was sat in an old threadbare armchair in a corner of the room. She was a petite and fragile-looking woman and looked older than anyone I'd ever seen before. I couldn't be sure, but I thought I saw her flinch as soon as Edith pointed at her. It was as though she lived in her daughter's shadow. Granny Wilson looked up and squinted as I took a step forward.

'That's it, child. Come into t'light where I can see yer.'

I anxiously made my way across the kitchen, watching where I placed my feet. Pig muck was all over the kitchen floor too, filling the room with the same nasty aroma that had hung in the backyard. I felt nervous because I was meeting my paternal grandmother for the very first time. Granny Wilson took my hands in hers and stared at me for what seemed like an eternity. Without warning, she turned and pulled something out from behind her chair.

'I've got yer a gift. Well, I've got yer two. I couldn't decide, see,' she said, handing me two parcels wrapped in brown paper and tied up with string.

I undid them, being careful not to rip the paper, as Edith looked on. I wondered what on earth they could be. I was thrilled when the paper fell open to reveal an Oxford Dictionary and a tennis racket.

'Thank you!' I said, beaming with delight.

'Do you like them?' Granny Wilson asked.

'I love them!'

And I did. I never received presents unless it was Christmas or my birthday but now I'd just been given two – and in the middle of summer!

'I s'pose yer 'ere about London trip, eh?' Edith said, breaking the moment.

'Yes, I am.' I said, nodding. 'I mean, I'd love to go, if you'd take me.'

Edith studied me for a moment and wiped a filthy hand across the front of her overalls.

'Aye, all right then. Yer can come. Yer can keep our Lucy company. 'Ere, wait a minute, I'll shout her. Lucy, LUCY!' she hollered like a man, standing at the foot of the stairs.

A pretty young girl came down the stairs. It was Lucy, Aunt Edith's daughter. She was three years older than me, and it was

27

obvious from the way she held herself and spoke that she was very well educated.

'Pleased to meet you,' Lucy said, shaking my hand formally.

After a little discussion, it was agreed I would meet them both later that week at Featherstone railway station.

'Thanks,' I trilled as I headed for the door. 'And thanks for my presents, Granny Wilson.'

The old lady smiled back at me.

'Yer welcome, lass.'

I left the house clutching my presents as though they were the crown jewels.

A few days later, Mam took me to the railway station to meet Edith and Lucy. Granny Wilson was far too old and weak to make the journey, so it would just be the three of us. As soon as she saw Edith approach, Mam gave me a quick peck on the cheek and said her goodbyes.

'Enjoy it, our Pat. And, whatever yer do, be careful of yer Aunt Edith. She's a strange one, her.'

Moments later, Aunt Edith had taken charge.

'Train leaves soon, so we better get our sens over t'right platform,' she grunted.

They were the only words either of them spoke to me throughout the entire journey. It made me question what I was doing there.

'Why have I been invited when it's quite clear I'm not wanted?' I wondered.

Hours later, steam billowed up from beneath the train as we climbed off it and down onto the platform at Kings Cross station. We boarded a bus to Finsbury Park, where Aunt Nellie lived. Nellie was my father's half-sister from Granny Wilson's first marriage. Her house was huge, but it was packed with people staying over for the victory parade. Another aunt and uncle were there, along with two other young women from Featherstone. There was a young girl called Dorothy who was the same age as me. She'd travelled down from Huddersfield with the couple. They had no children of their own so they'd brought along Dorothy – a friend's child – to enjoy the parade. Dorothy and I slept on the floor of the girls' room, while Edith and Lucy shared the bedroom next door. The walls were thin and, throughout the night, I heard Lucy and Edith talking in raised voices. The following morning there was an awful row between Edith, Nellie and my other aunt. I didn't know what it was about, but I was certain they were arguing over money. The front door slammed loudly, so I peered out of the upstairs window. I watched as Edith and Lucy stormed along the street, clutching their overnight bags. Edith had just upped and left me – a twelve-year-old girl – alone in London. Although I was staying with relatives, I didn't really know them. The first my parents knew was when someone in our village spotted Edith and told my mother she was back.

'Eh?' Mam said, scratching her head. 'Are yer sure? Because I've not seen hide nor hair of our Pat.'

Mam went into a blind panic as they attempted to track me down. She remembered she had Aunt Nellie's telephone number written down, so she called her from a public phone.

'It's Edith,' Nellie told her. 'She's gone and left the poor girl up 'ere with us in London.'

'I knew it!' Mam raged on the other end of the phone. 'I knew I shouldn't have trusted that bluddy woman wi' our Pat.'

Mam decided that, as I'd already made the trip, I shouldn't miss out because of Edith. She was determined her actions wouldn't cut short my treat. In the end, I was allowed to stay on and watch the parade. Once it was over, my aunt and uncle had promised to return me to Yorkshire, along with Dorothy. Mam and Dad had arranged to collect us at Huddersfield train station.

The parade itself was wonderful. We walked to the Mall to watch the events. Dorothy and I found ourselves pushed against a stand reserved for servicemen who'd received the Victoria Cross for bravery. The stand was pretty empty, so Dorothy, some other children and I were invited to sit in the empty seats to get a better view. I was particularly impressed by representatives of the Greek armed forces, who marched past wearing traditional national costumes.

'Look, Dorothy,' I shrieked. 'Their outfits look just like ballet costumes!'

Dorothy put a hand against her mouth and giggled.

'Shush,' a man sitting behind me scolded.

'The King's coming.'

The crowd fell silent as a carriage carrying King George VI approached. I was awestruck as I watched him pass right in front of my eyes. His complexion looked as perfect as if it were in a photograph.

'Blimey!' I gasped, turning towards Dorothy, who was equally as star-struck.

After the parade, we headed back to Aunt Nellie's, who had cooked up a delicious tea of sandwiches and cakes.

'It was a day to remember,' she declared, kicking off her shoes and rubbing her aching heels with the palm of her hand.

The following morning I caught the train with Dorothy and my aunt and uncle. Of course, once I'd returned home, Mam and Dad vowed never to speak to Edith again.

Not long after my London adventure, I entered a dance competition in Lytham St Annes. My mother travelled with me and we shared a room in a bed and breakfast. Dad couldn't come, because he couldn't get time off work. A few days after we'd arrived, Mam received a letter from Dad. He'd written to tell her that Granny Wilson had died.

'No!' she gasped as she read it out loud, perched on the edge of the bed.

Dad explained how Granny Wilson had been found dead in the allotment at the back of the house where Edith had kept her pigs. For once, Edith was in the clear because she was away in Ireland with Lucy. The police called at our house to ask Dad if he could identify the body of his mother – a woman he'd not seen for many years. It'd meant he'd have to go back inside the family home – a place he'd done his best to avoid for most of his married life. My father was suspicious it was a trap, so he took an independent witness along with him. However, as soon as he stepped inside, there was an even bigger shock in store – the entire place was stuffed full of banknotes.

'It were in cupboards, drawers, even under t'bedclothes. Yer should've seen it, Sarah. Money were everywhere,' he told my mam. 'I've not seen owt like that before in me life!'

Mam shook her head in despair.

'Well, no good will come of it,' she remarked.

When Granny Wilson's estate was eventually drawn up, it turned out she'd been sitting on a small fortune. Her estate was worth £40,000 – a king's ransom back then. As her eldest daughter, Aunt Nellie had tried to contest the will but with little success. Instead, Edith got the lot, which came as no surprise, least of all to Mam and Dad.

'I knew it!' Dad raged. 'I just 'opes she bluddy well chokes on it!'

But times were changing. The mines were nationalised the following year, in January 1947, and pit baths were installed. It meant the miners no longer needed to go home still wearing their pit muck. With nationalisation came pit canteens, which were introduced into each colliery. Canteens meant the men could now buy tea, bacon butties and even Woodbine cigarettes onsite. Wily old Aunt Edith had realised her shop days were numbered, so she put the property up for sale. She had the foresight to see that the little gold mine she'd built up over the years was about to dry up. Her books proved the business was healthy and a sound investment, so it had sold very quickly. However, with her old profits now going straight into the tills of the pit canteens, the business soon failed for its new owners. But Edith had long gone. With a pile of money in the bank, she bought herself a house in a smart and upcoming area of Pontefract. I just found it incredibly sad that Granny Wilson had died without ever really getting to know any of her other grandchildren.

CHAPTER 3

HUMPTY DUMPTY AND HIGH KICKS

One day, towards the end of my final year at school, my friend Sheila and I went into the school cloakroom to change for our PE lesson. We took off our gymslips so that we could exercise in our regulation brown gym knickers and cream, square-neck blouses. Being a little older, and supposedly wiser, we'd decided at the last minute to get changed in the sixth-form changing room – a place where we'd be at the start of the following term. The sixth-form changing room was for the sole use of the older girls and strictly out of bounds but we didn't let that stop us. The door was only half-shut when we heard the sound of footsteps outside in the corridor. Fearing someone was about to come in, we slammed the door closed. As we did so, there was a God-almighty scream.

'You fools!' a furious voice bellowed.

I prised it open so we could see what we'd done or, more precisely, who we'd hit. We were greeted by the head girl of the school, who was standing there fizzing with anger. She was holding a pair of spectacles in her hand, but the frame was all mangled and the two glass lenses completely smashed.

'Look what you've done!' she cried, pointing down at them.

'S-s-s-sorry,' we stammered in unison.

But our apology fell upon deaf ears.

'Well, you can pay for these to be repaired, that's for sure!' she snapped, before turning sharply on her heels and marching off down the corridor.

Spectacles were a very expensive item at that time, so Sheila and I were terrified about what our mothers would say when they found out. I knew Mam would be fuming but I was more concerned I'd have to forfeit my dance classes to pay for the repair. Sheila's parents weren't wealthy either, so she was in exactly the same boat as me.

'Pat, what on earth are we going to do?' she gasped as we sat there fretting.

We'd wandered back into our usual changing room. Moments later, our classmates began to filter in through the door.

'Whatever's the matter with you two?' a friend asked, plonking herself down on the wooden bench next to us.

Sheila and I told the class what we'd done.

'I thought she was going to flip her wig!' Sheila remarked as we recounted the whole sorry tale.

'No!' one girl gasped dramatically. 'You're going to be in so much hot water!'

I shook my head because I knew she was right. Just then, another friend stepped forward. She had a brilliant idea. More importantly, it was one that would help solve our problem.

'We should hold an auction,' she suggested. 'Sell off things that no one wants or needs anymore. I bet we'd raise lots of money – enough to pay for the head girl's spectacles anyway. What do you both think?'

Sheila and I looked at one another.

'What a fabulous idea! It's absolutely foolproof. What could go wrong?' I squealed with excitement.

Everyone in the class agreed that it was a fantastic idea, one that would reward us with pennies from heaven. All the pupils would bring in knick-knacks and ornaments from home and we'd sell them off to the highest bidder. All monies raised would pay for the unexpected spectacle repair. It was decided the proceedings would be run under the watchful eye of the class prefect, with me acting as auctioneer. Days later, we held our first sale. To my delight, it was a thrilling success. I couldn't believe quite how much money we'd managed to raise from other people's junk. Once I'd counted it all up, I placed the pennies inside a bag and hid it up inside the chimney breast at the front of the room. Our auctions continued for the best part of the week, until one morning the door flew open and in walked the head girl. The whole room hushed as she stood before us.

'I know what you've been doing in here,' she said, gesturing with her hand around the room, 'but don't worry because my spectacles have already been repaired and paid for.'

Sheila and I looked over at her. There they were – her

spectacles, perfectly repaired and perched upon the end of her pretty little nose.

My heart rose. This was the best day of my life! We had a small fortune stashed up the chimney, but now we could go and spend it down the sweet shop! But the smile was soon wiped from my face by the head girl, who informed us she already had plans for the money.

'Come on then,' she said, beckoning to me with her open palm. 'Hand it over.'

'Hand what over?' I replied, feigning ignorance.

'The money. I know you've raised quite a bit, so you need to hand it over to me now.'

I looked over at Sheila – and she at me – as the rest of the class looked on. We knew we'd been rumbled. Without thinking, I glanced over towards the fireplace, which was directly behind her, and she followed my gaze.

'Ah, is that where you've hidden it? Good! Now, go on then, go and fetch it.'

I reluctantly wandered over and knelt down on the hearth. I pushed a hand high up inside the chimney breast and rummaged for the bag of cash. As I pulled it out, I loosened some soot, which dusted both me and the hearth.

'But your spectacles have been fixed, so what will you use the money for?' I asked, sweeping the soot off my lap.

'School funds,' she announced, taking the bag from my hand. 'That way, everyone will benefit from your fundraising.'

My heart sank and not for the first time. I'd just handed over a small fortune. To make matters worse, I knew it would be used to pay for things in school – a place I planned to leave as soon as I could.

In spite of my desire to leave, I continued to work hard and soon I'd come to the attention of the headmistress, who was called Miss MacDermott – or Dour Scot Mac, for short. Due to my diligence, I'd been earmarked for a career in teaching. Of course, Mam was delighted when she was called to a subsequent meeting in the headmistress's office. She'd sat there proudly as the headmistress informed her I'd make a perfect candidate for Lady Mabel College of Physical Education – a teaching school in Harrogate.

'Garls such as Patricia make perfect teachers,' she said, her crystal-cut voice slicing through the air like a knife.

My mother beamed with pride. I think she was relieved her efforts hadn't been in vain.

But the headmistress hadn't finished with me: 'Garls such as Patricia are destined for greater things in life,' she declared. 'Indeed, she will make a fine young lady and a fine young teacher.'

She looked over at me, eyeing me up as though I was a prize horse. But I felt hollow inside. All I'd ever wanted to do was to dance and Mam knew it. Once we were outside her office, I tried to argue my case but my mother refused to listen.

'Look, I know yer love yer dance, our Pat, but teaching's a proper profession for a lady. Besides, yer'll never get anywhere in life if yer have to dance for yer supper.'

'But I don't want to be a teacher, Mam. I want to dance – it's all I've ever wanted to do.'

She realised how upset I was and her voice softened a little.

'I know, love. But yer dance, well, that's just a hobby, isn't it? It's not as though yer can make a career out of it, is it?'

I watched in despair as she buttoned up her overcoat and stepped out into the schoolyard. It was spitting with rain, which mirrored exactly how miserable I felt inside.

'No. Teaching is a proper job,' Mam decided. 'And that's what yer should do – a proper job. Yer could have a good career for a woman. Yer've worked hard enough, so now's time to reap t'rewards.'

She opened up her umbrella and held it up to shelter herself against the drizzle. The rain pattered softly against my face, helping to disguise my tears.

'But…' I said, trying to change her mind.

Mam turned and looked at me sternly, as though it was her final word on the matter. If the headmistress said I should become a teacher, that's what I would become. It didn't matter that she was just trying to turn me into a younger version of herself.

'*I want to be a dancer. It's all I've ever wanted to do,*' I thought bitterly, as we walked along the rain-soaked cobbled streets towards home.

Although my dance lessons had been a joy, I wondered how on earth I was going to find a job on stage that would convince both Mam and the headmistresses that dancing was, and could be, a solid career. My answer came sooner than I'd anticipated. One day, I was pottering about at home when I spotted a copy of the *Yorkshire Post* folded over on the kitchen table. Dad was an avid reader and took the paper every morning. I'd never read or even looked at it before now but something – a small ad at the bottom of the page – had caught my eye.

'Chorus Girls required for pantomime at Leeds Theatre Royal, in December. Applications in person, at Theatre Royal Leeds, between 5 o'clock and 7 o'clock.'

Underneath the advert was the address for the theatre – not that I needed it: I already knew where it was. Fate had handed me a chance. It was the answer to my dreams, and I knew I had to grab it with both hands. Instead of hanging around waiting to be discovered, I caught a bus to Leeds. Without telling my mother or dance teacher, I headed straight over to the theatre. The producers were already auditioning for the show when I arrived, so I took my place at the back of the queue.

Later that evening, I returned home, triumphant and completely exhilarated, clutching a signed contract in my hand.

'Yer looking pleased wi'yersen, young lady,' Mam remarked as soon as I walked in the back door.

'Guess what?' I shrieked, running up to grab both her hands in mine. I couldn't contain my excitement a moment longer.

Mam looked up at me, a little startled.

'Our Pat, whatever's got into yer?' she gasped. 'And what's that in yer hand?' she asked, pointing down at the sheet of paper.

'Mam, guess what?' I blurted.

'What?'

'I've just been chosen to dance in a pantomime at the Theatre Royal in Leeds. I'm going to be in Humpty Dumpty!'

But she didn't seem thrilled by the news.

'Humpty Dumpty!' she exclaimed. 'No, yer bloody not!'

She was so furious that she immediately took off her pinny, pulled on her overcoat and marched me off to see the headmistress to tell her what I'd done.

'Humpty Dumpty indeed!' she huffed, settling down in a chair as she repeated word for word what I'd told her.

The headmistress listened, sat back and placed her hands together in an arch. She thought for a moment and then she spoke.

'I think the best course of action is, when the pantomime is over, that Patricia take her higher certificate and train to become a teacher.'

A flicker of a smile flashed across her face as she continued. 'After all, I know Patricia, and I know that she will not want to dance in the chorus line at the back of the stage. That is when she will change her mind and become a teacher.'

The two women exchanged a knowing smile, but I didn't care because I'd just been granted permission!

The headmistress must have been psychic because she was right about one thing, although it wasn't the teaching. After a Christmas season dancing in the chorus line at the Theatre Royal, I decided that she was absolutely right – I didn't want to be in the back row anymore. I wanted to be right up at the front. I'd trained in classical ballet but chorus-line dancing felt basic and boring in comparison. We'd only been there a week when I spotted a dozen glamorous ladies striding in through the stage door.

'Who are they?' I whispered to one of the other dancers as, one by one, they filtered onto the main stage.

'Oh,' she replied, her eyes wide and her voice filled with awe. 'Those are the world-famous John Tiller Girls.'

I was still none the wiser, so I stood in the wings and waited as the music started up. I watched in amazement as the dancers' arms circled each other's waists, and they began to high-kick in unison, in one long straight line.

'Keep watching,' my companion whispered as they began to turn, supporting one another, high-kicking in time to the music and turning like a well-oiled machine.

As amazing as they looked en-masse, I was confident that I, too, would be good enough to join them. But first I knew I'd have to prove myself.

I kept busy with rehearsals, which ran from 10am till 8pm Monday to Saturday. We were expected to learn all the songs and dance routines. The producer gave me a script to read, and I was thrilled when I landed the part of understudy to the principal boy – although, with my blonde hair and shapely figure, I couldn't have been or looked more feminine. Each day I waited, biding my time until I'd summoned up enough courage to approach Miss Barbara, the Tiller Girls' choreographer. One day, during a break in rehearsals, I saw my chance and marched over towards her. The nerves rose inside me, but I tried my best to hide them because I knew she'd never take me on if she thought I was a nervous, giggling schoolgirl. A dozen pair of eyes followed as I walked right up to her, cleared my throat and began to speak.

'Excuse me, but I'd like to become one of your Tiller Girls,' I announced, my voice quivering slightly, betraying my nerves.

Miss Barbara looked me up and down. She was dressed in dark slacks, which made her look extremely slim and elegant.

She inhaled a deep breath of air as she considered the skinny, tall, blonde teenager standing before her.

'You're in the chorus line, aren't you?' she remarked, guessing correctly.

I nodded.

'Yes, but I've decided that I'd like to join the Tiller Girls up front.'

I flushed scarlet as I recalled what the headmistress had predicted only a few months earlier.

'But you've signed a contract with Mr Laidler,' she remarked.

And that's when it'd dawned on me. She was right. My heart sank to my boots as I realised I would be tied into it until the end of the panto season.

'But after that. What about after that?' I asked, suddenly picturing myself running across the freezing-cold fields at Lady Mabel College in gym knickers and a blouse. The thought alone was enough to send an icy shiver down my spine.

Miss Barbara sized me up for a moment.

'Very well, I'll audition you with a view to including you in our summer season. How about that?'

I was so thrilled that she was going to give me a chance that I thought I'd burst. I knew from that moment on that Miss Barbara would be watching me, so I vowed to try my best all the time. I was still living at home, so I'd leave the house around 11.30am, returning home eleven hours later. Mam would pack me up with something for my tea to keep me going through the long day, but she'd always leave a helping of stew and dumplings on the stove ready for my return.

The pantomime was a huge success. I loved everything about it: the buzz of being on stage, the costumes, the audience, the applause. At last, I felt as though I'd found my home – somewhere I truly belonged. I knew, from that moment on, that I wanted to spend the rest of my life on stage. At the end of the season, I marched up to Miss Barbara so that I could audition for her. With a new confidence gained from my stint on stage, I began. My audition involved a number of muscle kicks, which meant hopping about on one leg while kicking the other high in the air from the knee, without losing height between movements. I'd always been confident in my abilities as a dancer, but I was thrilled when she told me I'd not only got the job but I'd be travelling to Blackpool for a summer season with the Tiller Girls.

'You're tall, so you'd be perfect on the end of the line to hold it all together,' she decided.

Of course, Mam was disappointed and immediately made an appointment to see Dour Scot Mac. If Mam had been upset, it was nothing to how Mac felt about my chosen career.

'To say I had such high hopes for you, Patricia Wilson,' she said with a sniff. 'But now you've thrown it all away, all your fine education, and for what? For a life on the stage.'

It was obvious Mac looked down on showgirls. But to me, it seemed like the most exciting career in the world and now I was on my way. With six weeks to go until my Tiller Girl training, I signed on the dole. I soon learned that all the dancers did this. There wasn't any shame in it because we always knew work would come with the change in season.

If I thought I'd be bored waiting for my training to begin, I was mistaken. Weeks later I was chosen to be the Gala Queen for Featherstone's Purston Park. The park needed to be officially opened by the Gala Queen, so I was driven through the village in an open-top car, joined on board by two younger attendants.

'Are you nervous?' I asked a younger girl sitting on my left-hand side.

She looked up at me, gulped and then nodded. It was clear the sight of the gathering crowd ahead had left her rigid with fear.

'Don't be,' I whispered, grabbing hold of her hand. 'I'm right here beside you.'

My Uncle Alf had written a short speech, which I read aloud, before cutting the ribbon and declaring the park officially open. More importantly, I was given a dress allowance, which I used to buy a beautiful brown suit from a shop in Featherstone. The suit came in handy for my journey to London, where I'd train for the next few months and learn how to dance like a Tiller Girl. The only problem was, I was a typical naïve Yorkshire lass and our digs were based in central London. I was only seventeen years old, but I soon found myself living in the middle of a place called Soho. Unsurprisingly, over the next few months I grew up pretty fast.

CHAPTER 4

BLACKPOOL BELLE

'Look at that lady,' I said, peering from an upstairs window at the Theatre Girls Club in Soho.

It was my first evening there, and I'd been watching the woman in the street below for the best part of an hour.

'She was there earlier. What do you think she's doing?' I asked, my eyes wide with innocence.

One of the other girls approached, craned her neck to glance down at the pavement below and looked back at me with a surprised look on her face.

'What? You mean you really don't know?'

I shook my head.

'Don't know about what?'

I didn't have a clue what she was on about.

A smirk spread across her face.

'Why? What do you think she's doing?' The girl remarked, a hint of mirth in her voice.

I shrugged my shoulders.

'Well, I really don't have the foggiest idea but I've been watching her all afternoon. She meets a man in the doorway, takes him inside and then they both come out after a couple of minutes.'

'A couple of minutes?'

'Well, yes,' I said, looking down at my watch. 'It's usually a couple of minutes. But there was a man who went in earlier and he was a new record because he was in there for at least fifteen minutes.'

The dancer threw back her head and snorted with laughter as she clasped the edge of a tea towel against her face. She used a corner of it to dab away tears of laughter, before glancing down at me perched on the window ledge.

'Gosh, you really don't know, do you?' she said, shaking her head in pity.

'Know what?'

She bent down to get a better view of the street below.

'That lady there,' she said, pointing towards the woman standing in the shop doorway. 'Well, she's a brass nail.'

'A brass nail?' I repeated but I was still none the wiser.

'You don't know what a brass nail is, do you?'

I shook my head.

'It's cockney slang for tart. She's a prostitute; a lady of the night.'

I was bewildered. I didn't have a clue what she was talking

about. I came from a small Yorkshire pit village, so I'd never even heard the word 'prostitute' before.

'What's a prostitute?' I ventured.

I knew I sounded stupid for asking but, if Soho was going to be my home for the next few weeks, I'd jolly well better find out – and quick!

'It's a woman who charges men for sex,' the girl said bluntly. 'That's why she takes them inside. She has sex with them and they pay her. This is Soho. It's what happens, so you'd better get used to it. And,' she said, turning back to face me, 'whatever you do, don't go talking to any strange men!'

Although she was one of the new girls, it seemed she was so much more knowledgeable than me.

I watched in disbelief as another man – a decent and well-heeled gentleman – approached the lady on the street below. He tipped his hat in greeting as she smiled and led him inside.

'No! Don't go inside with her – she's a brass nail!' I shouted, banging the heel of my hand against the windowpane.

But he did. They all did. If anything, the daily comings and goings of Soho folk taught me never to judge a book by its cover. The woman, although distinctly middle-aged, had also looked quite normal. Her 'clients' even more so, almost as though they were coming back from a long day in the office. I could just imagine them heading home to their unsuspecting wives and children – respectable fathers and husbands but also men who visited prostitutes.

I lived in a shared dormitory with seven girls at the Theatre Girls Club. It was home to dozens of girls who were either in between shows or still in training. Our digs were situated in Soho's Greek Street in a very old and crumbling brick building, which looked and felt a bit like a workhouse. The accommodation had its own warden – a woman called Miss Bell. She was backed by an assistant called Emily, who was so prim and proper, she looked as though she'd just walked out of the pages of an Emily Brontë novel. Both women were Scottish and extremely serious. Miss Bell was much smaller than Emily and wore a dark cardigan and a skirt that skimmed her ankles. Her cardigan was always covered with wisps of grey hair that had escaped from a severe bun, which she wore tight at the nape of her neck. In many ways, with her dour personality, Sunday-school teacher outfit and strict rules, she reminded me of my old headmistress, Dour Scot. A lot of the time, it felt like being back at school.

'Rules and times are there to be obeyed, girls,' Miss Bell would scold if anyone was late for breakfast.

Outside, in Greek Street and the surrounding area, it was a little 'lively', which meant we weren't allowed to venture out after dark. Our curfew was a respectable 8.30pm and woe betide any girl who broke the rules because she would be immediately expelled from the dance troupe. Not that we ever did, because we were terrified we'd lose our coveted place in the Tiller Girls. However, the curfew meant we were unable to watch night-time shows. This annoyed me greatly because, being an Equity member since the pantomime in Leeds, I was able to go to any cinema or theatre completely free of charge.

Our evening meal was meagre, to say the least, and we were expected to clear away after ourselves and wash and dry our own dishes. The Theatre Girls Club was as far removed from the glamorous world of show business as you could imagine. Our day consisted of dance rehearsal at the John Tiller School, which was a stone's throw from where we boarded. We'd wake up around 8am to make rehearsals, which started at 10am prompt, with a short break for lunch. We were all responsible for our own lunch, so we'd feast on bits of bread and cheese because they were cheap. During rehearsals, we'd practise muscle kicks, where the knee was held at waist level, with the kick coming from the knee. We'd practise until our legs ached so much that they felt as though they were hanging on by a thread at the end of the day.

Cross, cross, tap heel to right, tap heel to left, muscle kick, kick, kick down…

It was a boring and monotonous routine but we had to rehearse until our timing was absolutely perfect. It was thoroughly exhausting, but I soon learned that the best remedy for tired calf muscles was to lie on the floor with my legs flat up against the wall. It wasn't very ladylike – I could just imagine my old headmistress shaking her head in despair – but it always seemed to do the trick. We wore black knickers, a white blouse and a black dickie bow for rehearsals and would dance for up to eight hours a day. As Tiller Girls in training, we were paid £5 a week, but we'd have thirty bob deducted at source to pay for our bed and board. We were all required to be members of Equity and were expected to pay our membership every season, which cost us another couple of quid each. If someone forgot to pay their dues or was late with payment, the Equity representative would come to the theatre looking for them. They'd literally chase them across London if they had to!

With my £5 weekly pay packet, I felt as rich as a queen. I had more money than I'd ever had in my life. I'd grown up in a poor, working-class family and I decided that I never wanted to live like that again. Determined to save a nest egg, I squirreled away ten shillings a week, which I very sensibly put in a post-office savings account.

One day, one of the older dancers – a girl called Mary, who was a heavy smoker and who also enjoyed a tipple or two – approached me. I'd warmed to Mary because, like me, she was from Yorkshire, although I soon realised we were polar opposites.

'Eh up, Pat.' Mary said, plonking herself down in the chair next to me. She plucked a fag from a sliver cigarette case, struck a match and lit it. The bluish-grey smoke swirled in circles in front of my face as she leaned in close to whisper something.

''Ere, Pat. I don't s'pose you could do us a favour and lend us 'alf a crown, could yer?'

I was a little taken aback because no one had ever asked to borrow money from me before, but then I'd never had any to lend.

Mary and I were sat in front of the dressing-room mirror but the whole room was buzzing around us. Dancers were chatting away, stretching muscles and swapping gossip, so I was surprised she'd asked me and not one of the others when, in truth, she barely knew me. But I also wanted to help.

'Erm, yes, of course,' I stammered. 'But I'm not that flush myself. When do you think you'll be able to pay me back?'

Mary seemed affronted.

'Oh, well, if it's too much trouble...' she said with a sniff, making me feel mean.

'No, no, it's not that. It's just that I like to put some savings away each week and—'

Mary butted in, plucked the cigarette from her lipsticked mouth and blew the smoke sharply to one side.

'Payday. Thursday, I promise, Pat. Cross me heart and all that. All right?' she said as more of an answer than a question. She quickly snatched the silver half-a-crown coin from my hand before I had a chance to change my mind.

Payday came and went but there was no sign of the money. I felt naïve, young and out of my depth. Suddenly, it became clear why Mary had asked me and not the others. They were probably already wise to her. They'd probably already had their fingers burned lending her money, never to see it again. At first, I was unsure what to do. I didn't want to fall out with her – or anyone else for that matter – because I'd just arrived. But at the same time, I thought that, if she had the cheek to ask for money, I had the cheek to ask for it back.

'Mary, about that half-a-crown,' I said, striding across the dressing room towards her.

She turned around in her chair and stared blankly back at me.

'The half-a-crown I lent you last week,' I said, my voice beginning to falter. 'I mean, I lent it to you and you promised to give it back on payday. Well, payday was Thursday and today is Tuesday. I need it, Mary. I need it to buy makeup and stuff. So, if it's all right with you, I'd like it back now, please,' I said, standing there with my hand held out.

Mary didn't quite know what to do or say. Looking back, I expect she didn't think a seventeen-year-old would have the gall to ask for her money back, but I had and now I wanted what was due to me. I'd played by the rules and I expected everyone else to do the same. Some of the other dancers had overheard and looked across at one another. It was quite clear to me that Mary was known to all and sundry as a 'late payer'. It was something I intended to learn a valuable life lesson from.

'Sorry, I completely forgot, Pat,' she replied. 'Look, erm, I'm not sure I've got it. Maybe I could pay yer this Thursday?'

But I was adamant.

'No, it's late. I need it and you owe it me, so I'd like it now, please,' I said with my palm still open.

Mary flushed red as she rummaged a hand around in her purse.

'OK,' she replied, pulling a coin from her purse. She snapped it shut in a temper. 'There yer go. Now we're completely straight and I don't owe you a penny.'

'Thank you!' I smiled as I turned and walked away, feeling jubilant.

I hadn't lied to Mary. I really did need the money for makeup because we had to buy our own for the show. The greasepaint foundation was so thick that we'd use a towel – a simple square of cotton – and liquid paraffin to remove it. The foundation came in a small stick that you smeared on your face. It was a brownish skin colour, which gave you a similar hue to that of a good holiday in the sun. Although it was thick,

I'm convinced the greasepaint was actually rather good for my skin. It must have nourished it because I only ever developed pimples when I hadn't used it for a while. We painted our eyes the same regulation bright blue and daubed red rouge on our cheeks to compliment our healthy glow. In short, we were all eyes and teeth!

After two short weeks, our time in London had come to an end. There was a lot of excitement at London Euston one Sunday as I caught the train with a group of giggling girls. We were bound for Blackpool, where we would dance the summer season away at the end of the North Pier. After wandering through the streets of Blackpool, two other girls and I – Edna, a Geordie from Newcastle, and Sheila, a Londoner – checked into our rooms. Our digs were in a small boarding house close to the seafront. Our rooms cost us £2 a week, which meant we had £3 to spare. I continued to put £1 a week away for a rainy day, which meant I was left with £2 to paint the town red. Our formidable landlady, Mrs Williams, was a large bosomy woman who had steel-grey, scraped-back hair and a large, dark-brown mole on her face, which I couldn't help but gawp at every time she stopped me for a chat. I was simply terrified of her!

'How are you settling in, girls?' she asked one morning as Edna and I came rushing down the stairs.

'Oh, fine, thank you, Mrs Williams,' I said, trying to avert my eyes so I wouldn't stare at the humongous mole protruding from her upper lip.

I felt Edna's elbow nudge against me.

'Good, good,' the landlady replied. 'Now, if you need more

towels, I'm just through there,' she said, pointing through to the kitchen at the back of the house.

'Yes, Mrs Williams. Thank you, Mrs Williams,' we chorused as we ran out of the front door and onto the street.

'Did you see it? Well, you couldn't miss it!' Edna said, laughing.

'Don't,' I said, giving her a playful push. 'I couldn't take my eyes off it.'

Despite our age, and Mrs William's stern appearance, she allowed us to visit Blackpool Tower Ballroom after the show. Unlike the other landladies, she never once locked us out and would often sit up and wait for us to return home.

Mam and Dad realised I'd have no transport in Blackpool, so I asked if they'd put my bicycle on the train so I could collect it from the railway station. After that, I used it to get to and from the theatre. Sheila and Edna decided to do the same because there was no such thing as taxis for poor showgirls like us: only public transport. Our bicycles saved us a small fortune on bus and tram fares. We continued with show rehearsals for another two weeks, but now we were rehearsing along with the rest of the cast. Sometimes, the routines seemed to drag on forever so, in a bid to cheer myself up, I decided to give my long blonde hair a pink rinse.

'Pat! What on earth have you done?' Sheila gasped as I emerged from the bathroom one day.

'I've put a rinse in my hair.' I said, rubbing an old towel a pale pink colour as I tried to dry it. 'Why?' I asked, noticing the look on her face.

'No! You're not allowed to!'

I pulled the towel from my head and looked up at her.

'It's in your contract,' Sheila explained. 'You're not allowed to change your appearance, otherwise—'

'Otherwise, what?' I asked. My pink, stringy hair dripped fat drops of coloured water onto the wooden floor below as I waited for her answer. But Sheila shrugged her shoulders.

'I don't know, but I wouldn't like to put it to the test. It's written in your contract.'

Needless to say, I spent the whole of that day and the next washing my hair to try to return it to its natural ash-blonde.

The Tiller Girl show opened to a packed house and our first routine included a beautiful and artistic ballet scene. Even though I was the new girl, I was delighted when I was chosen to play the part of cupid.

I can't believe I'm actually dancing with the Tiller Girls on a proper stage, in a beautiful theatre. At last! I've made it. I've dreamed of this moment for all of my life! I thought happily to myself as I pulled on my cupid's costume. The costume consisted of a tunic, thick dance tights and pair of pink dance knickers that covered my own. The larger, 'silky dance pants' fastened using an antique-looking hook-and-eye sewn on at the side. The voile tunic, which barely reached my hips, had a cord, which I tightened around my waist. Soon I was ready to go on stage. My routine consisted of pretty basic ballet moves – mainly standing on my left leg with my right leg extended. I was standing in this pose when the music started and the front curtain began to rise. The stage lights were bright and almost blinded me as I tried to remember my routine and timing. As the music changed, I began to bring my extended right leg inwards, as slowly and as gracefully as I could. And that's when it happened.

Ping!

I felt a sudden sense of 'release' as something gave way at the side of my right hip. Then I felt a horrible sliding sensation as my silky knickers fell to the floor, landing in a messy bunch around my ankles. I heard a muffled snigger from behind me as one of the dancers tried her best not to fall over. I laughed too but, somehow, I managed to contain my fits of giggles as the packed theatre looked on at me in horror, wondering what I'd do next. With a delicate tiptoe, I managed to step out of the leg holes and over to one side. With a deft flick of my ballet point, I kicked the silken pants across the floor so that they slid over towards stage left. An arm had extended from the darkness of the wings as a hand quickly grabbed the offending undergarments off the stage. I completed the rest of my ballet routine knickerless, apart from my underwear hidden beneath my stage tights. Afterwards, we all fell about with laughter.

'Oh, hello, Nicolasss!' Sheila teased as I ran off stage.

'Don't!' I said, clutching a hand against my chest. 'I thought I'd die laughing!'

'I loved the way you hooked it on your foot and flung it to one side, Pat,' Edna remarked as we wiped away the tears of laughter from our eyes.

Although I had my savings and £2 a week to spare, I didn't actually spend very much. Only a few weeks after I'd arrived in Blackpool, I was asked out by Rodney, a talented bass player who played for the theatre's orchestra. Rodney's father was the musical director, overseeing the whole show, so, in my eyes, he was a very powerful man. Rodney was my first proper boyfriend. Dark but not particularly tall, he'd just finished studying at the Royal School of Music in London. Oddly enough, his surname was Stewart, which I later became, although I didn't marry Rodney, even though he thought of himself as my boyfriend.

In reality, it was all very innocent, with most of our 'dates' spent sipping afternoon tea in the Pier cafe. Thanks to Equity, we were also able to enjoy the odd free trip to the cinema, although we always watched the matinee performance because we'd both have to work the show in the evening. I danced twice every night and three times on a Wednesday, when we held our own matinee. Sundays were strange because there was an odd law in place that forbade anyone to charge for dancing on the Sabbath. Bizarrely, the producers got around it by sending us out onto the stage dressed in full costume to just stand there. It was all very strange but we had a paying audience so, in many ways, it was business as usual.

One evening, we'd just finished a show when the stage-door manager, Harry, tapped on our dressing-room door.

'Oh, Harry, what are you knocking at our dressing-room door for?' one of the dancers teased.

She cupped his face fondly and blew him a kiss. Harry blushed and waved her away with his hand.

'Pack it in, girls,' Harry said, grinning. He poked his head around the door and scanned the room. 'Now then, I'm looking for two dancers.'

'Oooh,' the girls whooped in unison as Harry flushed again.

'Well, you've certainly come t'right place 'ere, 'arry,' Mary chipped in, as everyone hooted with laughter.

I was busy soaking my makeup cloth with liquid paraffin when I heard my name mentioned.

'No, I'm looking for a Pat Wilson and a Wendy Clarke,' Harry explained.

My head spun away from my reflection and I turned to face him.

'Me?' I asked, thinking I'd misheard.

I was one of the new girls. Whatever did Harry want me for?

'Go on, what have I done wrong?' I said with a laugh, recalling the knicker incident.

'No, it's not that,' Harry said, shaking his head and half-covering his eyes because we were all half-undressed. 'It's just there are two gentlemen waiting at the stage door. They want to speak to you and Wendy.'

'Really?' I gasped.

'Yes,' Harry said and nodded.

I glanced downwards. I'd already removed my costume, so I was sat half-naked in front of the dressing-room mirror in just my slip and dressing gown.

I can't go out dressed like this! I thought, as my eyes scanned the room looking for Wendy, but when I saw her, I realised that she was dressed exactly the same.

'Who is it, do you think, Pat?' Wendy asked, coming towards me.

I was as clueless as she was.

'I don't know,' I said standing up and grabbing her hand, 'but we're going to go and find out!'

With that, we ran along the corridor and headed towards the stage door, excited at what and who awaited us.

'Hey, maybe we've been spotted! Maybe it's Hollywood waiting for us!' I said, giggling.

'Oh, I hope so, Pat!'

We both let out a squeal of excitement as we ran towards the exit and the two men who were waiting to speak to us. Little did we know then but those gentlemen were about to turn our lives upside down with an opportunity that would follow us for the rest of our lives.

CHAPTER 5

THE GIRL IN THE SPOTTY DRESS

The men lifted their hats as we approached them at the stage door.

'Here they are,' one said, turning towards the other.

'Thank you for coming to see us, ladies,' the younger one began.

His hand fumbled around in his overcoat pocket and he pulled out a business card. He gave it to me.

Brian Dowling, Reporter
Picture Post Magazine

I looked down, trying to absorb the words as Wendy craned her neck to try to read it.

'Here,' I said, handing it to her. A look of surprise flashed across her face.

'Well, if we're doing introductions, I suppose I better give you my card too,' the other man remarked, dipping a hand inside his jacket breast pocket to pull out an almost identical card:

Bert Hardy, Photographer
Picture Post Magazine

I was a little puzzled. What did these two gentlemen want to speak to me and Wendy about?

Our confusion must have shown because Brian began to explain.

'You might wonder what brings us both here to the stage door asking for you,' he said.

We nodded our heads, although we'd both heard of the *Picture Post* because it was a best-selling magazine, shifting around a million copies a week.

'The thing is,' Brian continued, 'the magazine has been losing circulation so we came up with the idea of running a competition to get more interest.'

Wendy turned to look at me. We were unsure where this was all leading and what on earth a *Picture Post* competition had to do with us.

'Our boss decided we needed to run a photographic com-petition, and Bert here,' he said, gesturing over at his colleague, 'well, he's a photographer and he reckons anyone can take a good picture, as long as they have a good eye for a photograph. Isn't that right, Bert?'

'That's right,' Bert chipped in. 'You don't need a good camera or anything to take a cracking picture but people don't believe me, so I'm going to do it and prove them wrong. All you need is a basic camera. It's what or who you're taking the photograph of – that's the most important bit.'

'And that's where you two ladies come in,' Brian said, smiling broadly. 'Well, we hope it is, anyhow. You see, Bert here, well, he's one of the judges, so we came along to Blackpool to find something he could take a picture of and that's when we spotted you two girls up on the stage.'

I felt my face flush because I was flattered that, out of all the Tillers, they'd chosen us.

'You mean, you want to take a photograph of me and Wendy?' I replied.

'Exactly!' Bert said with a grin. 'You don't need a posh camera to take a good photo. If the photograph is good enough, it will speak for itself. It'll be the man behind the camera, not the camera that will be the winner.'

'So, what's the prize?' Wendy asked.

Brian looked at Bert and the two men smiled knowingly at one another.

'Actually, it's quite a lot of money. There's a large cash prize on offer to the winner.'

'Is there?'

'Yes, the first prize is £5,000.'

'£5,000!' Wendy and I gasped out loud.

A £5,000 prize was a life-changing sum back in the 1950s and more than enough to buy two houses, especially in Yorkshire. I was thrilled that we'd been asked to front such a huge competition.

The magazine's circulation was falling because it was 1951, and more people were choosing to watch television rather than sit and read. The editor had decided a prestigious competition was just the thing needed to lift both circulation and the magazine's profile. It made complete sense. They wanted to take a photo of two Tiller Girls because we were seen as part of that same glamorous showbiz environment. I was delighted that Bert had chosen us and I couldn't wipe the smile off my face. Then I looked down and remembered something. My eyes dropped to my dressing gown and I felt my heart plummet. I looked across at Wendy.

'Please tell me you don't want to take a photograph of us looking like this, do you?' I gasped.

Wendy looked at me and then at herself.

'I hope not, Pat. I'm not going in the *Picture Post* dressed like this!' she said as we both dissolved into a fit of nervous but excited giggles.

Bert raised a hand up to stop us.

'No, ladies, I wouldn't dream of it. But if you could meet us down on Blackpool promenade tomorrow morning, that would be marvellous.'

'But what should we bring? What would you like us to wear?' Wendy asked.

'If you could both come dressed in beachwear, I think that would work out just fine.'

We all agreed and a plan was formed to meet early the following morning.

'Oh, how exciting!' I squealed, clutching Wendy's hand as we ran back to the dressing room to tell the others.

'What did those fellas want?' Mary asked as soon as we ran in through the dressing-room door. The other dancers stopped in their steps and the chatter fell silent as everyone waited to hear what we had to say.

'We're going to have our photograph taken by a man from the *Picture Post*,' I trilled.

'Yeah, sure. Is that what they told yer?' Mary said, smirking as she pulled her dressing-gown cord tight around her waist.

'No, it's true! Look, they even gave us their business cards,' I said, digging a hand inside the front pocket of my satin dressing gown.

Sheila stepped forward and took the cards from my hand.

'It's true, Mary. Says here that one is a photographer and the other is a journalist.'

The whole room gasped as I turned and smiled in Mary's direction. It was obvious she thought we'd made the whole thing up.

'But what are you going to wear?' Sheila asked suddenly, breaking my thoughts.

'Beachwear,' I said. 'They want us to wear beachwear.'

'I bet they do,' Mary sniffed sarcastically.

The following morning, I put on my bathing costume, which was cut modestly low against my legs, and pulled on a brown-and-cream spotted dress over the top. I loved the dress. It had been a gift from my parents to wear during my first summer season in Blackpool. My mother had bought it from Roberts – a posh ladies' shop in Station Road, Featherstone. It had cost her

£3, which was quite a lot of money then, so it meant the world to me and was my absolute favourite.

I met Wendy at the North Pier just before 10am, as arranged, and we headed down to Blackpool Tower, where Brian and Bert were already waiting for us. Sure enough, Bert was standing there holding a Box Brownie camera in his right hand.

'Morning!' Brian called out chirpily, waving a hand in greeting. But the sea breeze was so strong that it blew his voice away almost instantly.

The skirt of my dress billowed up around my legs as we walked over towards them.

'Whoops-a-daisy!' I said and giggled.

I put both my hands down to try and make the flimsy fabric stay still and behave.

It was a blustery but lovely sunny morning – typical weather for Blackpool seafront.

'Right then, girls,' said Bert, taking control. 'I think I'd like to start off by getting a photograph of you each riding on a donkey.'

Wendy and I laughed and linked arms as we followed Bert down onto the beach below.

Our donkeys must have been used to having their photographs taken – well, more than Wendy and I – because they were ultimate professionals. Bert got his shot, so he suggested we strip down to our bathing costumes on the sand. It was all very innocent and proper. Wendy kicked off her shoes and I undid my sandals. We began to build sand castles on the beach as Bert snapped away.

'Pat, turn your head slightly to the right. That's it. Perfect!' Bert called. 'Hold it there. That's right. Wonderful!' he said, pressing the button. 'Right,' he said, looking around him and trying to decide what we should do next. 'I think I'll take a few more on the railings up there and then we're done.'

'You're doing great, girls,' Brian chipped in. 'These photographs are going to be smashing! Here,' he said, holding out his hand towards me as I struggled to my feet. 'Let me help you up.'

Brian helped us with our things as we pulled our dresses back over the top of our bathing costumes. I slipped on my sandals and waited for Wendy to fasten her shoes, before we both headed up to the promenade. Bert was already up there waiting. I watched as he turned, looking all around him, trying to frame the right shot in his head. By now, the wind had picked up. It was late May and, although the sun was still high in the sky, the wind made it feel a little chilly. Families and couples rushed past us, holding onto their hats to stop them from flying off in the wind. Children clutched buckets and spades, their faces happy and sticky with candyfloss and toffee apples, while seagulls screeched and swooped above our heads, looking for pickings. The breeze carried the smell of the sea, sand and nearby fish and chips, which people devoured hungrily while enjoying the sea view from their front-row seats of multi-coloured striped deckchairs.

'All right then, girls,' Bert said. 'I'd like you two ladies to position yourselves on the railings.'

I tried my best to smooth down the flimsy hem of my dress against the breeze.

'Do you want us to stand up straight against them or sit on them?' Wendy asked, pointing at the railings.

'I'd like you to sit on them but, whatever you do, don't hold on!'

We climbed up onto the pale-grey railings and looked down at the 12-foot sheer drop directly behind us.

'What, you mean we can't hang on at all?' I asked Bert, who already had the camera up against his face.

I feared one wrong move would not only be the end of my dancing career but quite possibly my life!

'No!' Bert instructed. 'Do what you have to do to balance yourselves, but I'd like you to keep your hands and arms free so it looks as natural as possible.'

With the breeze picking up, I was absolutely terrified I'd plummet to my death on the beach below. Bert must have sensed it because he added, 'But you can hold onto Wendy, if you like?'

'I hope we don't fall, Wendy!' I said and laughed nervously. I twisted my left foot around one of the railings to try and anchor myself down. 'Because if I do, I'm taking you with me!'

Wendy looked at me, realised I was joking and we both burst into giggles.

'Don't, Pat,' Wendy said with a smirk. 'I'll lose my balance!'

With both hands clutching my friend, the wind picked up once more, blowing the hem of my spotty dress up and out. I'd wanted to let go of Wendy so that I could grab it but I was terrified I'd slip back. Instead, I sat on the railings unable to do a single thing about it. Wendy realised what was happening and we both began to scream with laughter and terror. Bert pressed his finger on the button of the Box Brownie camera and the shutter fell at that precise moment. The image of my billowing dress on Blackpool promenade had been captured forever.

It was four years before Marilyn Monroe's skirt had fluttered up over the famous subway grating in the iconic film *Seven Year Itch* so, in many ways, me and my spotty dress had beaten Marilyn to it! I can't be sure, but I believe our photograph was later used as inspiration for the cult 1987 film *Wish You Were Here*, starring Emily Lloyd. Her character had a cheeky habit of lifting her skirt and flashing her knickers!

With the shoot finished, Bert packed away his camera and called the day to an end.

'Thank you, ladies. I think I've got some lovely photographs,' he said, satisfied with his morning's work.

'Do you think they will use them? The magazine, I mean?'

Brian and Bert both nodded.

'Oh, I'm sure they will. Bert's one of the best in the business. He's bound to have taken a winning shot,' Brian said, patting his colleague on the back.

Bert smiled modestly.

'Goodbye, girls, and thank you both for your time.'

'And don't forget to look out for yourselves in the *Picture Post*!' Brian called back as he turned to wave us a cheery goodbye.

'Do you really think they'll actually use any of those photographs?' I asked Wendy as we strolled along the prom and back towards the pier.

'I don't know,' she said with a shrug, 'but I suppose we'll soon find out.'

A fortnight later, our photograph was published on the

front of *Picture Post* magazine and it launched a nationwide competition.

'Oh, let's 'ave a look,' one of the Tiller Girls said as Wendy and I pored over the front page in the dressing room.

As I looked more closely at the photograph, I clasped a hand against my mouth in horror. With my skirt blowing up, it looked as though I had no knickers on at all!

'Oh no! What's my mam going to say, Wendy?' I gasped. 'And look at my legs... they look awfully skinny!'

'Don't show her!' one of the girls suggested.

But it was no good. *Picture Post* was a widely read magazine. I knew it was only a matter of time before my mother or father spotted me on the shelves of the local newsagent. When she did, Mam didn't even notice the 'no knickers' bit. She just saw her daughter on the front page of a magazine that was read by over a million people.

'I'm so proud of you, Pat. I could burst!' she later wrote in a letter to me.

All I could think was, *What will the neighbours say?*

Although we were perched on the perilous railings of Blackpool promenade, we looked like two young girls enjoying a day out at the seaside. We looked as though we were having the time of our lives, which we were. Underneath the photograph, the editor had called us 'The Blackpool Belles'.

It wasn't until many years later that I found out why I looked as naked as I did in the photograph. When Bert had developed the film back in the dark room, the black-and-white image had caught my spotted skirt blowing up in the wind to reveal my one-piece bathing costume. The only problem was that the magazine's editor presumed my costume, which was cut modestly low against my leg, was, in fact, my knickers! He was so worried that the picture would cause general outrage for its perceived 'indecency' that he immediately ordered Bert to remove both the costume and the offending 'knicker line'.

'We know it's not her actual knickers,' he'd told Bert. 'But what if the general public thinks it is?'

Bert did as he was told and, as a result – and to my ultimate horror – it looked as though I was wearing no knickers at all!

CHAPTER 6

DANCING
QUEEN

The show played all summer but, all too soon, the season came to an end. The day-trippers and holidaymakers returned home as Blackpool prepared itself for the autumn weather and the turning on of the town's famous illuminations. With the close of the show I packed up my trunk, kissed Sheila and Edna goodbye and headed back home to Yorkshire.

Mam was waiting for me at the station as the train pulled into Featherstone and I climbed down onto the station platform.

'Oh, come 'ere, our Pat. I haven't half missed yer!' She said, her eyes filling with tears of relief as she hugged me and refused to let go.

'Oh, yer too skinny!' she scolded, holding me at arm's length so she could take me all in. 'I hope yer've been eating properly while yer've been away. And I hope that lot haven't been working yer too hard.'

I smiled at her because, no matter what I said, I knew she was and would always be worried about me because I was her only child.

'Now,' she said, 'let's get back so yer father can see yer when he gets in from work.'

Mam explained that my luggage would follow us on. Dad had arranged for one of his mates to pick up my trunk from the station by horse and cart later that day.

Of course, my father was delighted to see me when he came walking in through the back door.

'Eh, yer aren't half a sight for sore eyes. Come here,' he said, gathering me into his arms. 'I aren't half missed yer, lass. We both 'ave, haven't we, Sarah?'

Dad glanced over at Mam, who couldn't stop looking at me. I felt quite choked up to be back home in the arms of my loving family.

I signed on the dole for the next six weeks because Christmas season was just around the corner and, after that, a second summer season in Blackpool with the Tiller Girls beckoned. I'd only been at home a couple of days when my mother announced she'd arranged for me to do the choreography for an amateur pantomime production to be held in the village hall.

'It's like this. I said to her, well, if our Pat can't help out, who can? Anyway, they want yer to do it.'

'All right, Mam,' I agreed. 'Of course I will. When do they need me?'

Mam straightened up, wiped both hands on the front of her apron and then rested them on her hips.

'Well I've told her yer'll start right away! They'll be there now waiting for yer.'

I chuckled because Mam was determined to keep me busy, if nothing else. I didn't mind because I loved to dance so it didn't feel like work at all. With no time to lose, I headed over to the Miners' Welfare Hall where I found a group of little girls waiting for me. I formed them into a dance troupe and called them the Sunbeams, which was a juvenile troupe based on the famous Laidler babes. I was given a troupe of older girls to train too. A few weeks later, we staged the show at the same hall in Featherstone. With adoring parents and grandparents making up most of the audience, we quite literally brought the house down.

Afterwards, I received a letter from one of the grandparents, thanking me for all my hard work. I already loved my job but the letter was warmly received. It made me realise there was no greater satisfaction than doing something you truly loved. It'd also convinced me I'd chosen the right job because I knew, without a doubt, that I would have hated being a PE teacher.

A few weeks later, I was at home when I suffered the most terrible stomach cramps and then developed a fever. Mam called for the doctor and I was rushed to the local hospital, where I had my appendix removed. I began to panic when I realised the rehearsals for the pantomime were just weeks away and I was worried I wouldn't be fit enough.

'She needs plenty of rest,' the doctor advised my mother.

'But I need to be back on stage in a few weeks,' I insisted.

The doctor looked at my mother and then back at me. 'You won't be going anywhere, young lady, if you don't rest!'

So for once, I did as I was told, if only so I could be back on my feet to start high-kicking my way through the festive season. I was called up to perform in the pantomime at the Theatre Royal in Leeds, only this year I wasn't in the chorus line but up the front with the glamorous Tiller Girls. Thankfully, my appendix scar had healed quickly, so I was deemed well enough to resume my dancing career.

I was much taller than the other dancers, towering above them at 5 foot, 7 inches in stocking feet, so my height was put to good use. Miss Barbara placed me on the end of the line to 'hold it all together', as she always said she would do.

Around the middle of November, I headed back to London and to the Theatre Girls Club in Soho, to practise for the upcoming panto. Once the panto had started in Leeds, I was luckier than most because I was able to live with my parents, which saved me quite a bit of money. The downside was that it involved quite a bit of travelling to and fro on the bus to Leeds, so I spent most of my time either dancing or travelling. It meant that I missed out on the social life, which I was really annoyed about.

'I wish I could go out with you lot but I'll miss my bus,' I would say to Sheila with a sigh.

'Never mind, Pat. We'll soon be back in Blackpool!'

I used to enviously board the last bus home, thinking of all the fun the other dancers were having without me.

The pantomime run came to an end in the New Year and

I signed on the dole for another six weeks. Soon the time had come to travel London for the summer season's rehearsals.

'Promise me you'll write, our Pat,' Mam sobbed as she waved me off from the platform at Featherstone railway station.

'I will. Love you, Mam!' I called out.

Steam from the train had billowed up all around, engulfing us both.

As the train pulled away from the station, I looked back through the carriage window. The steam that had risen up had now dispersed, revealing my mother. She was dabbing the corner of her eyes with a handkerchief.

After two weeks of rehearsals in London, we boarded the train at Euston and headed back to Blackpool. This time, I, along with four other girls, had decided to rent a house together instead of living under the watchful and disapproving eyes of our old landlady, Mrs Williams. However, in our excitement, we forgot it would mean we'd actually have to do all our own cooking and cleaning. It should have been a doddle but we spent a full night, and the occasional day, treading the boards at the end of the pier, so we were always rushing out to work. Once the show was up and running, our thoughts turned back to our social lives, which had been pretty non-existent up until that point because we performed twice nightly. During the summer season, lots of the famous big bands had visited Blackpool Tower Ballroom, which was a fabulous and beautifully decorated venue. My relationship with Rodney had fizzled out at the end of the last summer season, so I was a free agent again. After the final show of the evening had ended, the girls and I donned our glad rags and headed straight for the ballroom to dance on the arm of one of the town's eligible bachelors. One evening, the Ted Heath band was playing, accompanied by a handsome young singer called Dickie Valentine.

'Oh, isn't he dreamy?' one of the girls remarked as we all glanced over at him.

'He is, isn't he?' I agreed, taking a sip of my drink.

The following morning, I headed over to Blackpool's Winter Gardens for my usual cup of coffee. To my delight, I turned around to find Dickie Valentine standing right behind me.

'Hello,' Dickie said with a smile. 'I saw you at the ballroom last night with your friends. I was hoping I'd catch you here.'

The coffee bar was a well-known haunt for performers. It was where the theatricals called in for their early-morning cup of coffee, to chat and to swap gossip.

I sat down at one of the empty tables, unable to believe that Dickie Valentine had noticed me. Moments later, he asked if he could sit opposite me.

'You don't mind if I...' he asked, his hand gesturing towards the empty seat.

'Oh no, please do.' I replied, beaming.

My heart beat furiously inside my chest.

Dickie ordered us two coffees, which arrived quickly. I sat there stirring the spoon in my cup, my heart beating ten to the dozen and my mouth dry with nerves.

Dickie Valentine had noticed me. I could hardly believe it! 'Wait until I tell the others!' I thought happily.

'So what's your name?' he asked, staring at me.

'P-P-Pat.' I stammered. 'It's Pat Wilson.'

Dickie leaned back in his chair and lifted his cup of coffee off the table. Gripping the handle, he blew across the top of it in an attempt to cool it down.

'So, Pat,' he said, breaking the awkward silence. 'Do you have a boyfriend?'

I shook my head. I noticed Dickie smile and I felt my heart melt inside.

'Well, in that case, I was hoping I might take you out. Maybe to the cinema?' he suggested.

My stomach somersaulted with delight.

'I'd love to,' I replied, a little too quickly.

Once again, it was all very innocent and we were more friends than sweethearts, but at least I had a good-looking man to accompany me to the cinema.

One evening, Dickie was waiting for me after the show.

'Pat, do you fancy going out to dinner tonight?' he asked.

'Tonight?'

Dickie nodded. 'Why? Is there a problem?'

'Oh, no.' I said with a smile. 'There's no problem at all.'

I ran all the way back to the dressing room. It was empty, apart from another dancer called Hilda. She was busy hanging up her stage costume.

'Hilda, thank heavens!' I gasped, trying to catch my breath. 'I've got an emergency!'

'Whatever's the matter?' Hilda asked.

I placed a hand on her shoulder and began to explain.

'Hilda, it's Dickie,' I gasped.

'What about him?' She replied with a puzzled expression.

'He's asked me out to dinner!'

Hilda smiled. 'But that's good, isn't it?'

'Well, yes. I mean, I've said yes but the only problem is I've got nothing to wear!'

Hilda scratched her head. She didn't have a clue what I was talking about, so I wandered over to a corner of the room, where I picked up a pair of jeans, a shirt and some raffia shoes. Unlike the other girls, I preferred to wear the latest cutting-edge styles. Back then, jeans were considered very daring. I'd bought them during rehearsals in London and I loved them dearly. I also knew they turned heads but for the wrong reasons because they were seen as 'bohemian'. The jeans might have been fabulously outlandish at the time but they were hardly the correct attire to wear to dinner.

'Ah, I see,' Hilda said, the penny dropping.

She turned for a moment, went back over towards the clothes rail and pulled out a beautiful fitted red dress. She held it up in the air to show me.

'I suppose you could always borrow this?'

My face lit up.

'Are you sure? Do you think it'll fit me?'

'Of course it will,' Hilda said, holding the dress up against me. 'Although it might be a little shorter on you than it is on me because you're so tall.'

'Wonderful! Oh, thank you, Hilda. You're an absolute doll!' I said with a grin, planting a red-lipsticked kiss on the side of her cheek.

I pulled on the dress and Hilda helped me zip it up. But then a thought entered my head.

'But won't you need it? To wear tonight?'

Hilda sighed as she pulled on my jeans and buttoned them up. She was normally such a conservative dresser that she looked odd, standing there dressed in my 'bohemian' clothes.

'Oh, no,' she said with a wave of her hand. 'Don't worry about me – I'm not going anywhere special. We're not all as lucky as you, Pat!' she said, giving me a wink.

Dressed in Hilda's beautiful red dress and a pair of spare shoes that I (thankfully) kept inside the dressing room, I said farewell and ran to the stage door, where Dickie was still waiting for me.

'You look sensational!' he said and whistled as he saw me approach.

'Oh, this old thing,' I said, grabbing the hem of it. 'It's just something I threw on.'

Around half an hour later, Dickie and I were sat enjoying a meal when the restaurant door opened. I automatically glanced up and, to my surprise, I spotted Hilda standing with her boy-friend. Sure enough, she was wearing my jeans, top and raffia shoes. She looked awkward and uncomfortable, as though she wanted the ground to swallow her whole.

'Er, I won't be a moment,' I whispered to Dickie and I dashed over to have a word.

To my horror, the other diners were whispering and nudging each other as they gestured over towards the odd-looking woman wearing jeans standing in the doorway.

'Hilda. What on earth are you doing here?' I said, taking her by the arm and turning her away from her boyfriend.

Hilda's face flushed as she began to explain.

'He arrived unexpectedly from Bradford, didn't he? It was just after you'd left. He said he wanted to take me for a meal, but all I had to wear were these awful clothes of yours.'

'But why didn't you go home and change?'

'Didn't have the time. He said he has to get back off to Bradford, so he wanted to come straight here. Said he was starving,' she said, grimacing.

Hilda was usually such a prim dresser that her boyfriend had also seemed baffled by her odd choice of clothing. Her discomfort was clear for everyone to see.

'Pat, I think he thinks I've lost my marbles dressed like this!' she hissed.

I felt guilty because I'd ruined Hilda's big night out. But there was very little I could do other than pat her arm and watch as she was lead, mortified, to a nearby table. I crossed the restaurant and returned to Dickie.

'Friend of yours?' he said, raising an eyebrow as I sat back down in my seat.

'Yes, that's Hilda. She's one of the other dancers in the show.'

Dickie smiled and nodded his head.

'Well, I do have to say she has the most fabulous and interesting choice in fashion!' he quipped.

I grimaced as he raised his glass and chinked it against mine.

Sadly, my relationship with Dickie only lasted six weeks because he had to leave Blackpool for the band's next show in

Morecambe. It was hardly the end of a beautiful relationship but it had been fun while it had lasted.

As with the previous year, the North Pier put on a matinee every Wednesday afternoon. It did good business, particularly if the weather was poor outside, which in Blackpool it often was. If the audience was sparse, we'd ask fellow performers to turn up and 'put bums on seats' to make the theatre a little fuller. Of course, they were Equity members, so they got in for free.

One Friday evening, I was leaving the theatre in a rush when my foot slipped against some steps backstage. Both feet shot up into the air as I fell top to bottom, down ten wooden steps. I'd been wearing my jeans and a pair of flat ballet-style shoes, which were (and still are) very fashionable but that also had very slippy soles. My feet went from beneath me and I hit my spine against the edge of each step as I clattered down. I'd been badly winded and was in agony as I tried to straighten my back.

Hilda had been walking behind and so she'd witnessed it all. Surprisingly, she was still talking to me following the dress debacle, so she rushed to my aid.

'Pat, oh my goodness,' she gasped. 'Are you all right?'

She held out her hand to try to help me back up to my feet.

'Oww, I'm fine, Hilda, honestly. Ouch!' I cried. 'It... it just hurts when I stand up...'

'I think we need to get you checked out,' she insisted. 'I think you need to go to hospital.'

'No!' I cried. 'I don't think I'm that bad, honest.'

But Hilda refused to listen.

'Nonsense. You need to get it checked out, Pat. What if you've broken something? What if you can't dance? Then you'll be out of a job for the whole of the summer!'

The thought of not being able to dance was enough to shock me into action. Hilda was right. I needed to get it checked. I blinked back the pain as I stood next to her. She held out her hand and managed to flag down a taxi.

'Hospital, please,' she called out to the driver as I inched my way into the back seat.

Thankfully, there wasn't much of a queue in the hospital's Accident and Emergency department. Before I knew it, a young Irish doctor called me. He was a tall man, with dark, Brylcreemed hair which shone in the light like a mirror as he proceeded to examine me.

'You've bruised yourself quite badly there,' he said pointing down at my back and my exposed posterior. 'I think you'd better come back tomorrow and pay us another visit,' he decided, before pulling the sheet over me to protect my modesty.

'Is it bad? It's just that I'm a dancer – a Tiller Girl,' I explained, wincing as I tried to turn over onto my back so that I could face him. 'I'm in a show at the end of the North Pier and I've got to dance tomorrow night.'

His eyes widened a little.

'A Tiller Girl, you say?' He grinned.

He turned towards the basin and began to wash his hands.

I nodded.

'Yes, that's why I need to get up on my feet as soon as possible. Why? I've not done any real damage, have I?'

The doctor smiled warmly.

'No, there's nothing broken. Don't worry, we'll soon have you up dancing again. You just need some heat treatment on your spine, then, once the bruising has gone, you'll be as right as rain.'

The following morning, I returned for my heat treatment. I waited to be called in by the Irish doctor but a nurse approached and led me through to another room.

'But I thought I was seeing that doctor,' I said, pointing back towards his consultation room.

She shook her head.

'No, he's referred you to Mr Smith, so he will see you now.'

I was puzzled.

'But why am I seeing a different doctor? I saw that one yesterday and he told me to come back today. It just doesn't make sense.'

The nurse shrugged. It was clear she didn't know either.

'I'm sorry. I've been told to tell you that Mr Smith will be treating you from now on. So if you'd like to take a seat, I'm sure one of the other nurses will come along and collect you soon.'

With that, she turned and walked off down the hospital corridor. I was confused but I let the matter go. I didn't care who treated me as long as I was able to go on stage later that evening. In the end, Mr Smith examined and treated my injured back using a heat lamp. The heat eased the damaged and pulled muscles around my spine, although the bruising remained.

'You should be all right to dance. Just watch yourself on those steps, young lady.' Mr Smith warned.

'Oh, I will. I have no intention of talking that little trip again!' I said and smiled as I gingerly climbed down from the examination bed.

'Goodbye, doctor. And thank you.'

'Just mind how you go,' he said as I closed the door.

I arrived home to find Sheila sat waiting for me.

'How's the back, Pat? How did you get on? Do you think you're going to be all right for tonight's show?' she asked, firing one question after another.

I rubbed my back and gently lowered myself down into a kitchen chair, trying to keep my back as straight as I could.

'It's not too bad. It's a little sore but I think I'll live,' I said with a grimace.

'Well, thank goodness for that!'

'Do you know, the strangest thing just happened at the hospital,' I said, and I began to tell her all about the Irish doctor who'd refused to treat me for my follow-up appointment.

'That's strange,' she agreed.

'It is, isn't it?'

Soon it was time to leave for the theatre, so I forgot about the doctor and the mystery appointment. The final show of the evening was a sell-out, so I was just glad I was fit enough to go on stage at all. I was sitting in the dressing room, putting the final touches to my makeup, when Harry, the stage manager, knocked at the door.

'Is Pat in?' he asked.

'It's not the *Picture Post* calling again, is it?' one of the girls said with a laugh.

Harry shifted awkwardly from one foot to the other. 'No, no, it's nothing like that. I've got a note for her, that's all.'

Sheila took the note from Harry's hand and brought it over to me. I was sat in front of the dressing room mirror when she handed me the envelope.

'What is it, Pat?' Hilda asked.

I shrugged my shoulders.

'Haven't a clue. Maybe it's fan mail,' I joked.

Hilda watched as my expression turned from one of joy to one of complete shock when I tore open the white envelope and read the note inside.

'Oh, Hilda,' I gasped, putting a hand against my mouth. 'It's from that doctor. You know – the Irish one I saw at the hospital; the one who refused to treat me when I went back this morning.'

'Is it?' she gasped, leaning over my shoulder to look. 'Why? What does it say?'

The others dancers overheard and stopped what they were doing. Soon everyone had crowded around to listen.

'It says, oh, blimey, I can't believe it!' I gasped with my hand still against my mouth.

'Go on, Pat. Tell us what it says,' Sheila urged.

I cleared my throat and began to read it aloud: 'It says: "Your doctor is in to see you dance."'

I looked up from the note to the others, to try to gauge their reactions. Their faces were a picture.

'Look,' I shrieked, pointing at the bottom of the note. 'He's even written down his seat number and the row he's sitting in!'

The note was passed around the dressing room and everyone chatted about it as I decided what to do. We were only minutes from going on but I knew he'd be out there, sitting in the audience and watching my every move.

'Eh, you can do much worse than 'aving a doctor as a beau,' Mary chipped in, stubbing out her cigarette in an ashtray.

A few of the girls nodded in agreement. But I wasn't convinced.

'I just don't fancy him, Mary. Besides, don't you think it's a bit strange? I mean, he's seen me undressed!'

A ripple of laughter filtered across the dressing room, but I failed to see the funny side.

'I could just see you as the next Mrs Dale,' one girl teased, pouting her mouth and blowing me a kiss.

Mrs Dale was a popular radio programme, where the leading lady was married to a fictional doctor called Dr Jim Dale. Her quip made the whole room erupt with a roar of laughter. I didn't find it funny; in fact, the whole thing had left me feeling decidedly on edge. Instead of breezing through my dance routine, although I had a smile painted across my face, I spent the rest of the evening plotting my escape.

Moments later, we made our way onto the stage and circled our arms around each other's waists. A dozen pairs of legs began to kick high into the air, as a dozen pairs of eyes searched through the footlights into the darkness of the stalls where we knew the doctor would be sitting. Soon I'd worked myself into a bit of a lather because I didn't want to have to face him at the end of the show. As each routine closed to a round of applause, I realised I was one step closer to coming face-to-face with a man who'd come face-to-face with my bottom! It was only towards the end of the evening that I had a brainwave. In fact, it was such a fantastic idea that I couldn't believe I hadn't thought of it earlier.

'I've got a plan.' I whispered to Sheila, although I didn't have time to tell her what it was.

I was eighteen years old and, like most teenagers, I hadn't thought my brilliant plan through at all. After the show, I decided I would leave the theatre but I wouldn't exit by the stage door – I'd use the fire exit, which was situated just inside our dressing room. The only problem was that the theatre was right at the end of the North Pier, which meant it was well out into the sea. But I hadn't thought that far ahead.

Once we'd taken our final bow, I dashed off stage as fast as my injured back would allow, removed what makeup I could and quickly changed into my own clothes. Without telling a soul, I sneaked through the fire exit. To my dismay, I realised it was surrounded by railings and very little else. With no room to manoeuvre, there was only one thing for it – I'd have to edge along the outside of the pier on the railings. If I thought I'd had a close brush with death when Bert had taken our photo for the *Picture Post*, it was nothing in comparison to dangling with one leg over the end of the pier and the other over the choppy North Sea, a hundred feet up in the pitch dark!

Clinging to the railings, I carefully pushed myself along, inch by inch, until I was able to plant both feet back on the wooden decking. I dashed away from the theatre and the pier as fast as my bruised posterior would let me.

Unfortunately, the poor doctor remained there, standing at the stage door, awaiting my imminent arrival. I never did show. I stood him up and in quite a style, risking life and limb and my already injured back in the process. But he must have got the hint because, after that, the young doctor never called on me again.

CHAPTER 7

DOUBLE ACT

The show was six weeks into its run when I got another call to go to the stage door. We'd just finished the Wednesday afternoon matinee, so I wondered who on earth it could be waiting to see me on a wet, cold day in the middle of the week.

'Who is it, Harry?' I asked.

'Dunno,' he replied, shrugging his shoulders. 'It's just some fella. Said he'd stand and wait for you after the show.'

I pulled a face.

'Maybe it's another admirer. Or the *Picture Post*,' Harry joked, his voice trailing behind me as I walked down the corridor and headed towards the stage door.

'I hope it's not that doctor!' I said and laughed.

As I turned the corner, I spotted a young, smartly dressed gentleman standing with his overcoat draped across one arm, shaking the rain off his suit. I'd never seen him before in my life.

'Hello,' he said, his face breaking into a wide smile. 'You must be Patricia Wilson.'

He held out his hand so I could shake it.

'Yes, but everyone calls me Pat,' I replied warmly, taking his hand.

'Pat, oh, right you are,' he said, pointing a finger against his temple as if to make a mental note. 'Sorry, where are my manners? My name is Bernard. Bernard Bresnick, but everyone calls me Nick Bernard. That's my stage name and that's what everyone calls me here in Blackpool.'

I nodded my head to show I'd understood but, actually, I was still none the wiser.

'I'm a dancer too,' Nick explained. 'I dance in a show called *Life with the Lyons*. We're currently performing at one of the other theatres in Blackpool. Anyway, listen, could I take you out for coffee?'

I backed away, a little startled by his forward suggestion. Nick laughed and waved his hand in the air.

'No, sorry. Nothing like that. It's just that I have a business proposal for you.'

I was intrigued. What would someone like Nick Bernard want with someone like me?

'All right then. Give me five minutes. I just need to get out of my stage costume.'

'Sure. I'll wait here for you, if that's all right?'

'It's fine.' I smiled. 'I'll only be a moment.'

I changed back into my own clothes, removed what makeup I could with a dab of liquid paraffin and met Nick back at the stage door.

'Why don't we grab a coffee inside the theatre bar?' I suggested as he followed me inside.

'The thing is,' he said, pouring a heaped spoonful of sugar into his cup and giving it a stir. 'I've been coming to the Wednesday matinee every week since the show opened.'

I sat back in my chair in surprise. The show had been going for six weeks.

'You have?' I gasped.

Nick nodded.

'Yes, and I've noticed you. I don't know what it is about you – maybe it's the blonde hair or the fact you're tall but I think you're good. What I mean is I think you're a great dancer.'

I bowed my head. I was still young and a little unsure of myself. Despite my stage bravado, I felt awkward because I didn't know how to accept a compliment.

'It's true, Pat.' Nick continued. 'Anyway, I don't know about you, but I've had it with being in a chorus line. I want to start up a double act and I hope that's where you'll come in.'

'Me?' I said, startled.

'Yes, you. You see, I'm looking for a female dance partner and I think you'll be perfect. So... do you think you'd be interested?'

The thought of being in a double act without having to share the stage with eleven other Tiller Girls sounded idyllic. I didn't even need time to consider it.

I leaned forward and looked Nick directly in the eye.

'When do we start?' I asked and laughed.

Nick grinned, held out his hand and we shook on the deal.

'Welcome, partner.'

I ran straight back to the dressing room to tell the other girls.

'I've just agreed to become part of a double act with a dancer called Nick Bernard,' I blurted out, the words escaping my mouth as soon as I'd entered the room.

Hilda gasped.

'Since when?'

'Just now,' I said, pointing back towards the door. 'I've just met him in the theatre cafe. He's been looking for a female dancer, so I've agreed to become his partner.'

The whole room whooped with collective delight. We were a close team and I considered them more family than colleagues, so they were almost as excited as I was by the news.

'So when will you start?' Someone piped up from the back of the room.

'At the end of the summer season when they switch on the illuminations, I suppose,' I answered, although I'd not really thought that far. 'But I expect we'll have to start rehearsing soon so we can get some bookings.'

As much as I loved being a Tiller Girl, after two long summer seasons, it had lost its shine. I just didn't find it as fulfilling anymore. In fact, the monotony of the dance routines had driven me to frustration and to a point where I felt as though my standard of dancing was beginning to slip.

Nick and I began rehearsing almost straight away. I asked, and was granted, special permission to practise every morning on the

North Pier stage. I was still living in a shared house with Edna, Sheila and two other girls, but I'd become good friends with a girl called Doreen. Like me, Doreen was tall but she was a little slighter in build and wore her dark hair short. She was also a North Pier Tiller Girl but, unlike the rest of us, her parents lived in Blackpool. Doreen had invited me over for dinner where I met her mum and dad, who were warm and friendly. In fact, they were so welcoming that they'd invited me into their home like a long-lost relative.

'Just call me Aunt Mary,' her mother said, spooning a huge helping of stew onto a dinner plate for me. She pointed over at her husband, who was sitting opposite us at the dinner table. 'And you can call him Uncle Jim.'

Before long, I was spending so much time there that I was asked if I'd like to stay in the spare bedroom. It was lovely to have my own space, my meals prepared and my laundry taken care of by Aunt Mary. Although I continued to pay my share of the rent back at my old digs, I loved spending time at Doreen's house.

Back at the theatre, it was decided the Sunday concerts, with the silly no-dancing rule, should be scrapped altogether. So after the close of curtain on Saturday night, Sunday became a free day for us all. One night, in a bid to repay her kind hospitality, I invited Doreen to travel with me to visit my parents at their house in Featherstone.

'Come on, Doreen. Hurry up, otherwise we'll miss the last train,' I said, grabbing my coat and my bag as I ran out the dressing-room door.

'Coming!' Doreen called and we dashed along the rain-soaked North Pier boards towards the town's railway station. By the time we reached Blackpool station, we were out of breath. We realised it was so late that there wasn't a direct train back to Featherstone that evening. Thinking on my feet, I booked a train to the nearest station: a place called Sharlston, which was four miles east of Wakefield, in West Yorkshire.

'But how will we get from Sharlston to Featherstone so late at night?' Doreen asked, beginning to panic a little.

I tapped the side of my nose with a gloved finger.

'Don't worry, Doreen, I've got a plan.'

The train pulled into Sharlston railway station around midnight and we disembarked onto a deserted platform.

'What now?' Doreen asked, looking all around us.

'Follow me!' I said and grinned.

I marched out of the station and towards the local police station. As we approached it, Doreen put a hand against my shoulder to try to halt me.

'Wait a moment. The police station?' She gasped. Her face was clouded with worry.

'Don't fuss, Doreen. We're two young girls, stranded late at night in the wrong town. They're bound to want to help.'

With that, I grabbed the door handle and stepped inside the warm reception area. I spied a brass bell on the side of the counter, so I pressed it and waited for assistance. Moments later, a lovely young constable came to the front desk to ask what the matter was.

'We've got ourselves in the most awful pickle,' I began, taking a lace-edged hanky out of my handbag, dabbing it at the corner of my eyes. 'It's my friend and I,' I said, gesturing over towards Doreen, who was standing behind me. She looked up at the officer and pulled a sad face. 'We've found ourselves stranded. We've missed our connection and now we're stuck here, in the middle of Sharlston, with no money and nowhere to stay for the night.'

I let out a little sob and looked down as I waited for the constable to take the bait. Unsurprisingly, he seemed alarmed at the sight of two young distraught women standing in front of him.

'Where is it you were trying to get to, Miss?' he asked gently.

'Featherstone. My parents live there. But we didn't realise when we set off from Blackpool that there wasn't a late-night connection...' I sobbed.

'Blackpool?' The constable repeated, scratching his head. 'Have you been on holiday?'

'No, we're both professional dancers. We're Tiller Girls, you see. Perhaps you've seen them on the stage? We high-kick and dance at the end of Blackpool's North Pier. We're dancers in a show.'

'Dancers, you say?' the officer replied, straightening his tie a little. He ran his fingers through his Brylcreemed hair. Now I had his full attention.

'Yes. My friend and I, we're both Tiller Girls.'

The officer looked from Doreen to me and back again.

'Tiller Girls? Right you are. Well, in that case, I'm sure we'll have an officer available who would be willing to give you two ladies a lift home. I mean, we can't have two young girls walking the streets on their own late at night, can we?'

I shook my head.

''Ere, give us a moment. I'll get Charlie to take you.'

With that, the constable did, indeed, go off to find Charlie, who took us by police car all the way back to my parents' house.

The neighbour's curtains were still twitching as Doreen and I climbed out of the back of the police car and bade our driver goodnight.

'Thank you ever so much, Constable... Sorry, I didn't catch your last name.'

'It's Charlie Jones, Miss, but everyone calls me Charlie. And it's been a real pleasure making sure you two young ladies got home safe and sound.'

We smiled sweetly at the officer, closed the car door and waved him off. After his taillights had disappeared off into the night, Doreen nudged her elbow hard against my arm.

'You'll be the death of me, Pat Wilson!' she hissed as we giggled, turned and made our way inside, where Mam was sat up waiting for us.

I don't know if Mam ever cottoned on, but I don't think so because she was always at the back of the house, waiting in the kitchen. Although the neighbours' curtains continued to twitch as we were dropped off by different police officers every other weekend. I could just imagine the gossip.

'Have you heard about Pat Wilson? I thought she was supposed to be dancing in Blackpool? Blackpool, my foot! If so, then why does she keep coming home late at night in a police car?'

We played the same trick every Saturday night in a different town or village until we'd exhausted all the police stations in the area. It was a winning formula – two stranded showgirls, miles from home. Plus, we saved a fortune in taxi fares.

A few weeks later, I received a letter from Miss Barbara, offering me a contract to dance with the Tiller Girls at the London Palladium in the Billy Cotton show, which would later become the Royal Variety show. But I was already committed to the double act with Nick so, reluctantly, I declined the offer. It pained me greatly because I've often wondered since how many people have turned down a chance to perform at the London Palladium.

In the meantime, Nick and I rehearsed five mornings a week on the pier stage until our routine was almost faultless. We'd decided to call ourselves Nick and Pat Lundon and had planned for a whole new dancing career. Around the same time, Doreen was thrilled when she received a prestigious contract to dance with the Bluebell Girls in Paris.

'I'm so delighted for you, Doreen,' I said, hugging her for all I was worth. Suddenly, it felt as though we had come to the end of a special time in our lives.

Once the second summer season had drawn to an end, Doreen and I travelled down to London together. Doreen had to train with the Bluebells before she left for France, and I needed to rehearse my act with Nick. Doreen and I stayed at the Theatre Girls Club in Soho because the digs were cheap and cheerful but, more importantly, they were also very central. Miss Bell, the old warden, had heard I'd formed a double act, so she allowed me and Nick to use the club rehearsal room free of charge.

'Thank you!' I gushed, moving forward to give her a grateful hug.

But Miss Bell had remained a dour woman, who didn't go in for such public displays of affection.

'No matter,' she said, brushing me off. 'It's not being used. Just mind you keep it tidy.'

Having a free rehearsal space was a tremendous saving, especially living in the West End. Miss Bell bent her own strict house rules and even allowed me to stay out later than the other girls. This meant I was able to go to watch some of the late-night shows in London. Meanwhile, Nick stayed with his parents in the East End, so I'd often get invited over for dinner. But it didn't stop Mam from worrying about me.

'You looked skinny the last time I saw you, our Pat. So I'm sending you a little something to keep you going,' she wrote in a letter one time.

I unwrapped the accompanying package and beamed with happiness when I saw what was inside. To my delight, she'd sent me a food parcel of cheese and crackers. She'd put them in a box and wrapped it up in brown paper. There was more than enough to keep me going over the next few weeks. Although bed and board was included in the rent, the portions they served up would have starved a mouse. With the extra rations from home, I was able to spend all my spare cash on stage costumes. I'd already bought a vibrant spotty, yellow-circle dress with a black velvet top before leaving Blackpool, but the shops in London were so much more expensive. Instead, I found dressmakers that made things up to my own designs. It not only saved me a fortune, it meant my costumes were truly original. With our act fully rehearsed and polished, our stage costumes hanging up in the wardrobe and our studio photographs printed, all we needed now were some bookings.

CHAPTER 8

THE SHOW
MUST GO ON

I held the studio portrait photograph in my hand and considered it.

'Do you think it looks a bit...'

'A bit what?' asked Nick, looking down at it.

'I don't know. Do you think it looks a little bit staged?'

'No, I think it's perfect, Pat. I think we look really good. We look employable, professional and reliable. It's just right,' he said, prodding it with his finger.

The luxury black-and-white photograph certainly screamed quality. It'd been taken by a London-based photographer by the name of Lanseer. The photographs, which showed us in different dance poses, looked expensive because they were. They'd cost around £20 — a small fortune — but Nick and I had split the cost of reproduction prints between us, so that we could keep the originals for best. We'd planned to use the reproductions at the front of house if and when we ever got any bookings. Later that day, we trailed around the best and worst theatrical agents London had to offer. We did this for the best part of a week. All the traipsing around left me exhausted. The balls of my feet stung inside my high-heeled shoes and my permanent fake smile made my face ache. But the worst part was the constant rejections, which had been utterly soul-destroying.

One morning, we arrived at another agent's office and knocked on the door. Quite often, it was a job in itself just to get past the secretary, let alone to get an appointment with the man himself. The agent in question happened to be Joe Collins, who was the father of Jackie and Joan, and he'd very kindly agreed to see us.

'Enter!' a loud voice boomed from behind the closed door.

I looked over at Nick and took a deep breath for courage as he pushed open the door.

'Hello!' Nick began in his well-versed pitch. 'We're Nick and Pat Lundon and we are a fantastic double act from—'

But Joe Collins had heard it all before. He put a hand up to halt Nick's patter.

'Where can I see you work?' he grunted.

Nick shrugged his shoulders.

'Well, that's the thing, you see.'

Joe stopped him once again and looked up at us both.

'So, let me get this straight. You're not actually working at this present moment?' he said, prodding a finger against his desk.

Nick and I looked down and shook our heads.

'Well, in that case, how can I take you on if I can't see your work?'

I sighed. We'd had the same response from every single agent we'd visited that week. Talk about a chicken-and-egg situation. But without one, it seemed you couldn't have the other, or even get close to it. Joe was pleasant enough, but he was also a businessman and neither Nick nor I had an answer for him.

Once we were outside, I leaned up against the wall, pulled off my stiletto, and rubbed a hand against my heel.

'It's no good, Nick. I'm going to have to sign on the dole. If we don't get work soon, I'll be broke,' I admitted.

'You and me both, Pat.'

Afterwards, we headed down to the West End to sign on. In many ways, it had turned out to be quite an experience because, in time, that little dole office became a who's who in show business. All show-business types have been out of work or 'in between jobs' at one time or another during their careers. What I didn't expect, however, was to be queuing next to some of the greatest actors of our time. My dole queue included the actor Sir John Mills, who went on to star in classic films including *Ice Cold in Alex* and *Ryan's Daughter*, for which he later won an Academy Award. But back then, we were all in the same boat.

'Sorry,' I said, accidently bumping in to him.

'It's quite all right,' he replied as we queued together.

It sounds laughable now – the stars of tomorrow all waiting to be paid dole until they landed the next big gig. Meanwhile, we just wanted to land our first gig! After exhausting all the agents' offices in London, we found ourselves standing outside the office of a club and publishing entrepreneur called Paul Raymond. Paul Raymond had a notorious reputation after he'd opened the UK's first strip club in Soho – a stone's throw from my digs in Greek Street. But he was also a young and up-and-coming agent and beggars can't be choosers, particularly Nick and I. I stepped forward and handed Mr Raymond our photos as Nick started up his usual patter. I held my breath as he flicked through our photographs.

'Where can I see you work?' he asked suddenly.

Nick and I shrugged, gave the same answer and prepared to gather our things and leave. But Mr Raymond stopped us.

'Listen, I might have an opening for an act like yours,' he said, still studying the pictures.

We looked at each other and stopped dead in our tracks. Work at last!

'It's a touring review show, playing the number-two and three theatres,' he explained. 'I'm calling it *This Is The Show*,' he said, grinning oddly, although I had absolutely no idea why.

'It sounds wonderful!' I chirped, relieved to finally have a work offer on the table.

Mr Raymond lit a cigar and took a long drag on it as he sized us both up.

'Yeah!' he replied, pointing his cigar in our direction.

He was a small man of slight build and he sported a little moustache that twitched every time he spoke. I watched as ash from the cigar fell and scattered against the plush carpet below.

'Everyone is so obsessed with television these days,' he complained. 'So I've devised a show, which I hope will put bums back on seats. You see, people won't pay to come and watch just anything when they can switch on a little black-and-white box in a corner of the room,' he said, twiddling his fingers against an imaginary television switch. 'So I've thought of something a bit... well, it's something a bit different. Some might say it's groundbreaking.'

'Well, we'll certainly do our best to help the show become a success!' Nick chirped up.

'Good! Right, I'll get the contracts drawn up and then you can sign them,' Mr Raymond decided. He propped the half-smoked cigar against the side of an ashtray and turned his head sideways to face us. 'Now, when can you start?'

Nick and I glanced at one another, brimming with excitement at the prospect of real work.

'Right away!' we chorused, quite unable to believe our luck.

It was only much later, well after the ink had dried on the contracts and we'd started rehearsals, that we realised the show featured nudity. Not only that but, when you took the first letter of each word and reduced the other letters, which is precisely what Mr Raymond did on theatre posters, the name of the show, particularly from a distance, read as *TITS*.

'That's why he laughed when he'd said the name of it in his office that day,' I remarked to Nick.

I shook my head as I wondered what on earth we'd got our-selves into. Thankfully, despite the lack of clothes on the other girls, I got to keep mine on so, to a certain extent, my reputation remained intact. The nudes were forbidden to move on stage and had to remain static so, all in all, it made for quite an odd show.

The only thing that seemed to get up people's noses, besides the nudes, was the fact the show was called *TITS*.

Revelling in the general shock and outrage, Mr Raymond took the show on tour around the country. To my horror, we were due to appear at the City of Varieties, a theatre in Leeds. Mam was ecstatic, of course, because I was going to perform close to home. She wrote to tell me that she, my cousins, friends and neighbours had all planned to come to watch me. I almost died at the thought of her turning up with half of Featherstone to such a tacky show. I had to think of an excuse and quick! In the end, I conveniently pulled a muscle in my thigh before the Leeds show. With a doctor's note to back me up, I was excused from the whole performance. I wrote to tell Mam that I wouldn't be performing in Leeds after all, due to illness.

'I've pulled a muscle, so please don't bother coming to see it in Leeds because I won't be in it,' I wrote.

It was only a half-truth but it seemed to do the trick because, thankfully, no one I knew turned up to see me dance in *TITS* on tour.

The show continued and my leg recovered. After Leeds, we played several more shows, including one in Oxford. Unfortunately, the students didn't agree with Paul Raymond's take on nudity, so they turned up armed with dozens of ripe tomatoes that they threw at the stage. The poor girls bravely held their poses as their bodies were splattered with ripened tomatoes. It looked like a bloodbath and, in many ways, it was. With tomato juice dripping down them, pooling across the stage, it was possible to hear them cursing the students from the stage.

'Bastards,' one of the nudes hissed, as the show farcically rumbled on.

I'd inherited the genes of a bare-knuckle fighter, so no one messed or tried to throw rotten fruit at me.

After a three-month tour, the show ended in London, where we performed at the Collins Music Hall in Islington. The theatre was an absolute fleapit. It was an extremely old theatre with damp dressing rooms and a rickety old wooden stage. There was running water but, unfortunately, it ran down the dressing-room walls instead of from the taps. Even the musicians in the orchestra pit looked and sounded well past their sell-by date. But the Collins Music Hall had one advantage – it was where all the good and great agents in London came to search out new talent. As we danced our way across the stage, taking our lives in our hands as the floor bowed and creaked beneath us, I spotted a few familiar faces sitting in the stalls.

'Did you see them?' I gasped after Nick and I had taken a bow.

'Who?' he asked.

'The agents. The ones who said, "Where can we see you work?" Well, they've just seen us, haven't they?'

If the stage was bad, the dressing rooms were absolutely dire. To make matters worse, the theatre backed straight onto a graveyard. It was hardly glamorous showbiz living but at least it was a foot in the door. Besides, the theatre cat kept all the rats at bay. I found myself surrounded by cats at home too. As a 'working girl', I was no longer allowed to board at the Theatre Girls Club. Instead, I found a room in a theatrical boarding house in Islington. The only problem was I was the only lodger daft enough to stay there.

The landlady was a widow called Lizzie, who owned around a dozen cats. I couldn't be sure how many creatures there were because they roamed freely around the house, including the kitchen table from which we ate our evening meal. Everything was covered in cat hair, which wasn't very hygienic or, indeed, very pleasant. But I paid Lizzie £2.10 a week for the privilege of living there.

Nick and I danced to a lot of American swing music, but the orchestra was terrible and produced a terrible caterwauling instead of a smooth swing beat. It was impossible to try and move, let alone to try and dance in a sexy fashion to such a terrible racket. However, in spite of the awful orchestra, we were spotted and booked by a man called Richard Stone, who was the agent for a rising comedian called Benny Hill. Richard must have covered his ears because he saw something in us that evening and booked us up for a sixteen-week season at Butlin's in Clacton.

'At last!' I announced to Nick as I looked around our damp dressing room with its peeling paint and sodden walls. 'Finally, we've got a ticket out of this fleapit!'

Our first show at Clacton was written in conjunction with two upcoming writers called David and Peter Croft, who were brothers. They both later found fame, with David going on to produce hit TV shows such as *It Ain't Half Hot Mum*, *Are You Being Served* and *Dad's Army*.

Before we left London, we were also talent spotted by a company secretary called Veena Rochefort, who helped run the Issy Bonn agency based in London. She recommended us for future work with the boss, who trusted her judgement. On the strength of her word, Issy Bonn booked us to appear in variety – mixed with all different types of acts – following our stint in Clacton. It finally felt as though we were on our way!

'Thank heavens we'll be leaving this behind,' I whispered to Nick as we performed one last time at the Collins Music Hall.

'I know. I don't think I could have stood another week,' he agreed.

I don't know if it was fate but less than five years later, in 1958, the Collins Music Hall burned to the ground and had to be demolished. I don't know what happened or what had caused the fire. Only one thing was for certain: it had probably helped save the lives of countless performers who'd risked life and limb every time they stepped foot on its death trap of a stage.

CHAPTER 9

BREAK A LEG

A few weeks later, we were called to the offices of Issy Bonn, or the Langham agency as it was also known. Issy Bonn told us he'd planned to take a variety show on tour and asked if we'd like to open both halves of it. Of course, we didn't take too much persuading. The first routine lasted seven minutes, while we opened the second half with a three-minute dance. As a result, Nick and I ended up working all the number-one theatres, which were the very best the country had to offer.

On the same bill as us were acts such as Des O'Connor, Ray Allan with his puppet Lord Charles and two female singers called the Coppa Cousins. The Cousins were two girls called Joyce and Greta. The latter was Ray Allan's girlfriend, who later became his wife. Also in the show was a South African trumpeter called Eddie Calvert, who had just reached the top of the hit parade with his recording 'Cherry Pink and Apple Blossom White'. Eddie was booked to close the first half of the show, which he wasn't very happy about because he felt he should be higher up the bill.

'But I'm number one! I should be top of the show,' he complained.

But the problem was, number one or not, there was always a much bigger and better act waiting in the wings because that was showbiz.

The variety tour lasted several weeks, visiting towns across the country, including the Alhambra Theatre in Bradford. Unlike before, when the *TITS* show had arrived in Leeds, this time I invited the whole family. I was respectable once again, with no more nudes to worry about! After a stint up north, Nick and I were booked to appear at the Finsbury Park Empire in London. The theatre was gorgeous and was regarded as the biggest variety theatre, next to London's Royal Palladium. Topping the bill was the world-famous Hollywood double act Laurel and Hardy. It was 1953 and the comedy duo had pretty much finished in film. Times and, indeed, audiences had moved on with the introduction of television. More and more people were hiring television sets for their homes, which had a knock-on effect on theatre audiences. Like many stars of the silent movies, Laurel and Hardy had been left behind. Instead, they made their living touring the country with their classic slapstick routines, which always made the theatre audiences roar with laughter.

Oliver, the larger of the two, was the nicest gentleman you could ever wish to meet. Despite their stage persona, neither of them ever talked very much about themselves. I often found that the bigger the star, the less of an ego he or she would have. Oliver Hardy, in particular, was a thoroughly nice chap, who always seemed to have time for the younger performers, including me.

'You did swell there, Pat!' he said one night as I came running off stage.

'Oh, do you think so?' I said, trying not to sound too star-struck.

'Yeah. You knocked 'em dead!' he said, swiping the air with his fist. 'You really did. That's it, we'll all have to up our game if we want to follow you!'

I laughed and blushed. By now, I'd learned how to accept a compliment, especially when it had been genuinely given.

'What's it like,' I asked, 'to be such a household name; to be recognised everywhere you go?'

Oliver shrugged his big, meaty shoulders and held out the palms of his hands as though he didn't have a clue.

'I don't think of myself as anything special, Pat,' he whispered. 'You see, the moment you start believing your own fame is the day you're a goner.'

The following night, Oliver was back there again, standing in the wings.

'What's the audience like tonight, Pat?' he asked as I ran off.

'Yes, they seem very friendly,' I gasped, trying to catch my breath.

'Good, good.' He nodded. 'Makes it easier for us all if they're in for a great show.'

I admired Oliver. He was friendly, decent and refreshingly

honest. Also, unlike some of the other men in the show, he never once tried to look at my legs.

On the same bill was a ventriloquist called Arthur Worsley, who had a doll with the catchphrase 'gottle of geer'. The doll, called Charlie, would repeat that same sentence over and over again and, because we were in a swanky number-one theatre, the tannoy fed directly into the dressing rooms. We couldn't shut it off, so we were forced to listen to the routine every night. That bloody doll squawked the line, night after night, as Charlie the doll teased, 'Go on, say it. You can't say it, can you, son?'

The act was that Arthur would look back at his doll blankly and pretend to be the dummy.

But I wanted to get a gottle of geer and wrap it around both their bloody necks! Strangely, many years later, Arthur, my husband and I all became good friends. However, I always insisted that he never brought Charlie with him!

As the show continued to tour, Oliver Hardy also became a good friend. Stan was very polite but a little shy, so he tended to keep himself to himself. Although I was still on the bottom rung of the ladder, Oliver had treated me as an equal, which he did with all the performers. One evening, as the show drew to a close, Oliver tapped on my dressing-room door.

'Is this where the lovely Pat lives?' he enquired, popping his head around the edge of the door with a smile.

'Hello, Oliver, come in,' I said, gesturing for him to sit down.

Oliver sat opposite me, clutching something flat against his chest.

'What have you got there?' I asked.

'It's a present. For you.'

'Me?' I gasped, putting my hairbrush down on the dressing-room table. 'Whatever is it?'

Oliver smiled and turned it around in his hands. It was a signed photograph of him and Stan.

'From me, to you,' he said sweetly. He gently prodded me on my shoulder with his finger.

The black-and-white photograph showed Laurel and Hardy standing next to each other. At the top, Oliver had written,

To Pat,
With love,
Stan Laurel and Oliver Hardy.

I was so thrilled that I couldn't wait to see Mam's face when I showed her. Many years later, I was sat at home watching the *Flog It* programme on TV. It had featured an old variety professional who had the exact same signed photograph, which had been valued at over £200. I went to look for my photograph but, sadly, it had disappeared, probably lost in a house move.

A year after the show ended, I was deeply upset when I heard that Oliver had suffered a mild heart attack. Both he and Stan were heavy smokers but, following his near brush with death, Oliver decided to look after his health. He lost an awful lot of weight, which completely changed his appearance. Sadly, it had all been in vain because only four years later he died. He was a true professional and it had been an honour to have worked alongside him. Along with the rest of the world and my show-business colleagues, I mourned the passing of a great man.

With our next job booked, Nick and I travelled to Clacton for a summer season at Butlin's. We did a couple more shows at Butlin's – one at Filey and another at Pwllheli in north Wales. Mam and Dad came to Wales as part of their summer holiday, so I went to stay with them. One day, my mother insisted on buying me a new summer dress. I knew there was only one good dress shop in the area, so we decided to visit it the following morning. After trying on a few dresses, I settled on one and Mam paid for it. We'd both been speaking English but the assistants continued talking to each other in Welsh. As Mam and I left the shop, the assistants turned to each other and said something we didn't understand. They began to giggle like a pair of schoolgirls. It was quite obvious we were the butt of their joke.

'I'd love to know what they were saying just now,' Mam huffed as we walked away.

My mother may not have been wealthy, but she was polite and extremely proud. The poor service had left her furious because the assistants had been very rude.

'I think they were laughing at us because we were speaking English. They thought they could talk about us,' I said.

After Wales, Nick and I travelled to Brighton, where we danced in a series of summer concerts on the south coast. We'd been asked to perform by the impresario Harold Fielding, who was the sole agent of Tommy Steel. Bizarrely, we ended up appearing and working alongside the Billy Cotton band show – the very act I had turned down along with the Palladium and the Tillers, a year or so before.

Although I was only nineteen years old, it was during this time that I met British blonde bombshell and pin-up Diana Dors. We were appearing in a variety show together at a theatre in Hull. One morning I was sat having a much-needed cup of coffee in the theatre bar when a very glamorous blonde lady sashayed in. All the men stopped in their tracks and had turned around to look at her with their mouths hanging open. It was Diana – Britain's answer to Marilyn Monroe. With her voluptuous figure and curves to die for, there was absolutely no mistaking her. I was only a teenager and a natural blonde to boot, but I felt extremely dowdy sitting next to the film legend.

'I wish my hair looked like yours,' I remarked.

I looked on enviously at her snow-white curls.

Diana glanced over at me. She cast her eyes over my hair before turning her attentions back to my face.

'Mine's all bleach. But if you want to be a brighter blonde, I'd say go ahead and do it. What have you got to lose?'

Diana had been booked to sing in the show but she wasn't very good because she didn't have a strong voice. Still, I suppose the men in the audience hadn't come to hear her sing.

As soon as I returned to London, I took Diana's advice and bleached my hair platinum blonde. I only wished she'd warned me about all the upkeep it would take. Afterwards, I found myself chained to a bottle of hair bleach as my natural blonde roots darkened with each month that passed.

Issy Bonn continued to supply us with work to keep us off

the dole. A short time later, he won a contract to send acts to dance in the American Zone in West Germany and asked if Nick and I would like work out there. At that time, Germany had been zoned between the Americans, the Russians and the British, following the end of the war. It was 1953 and I would be going abroad for the very first time. Back then, Germany seemed a very intimidating place to visit. Of course, Mam flipped when I told of her.

'Where? Germany! No yer not, our Pat! Yer know what them Germans are like!' she raged.

'Mam, the war's over,' I argued.

But it fell on deaf ears.

'I don't care! A daughter of mine, dancing right into t'arms of Hitler and his mob? Whatever next?'

She was so angry that she couldn't have been more upset if I'd told her I was travelling to the moon!

'But, Mam, I'll be safe.'

'Yer not going and that's that. Over my dead body!' she huffed, snapping her pinny off and looking to Dad to back her up.

However, my mother had done one thing right – raise a daughter as determined as she was.

'I am, Mam. I am and I will. I'm not dancing for the Germans; I'm dancing for the Americans. I'm an entertainer now and someone has to go out there and entertain the troops. It keeps morale up and I want to do my bit.'

Mam stopped folding clothes into the washing basket and looked up at me.

'But t'war's ended,' she repeated, trying a different tack.

'I know but those soldiers are still stuck there, miles away from home. And I reckon they could do with a bit of cheering up.'

Although I didn't like to admit it, I'd felt a little apprehensive about my visit to Germany. I'd seen photographs of what the Nazis had done and I recalled the air raids and bombings from my childhood. However, I didn't share any of these concerns or worries with Mam, Nick or Dad because work was work.

With my mind firmly made up, we asked the agency to book our travel tickets. Nick and I caught the boat train from Liverpool Street to Harwich, where we travelled on a ferry bound for the Hook of Holland. The boat sailed through the night so, by the time we arrived in the early hours of the morning, I was parched and in desperate need of a cup of tea.

'Oh, let's find a café, Nick. I could murder a cuppa!' I gasped as we stepped off the ferry and back onto dry land.

We found ourselves a British Rail café, where we'd decided to stop off for breakfast. But as soon as we walked inside, my mouth fell open. The café was nothing like the British Rail cafés in London. Back in Blighty, they were dull, cold and sparse in comparison. The Dutch version looked more like a four-star hotel than a regular cafe. The dining room was ultra plush, with proper dining-room chairs, silver service and white linen tablecloths covering the tables. As a showgirl, I was used to cafés in London, which had a terrible habit of tying teaspoons to the counter with a piece of string to stop them from being pinched! Tablecloths were unheard of back home and as for napkins, well, there was no such thing. Here in Holland, I felt as though I'd walked into the restaurant of the Savoy, not a railway café in a country that had been occupied for years.

'Eh, it's a lot posher here, isn't it?' I whispered to Nick, holding up the untied teaspoon in my hand.

'I know. I can't believe they give these out here!' he said, taking it from me.

We stirred our tea and tucked into a continental breakfast. It was the first time I'd ever tried one, so I was a little bemused when the waitress had brought it over.

'Pastry, for breakfast,' I scoffed. 'I wonder what my mam would have to say about this.'

After an hour, we boarded a train bound for Germany. We'd been warned by Veena, Issy Bonn's secretary, to keep an eye on our luggage because the Germans had a habit of offloading it at the wrong station. I was terrified we'd lose our stage costumes because they were our entire worldly goods. I heard the sound of a whistle and the train pulled out of the railway station bang on time. As we travelled along through the flat countryside, I was shocked at how many people were riding bicycles. It looked as though the world and his wife were all on their way to work by bike.

'They love their bicycles out here, don't they?' I said to Nick as we both stared out of the train-carriage window.

'It's Holland, Pat. Everyone owns a bicycle.'

After a day's travelling, we arrived in Stuggart with our luggage and stage props still intact. By now, it was dark, so we threw caution to the wind and caught a taxi straight to our hotel, which had been booked by the agency. Once again, I looked out of the window in wonder as we passed building sites. There were men toiling throughout the night, working by floodlight, trying to rebuild a city ravaged by RAF bombs. It seemed odd because, back in London, we'd left behind a city in ruins. Back home, curtains flapped in the breeze from broken windows, trapped in half-demolished houses and offices.

Although our hotel rooms were pretty basic, I noticed that every single one had central heating and a shower too. Again, central heating was considered a luxury back home and wasn't widely available, not even in London.

'Blimey, Nick. Look at this,' I said, holding my hand flat against the radiator in my room.

'I know. I've got one too. They're everywhere!'

'I can't believe it,' I said, shaking my head. 'And a shower too. You'd think, judging by this and what's going on out there, that Germany had won the war, not the other way round!'

Nick nodded his head in agreement. It was astonishing to see.

The following day, I was walking down the road trying to get my bearings when I stopped a lady in the street to ask for directions. As soon as she heard my English accent, she stopped smiling and her whole demeanour changed.

'English pig hound!' she spat and she turned sharply on her heel and walked away.

I felt shocked and upset because I'd never been spoken to like that before. All the Germans we'd met had been so welcoming. But it'd only been eight years since the end of the war and it was apparent that feelings still ran high.

The hotel management had pinned up a notice in the reception, which they did at every hotel where the professional entertainers were staying. The notice announced when and where the next auditions would take place. However, it wasn't an audition as we knew them. Instead, we were herded like cattle at the camp base. The soldiers watched the 'audition' and, if they liked you, they gave you the nod and you were booked on the bill.

The financial arrangement was equally as chaotic, with the Americans arguing the fee. Despite this, the Americans always paid more than their British counterparts, which was one of the reasons we'd travelled to Germany to work the American zone. We were dancers, so we did quite well with our bookings. But the comedians weren't quite as blessed. Unlike singing or dancing, jokes aren't always universal, as the comedians found out to their cost. Thankfully for us, work continued to flourish and we worked a variety of clubs inside the army camps. The best gigs were the officers' clubs, which were very smart and sophisticated and similar to a floor show in London's West End. The next ones down were the Non Commissioned Officers' Clubs, which were family orientated, with children running all around. Last but not least, there were the Enlisted Mens' Clubs, which were real spit-and-sawdust dives, and akin to working in a Wild West saloon.

'You've got to be kidding me,' I whispered to Nick as we turned up at one to perform in that evening's show.

'This is it, I'm afraid, Pat. Like it or lump it. We've got to go on tonight, otherwise they might turn nasty.' Nick then warned, 'More importantly, we won't get paid.'

I peered out from the side of the stage. Nick was right. I knew we'd be taking our lives in our hands if we dared to cancel at the last moment.

'I suppose it's all the same bread and butter,' I said, disappearing off to get changed.

The evening show had been billed as cabaret and we were working the floor. One of the soldiers went on stage, grabbed the microphone and began to introduce us.

'So, without further adieu, here they are, folks. Put your hands together for Nick and Pat Lundon.'

As the applause rippled throughout the club, I glided onto the stage elegantly with my arms outstretched. The music kicked in but, before the first four bars had finished, I slipped and fell over, landing hard on my bottom with a thud. I looked up to see the male audience erupt in a series of cheers and catcalls.

'Hey, you see that?' one soldier called out with his hand cupped against his mouth so that the whole room heard. 'That's one slippy dame!'

I felt myself flush scarlet as Nick turned towards me with a horrified look on his face. I was wearing three-inch stiletto heels but I'd never fallen before. Nick seemed as shocked as I was.

With nothing more than a damaged ego, I clambered to my feet to continue with the routine but, moments later, I was flat on my bottom again. I fell into a pose to make it look as though it was all part of the act but the audience wasn't buying it. Instead, there were more jeers, calls and wolf whistles.

Nick turned to me again, his teeth gritted together in a fake smile.

'Pat, what on earth is going on?' he hissed.

123

I flushed with embarrassment because I was mortified.

'I haven't a clue,' I whispered.

The horrific dance routine lasted for ten minutes, during which time I'd fallen over at least another eight times. By the time we'd taken a bow, I fled the stage and ran to the dressing room in floods of tears. Nick and I had worked on countless ballroom floors but nothing like that had ever happened to me before. I picked up one of my shoes and checked the sole. I'd fitted it with rubber to stop exactly this sort of thing from happening. The rubber was intact, so I pulled off the other and checked that too but it was exactly the same.

Moments later, the door opened and in walked Nick.

'Pat, what just happened out there?' he asked, throwing his arm behind him, pointing back towards the stage.

'I haven't a clue. Look, my shoes still have the rubber on them,' I said, turning them to show him. 'I just don't know, Nick. I did everything the same as I always do.' I suddenly began to sob. I couldn't control my tears a moment longer. 'I just feel... well, I just feel so stupid!' I sniffed. 'Did you hear them? They were all laughing at me.'

Nick nodded his head. It was clear that he was as upset as I was.

'Yes, I did. They certainly aren't gentlemen, that's for sure.'

I was still sat there weeping when the duty sergeant knocked at the door. Nick answered it and invited him inside.

'Y'all did well out there,' he said with a grin, gesturing back towards the stage.

'Well?' I shrieked, still upset by my series of falls. 'I've never felt so stupid in my life. I don't know what on earth just happened out there, but I've never fallen on stage before – not ever. Yet tonight, out there,' I said pointing towards the door, 'I fell over more than eight times.'

'Y'all did well though,' he said and smirked.

I turned to face him and so did Nick.

'Well? How can you say falling over eight times during a dance routine is doing well?' I said, my voice incredulous.

The sergeant removed his hat, scratched the back of his head with his fingertips and began to chuckle.

Nick smelled a rat.

'What's so funny?' he asked, looking over at the sergeant.

'It's just the little lady over there, well, we knew you were both coming so the janker (a punishment dished out to a misbehaving soldier) was to polish the floor as much as the soldier could. It's the guys, you see,' he said, looking up at me. 'Aw, shucks, little lady, don't you see? He polished the floor so the fellas out there could place a bet on how many times you'd fall over…'

Now it was time for Nick's mouth to gape open in horror. He turned back to face me.

I was boiling with rage and about to explode.

'What? Let's be clear about this. You mean he polished the floor so that I would fall over?' I repeated, thinking I'd misheard the soldier.

The sergeant threw his head back and laughed.

'He sure did!'

I was furious. In fact, I was so angry that Nick had to stop me from throwing my shoes at the sergeant, who beat a hasty retreat from the room.

Nick stood there with his mouth open as I continued to use swear words I didn't even realise I knew.

'You're just bloody lucky that I didn't fall over and break my neck!' I screamed as the sergeant ran from the dressing room.

'And as for that lot out there,' I bellowed through the door after him, 'you can tell them they're nothing but a bunch of ANIMALS!'

Needless to say, it was the last time we ever performed at an Enlisted Mens' Club.

CHAPTER 10

LET'S FACE THE MUSIC AND DANCE

Our tour of West Germany lasted for two months. Following our disastrous last show in Stuttgart, Nick and I had travelled to Mannheim, finishing up at an American base camp in Wiesbaden. Afterwards, we returned home and wondered where our journey would take us next.

We did a few seasons here and there but nothing definite seemed to be on the horizon. That was until a gentleman called Richard Stone approached us. Richard had been the one who'd spotted and rescued us from the rat-infested Old Collins Music Hall. He also turned out to be our knight in shining armour in more ways than one. By this time, television had really caught on in England, as more and more people hired their own television sets. Soon there were lots of variety shows popping up in the television-programme schedule. Richard was the agent for the comedian Benny Hill, who had not only become very popular but had also landed his own television show with the BBC in a prime-time slot.

'So I was wondering if you and Nick would like to come and perform on the show,' Richard asked.

'On television? You want us to perform on television?' I gasped, thinking how excited Mam would be when I told her.

'Yes. But it'll be live,' Richard warned. 'Do you think you'll be all right with that?'

I nodded. This was television. It was also the chance to perform to all those families watching at home. Show business didn't get much bigger or better than this.

The *Benny Hill Show* was screened live from Shepherd's Bush Empire's BBC theatre. The show had started at the BBC in 1955, with Benny writing nearly all his own material. Nick and I had been asked to perform a three-minute dance routine, which didn't sound very long but, then again, this was live TV. The more I thought about it, the more terrified I became.

It had been agreed that we would follow Benny Hill onto the stage. He was performing a comedy sketch called the cinema routine, where he would pretend to sit down just as the seats tipped up. I remember standing in the wings feeling horribly nervous. I'd never seen theatre lights so bright in all my life. In fact, they were so blinding that I half-expected the Angel Gabriel to come down from the heavens above. By the time we were ready to go on, my nerves had reached fever pitch.

'What if I forget the routine?' I panicked.

'You won't, Pat. You'll be great,' Nick replied, resting his hand against my arm.

'But... but... what if I fall over or something?'

'Pat, you'll be just fine. Now just take a deep breath.'

I did as Nick had said and breathed slowly and evenly to try to calm my jittery nerves.

I tipped my head forwards and sneaked a look at the studio audience. They absolutely loved Benny. His cinema sketch was going down a treat.

'They seem friendly enough,' Nick said, breaking my thoughts. He nodded his head towards the crowd.

'Yes, but it's not them I'm worried about. It's the cameras and everyone else watching back home.'

I felt butterflies rise inside my stomach as it flipped inside, making me feel queasy. I rested my hands against my diaphragm and breathed in deeply.

You can do this, Pat Wilson. Just keep calm and stay focused, I repeated inside my head.

Just then, Nick held out his hand.

'Ready?' he asked.

'As ready as I'll ever be,' I said, taking his hand.

In spite of my nerves, as soon as we'd glided onto the stage, I forgot all about the cameras, the audience and even the millions of people watching back at home. Instead, I felt as though I was floating on air. It was the most fantastic feeling and probably one of the highlights of my entire dancing career.

Mam was watching me back home in Featherstone. We couldn't afford to hire a television set, so she'd gone around to her sister's, my Aunt Alice's house, so she could watch it there. In fact, half the street had ended up inside Alice's tiny front room just to watch my TV debut, although I'd only found out about it afterwards when Mam wrote to tell me. It was as though I'd done something extraordinary, when all I'd done was dance inside a television studio.

'Yer shone, our Pat. We all said, even Aunt Alice. Yer danced like a film star. Me and yer dad are so proud of you.'

My eyes filled with tears of happiness. Even though my mam had wanted me to become a teacher, she'd realised I'd chosen something I loved to do. But the biggest reward was that I'd made her and Dad proud.

While Benny's show had soared variety entertainment to dizzy new heights on TV, back in the country's theatres, audiences were dwindling. Benny himself had been brought up in theatre. Like us, I guess he must have experienced lean times himself because he was, and remained, one of the tightest performers I'd ever met. Despite his fame and considerable fortune, Benny never once put his hand in his pocket. In many ways, he was refreshing because he never came across as the big star and treated everyone exactly the same. Sadly, this also applied when he was buying drinks at the bar because he never bought a single a pint, although he was always happy to accept one.

After the high of appearing on live television, I soon came back down to earth with a bump as we returned to perform in a summer season at Butlin's in Clacton. We were still at Butlin's when we were approached and offered work by a man called Barney Colehan. Barney was a well-known producer for the

BBC. I'd first heard his name as a schoolgirl listening to the *Wilfred Pickles Show* on the radio.

'Give him the money, Barney,' had been a well-known saying back in the day.

Barney was producing a television show called *The Good Old Days*, from the City of Varieties in Leeds, where I'd narrowly escaped starring in Paul Raymond's *TITS* show. Barney had seen us perform on the *Benny Hill Show*, so he'd invited us to appear on his show.

'More television work means more experience under our belts,' I remarked to Nick, who agreed with me.

Work was work, although the audience of *The Good Old Days* was totally different to the type we'd been used to dancing in front of at Butlin's. The show was also different, so we had to scrap our old routines and arrange a new act suitable for the Edwardian period.

The Good Old Days went so well that I was asked to sing one of the songs on the show but a singer I am not. As I belted it out, I glanced over at the audience. They were all dressed in Edwardian costume, swaying and singing in time to the music. It was the most surreal set up I'd ever seen, but it was also an extremely popular television show and the audience were an integral part of it.

'They're a friendly bunch, aren't they?' I remarked to one of the stagehands after I'd finished my routine.

'Oh, them lot,' he said, nodding his head towards them from the stage wings. 'They turn up in their droves. They're all shipped in from the local amateur dramatics groups – that's why they're so up for it.'

'Ah, I see.'

And I did. No doubt they were sat there waiting for their moment in the spotlight, dreaming of fame and fortune as I had once done.

I loved doing the show. Nick and I performed in so many of them that it almost felt like a family party. Barney asked if we could perform in another TV show called *Entente Cordele*. The show wasn't staged in a theatre but a type of floral hall in Harrogate. Nick and I danced an adagio routine, which was acrobatic to say the least. I wore a black skirt with a long split up the side, as Nick proceeded to throw me around into all sorts of dance poses.

Barney's friend and sidekick was a man called Jess Yates, the supposed father of Paula Yates. Jess was a photographer, so he was always knocking around the television studio with Barney. One day, they were just heading out to lunch when Barney turned to me.

'Have you eaten yet, Pat? Would you like to join us?'

'I'd love to!' I replied.

Jess and Barney explained they were on their way to a Chinese restaurant that was one of their favourites. The only problem was I'd never had Chinese food before, so I didn't have a clue what to order.

'What are you going to have then, Pat?' Jess asked.

I shook my head as I stared at the strange dishes listed on the menu.

'I'm not sure,' I told him. 'It all looks Chinese to me.'

The two of them fell about with laughter as I realised what I'd said.

In the end, I followed Jess's lead and ordered what he did – sweet-and-sour chicken.

'How's the food, Pat?' he asked as I tucked in.

I closed my eyes and held my fork in mid-air as I savoured the beautiful taste bursting against my tongue.

'This,' I said pointing with my fork at the plate of food in front of me, 'is the most delicious thing I have ever tasted in my life.'

It was around this time that a new music had exploded onto the scene. It was called rock 'n' roll. Along with it came a whole new audience – a type the theatrical world had never seen before. Instead of being faced with a prim-looking bunch, we'd be greeted by men dressed in drainpipe trousers, drape jackets and slicked-back hair. They wore winklepicker shoes that looked so sharp they could've stabbed someone.

After our TV stint, Nick and I were invited to appear in a show that featured a rock 'n' roll band. Our first performance was at Wood Green Empire, in London. A week later, we took the show on tour up and down the country. Topping the bill was a rock group called Art Baxter and his Rockers. Art Baxter himself fronted the group but there was a bass player, a pianist, a drummer and a guitarist. The guitarist was like no one I'd ever seen before. Once the music was in full swing, he'd lay flat on his back in the middle of the stage playing his guitar. The pianist was the same and never sat down. The audience couldn't get enough of it. Instead of staying in their seats, they'd rock 'n' roll in the aisles the whole way through, dancing to the beat.

'Have you seen them?' I whispered to Nick from the side of the curtain. 'They're all joining in!'

'I know,' he said grinning at me. 'It's great, isn't it?'

And it was. Instead of sitting there just watching what was happening on stage, they'd become part of it, only in their own way. It felt exciting and fresh but, more importantly, it made for a fun show.

Nick and I would open with a range of dances, from the Charleston to the tango, before a handful of other acts took to the stage. We'd open the second half with an 'Apache' routine that lasted three minutes and then Art and his boys would come on stage right at the end of the show and lift the roof off. They rock 'n' rolled for around half an hour before inviting us back on stage. We'd dance at the front, jiving to their music, and the audience would get up and join in, rock 'n' rolling in the aisles of the theatre. The atmosphere was electric.

A few weeks after the show had been on tour, I was approached by the band's pianist: a lovely looking chap called Phil Phillips. Phil was from London and he was tall with blond hair that he'd Brylcreemed into a teddy-boy quiff. I immediately liked Phil because, unlike other men I'd met in show business, once he was off stage, he was just a regular bloke.

'Do you fancy going to the pictures one afternoon, Pat?' he asked.

I readily agreed. Soon one date had followed another until we were officially 'courting'. At just twenty-two years old, we were both still very young. So when Phil got down on one knee and proposed to me, I didn't know what to do, so I said 'yes'. We travelled to Manchester later that same day, bought a ring from a jewellers shop and became officially engaged. I'd only known him three months, but I thought it was the right thing to do. Mam and Dad didn't say much; they just accepted it was what I wanted.

'It's what I want,' I said, showing Mam my engagement ring as Phil grinned behind me.

Even though I was young, I'd come a long way from being a little girl in Featherstone. I was a professional dancer now, dealing with agents and contracts, and I'd travelled and seen more of the world than my parents could ever hope to see.

But if I thought I'd seen it all, I was wrong. The Issy Bonn agency had secured a six-week contract for us to perform in a show on West Africa's Gold Coast.

'Africa! Gold Coast!' Mam shrieked as soon as I told her where I was going. 'Oh my Lord. Yer know what they call that, don't yer? They call it White Man's Grave and they wouldn't call it that for no reason would they?'

But I was adamant. Work was work. Deep down, I knew my parents trusted my judgement – besides, they also knew how headstrong I was. If they told me not to do something, I'd only do it more.

'Just keep yersen safe, lass,' Dad said, as Mam fretted over in her chair in a corner of the kitchen.

'I'll be fine, Mam. I promise.'

'I know, but I'm yer Mam and it's my job to worry about yer,' she said, cupping my face in both her hands.

Despite my mother's reservations, Nick and I boarded a plane at the airport. The aeroplane left the tarmac of London far behind as we took to the skies and headed off on our very own African adventure.

CHAPTER 11

AFRICAN ADVENTURE

Issy Bonn arranged for us and five other acts to fly out to Accra, the capital city of Ghana, in West Africa, to celebrate the country's independence from Great Britain. Back then, there were no long-haul flights, so we were told there would be a stop-off in Algeria, with another quick stop to refuel before we landed in Nigeria. What I wasn't expecting to do was to refuel in the middle of the Sahara desert!

During the flight, we hit a terrible electric storm and I was frightened to death. Before we'd left England, I'd taken some Quell tablets to try to combat any travel sickness. I'd hoped they'd see me through to the second day but I was wrong. By the time we hit the storm, I had my head inside a brown paper bag because I couldn't stop being sick. The plane felt pathetic and lightweight against such a raging storm and we bobbed around like a cork in water.

'Why on earth did we agree to this?' I wailed to Nick. 'I hope we don't die out here, thousands of miles away from home!' I said, grabbing his hand for courage.

'It'll be fine, Pat. Try not to worry,' he said, although I could tell he was scared to death too.

It was only March but the plane had become red hot and it'd felt like an oven inside. It was the middle of the day but we could see the clouds being struck by lightning. They lit up all around us like baubles on a Christmas tree as thunder shook the sky.

'I wish I was back in Featherstone. What on earth possessed us to take this blasted journey?' I whined.

For the best part of an hour, the aeroplane continued to bounce up and down like a yo-yo. Eventually, though, we flew through the eye of the storm and into calmer skies. Some hours later, the plane dipped as we prepared to land at what looked like a glorified petrol station in the middle of the Sahara desert. All the performers were asked to disembark the plane and were taken to an area at the side where we sat down on woven rugs. Men wearing baggy trousers that fastened tightly around the ankle came over to serve us lemon tea in china cups. If I thought *The Good Old Days* Edwardian-themed audience had been bizarre, I realised I'd not lived because sipping tea in the middle of the Sahara desert had to be one of the most surreal things I'd ever done in my life. Still, I couldn't take my eyes off the men and their bizarre baggy trousers.

'Why do they wear those trousers?' I asked a member of the cabin crew as he settled down next to me. 'They're just so odd.'

'It's because they think the next saviour is coming,' he explained, taking a sip of his tea.

I listened to what he'd said and shook my head.

'Yes, but why do they wear those strange trousers?'

The man smiled. 'That's it, you see. Local folklore has it that the next saviour will be born of man, not woman.'

'Right, I see,' I said with a nod, although I didn't at all. 'But what has that got to do with the trousers?'

The man nodded. 'Well, they wear the trousers so that when he is born, he will be caught and won't fall onto the floor.'

I turned to look at him.

'Are you being serious?' I asked, half-expecting him to burst out laughing. But he didn't.

'Yes, I am. Well, that's how it's been told to me anyway.'

After that, I looked at the men differently. They were obviously deeply religious, and it wasn't up to me or anyone else for that matter to make judgements on what they did and didn't wear.

We boarded the plane and set off once more. My stomach lunged as we finally lifted off into the sky.

'I hope we don't hit another storm,' I whispered to Nick. 'I don't think my stomach can take it, not with all that lemon tea sloshing around inside.'

Several hours later, we arrived in Accra. As we stepped down onto the tarmac, a tall and authoritarian man called Major Brown met us. Major Brown worked in conjunction with Issy Bonn, which had gathered the entertainers together and devised the variety show. But it was down to the major to cover our expenses, including travel, accommodation and our wages.

'Good evening,' he said, holding out his arms to greet us as though we were his long-lost friends, 'and welcome to Africa!'

I looked all around me, but it was dark and so impossible to see the landscape. A bus picked us up and the major directed it and us to our hotel. Although we each had our own room, they were pretty basic, even by entertainers' standards. I ran my fingers along the mosquito net shrouding my bed and, to my dismay, discovered a few holes. I wondered what had happened to the last occupant of the bed and fretted that he'd died of malaria.

'It's not exactly the Hilton, is it?' I remarked to Nick, who'd helped me in with my case.

'It's work, Pat,' he said, lifting my bag onto the bed. 'And work is work.'

The show was due to open the following night at a club in Accra. The first evening was pretty uneventful and, although the place wasn't exactly packed to the rafters, the audience was extremely welcoming. I also spotted something else. That evening, we'd played to a sea of white faces – there were no Ghanaians to be seen.

'They must be all ex-pats,' I remarked to one of the other performers after we'd taken our final bow.

'Yes, but aren't we here to play to everyone?' she replied.

It struck me that she was absolutely right.

Nick and I performed two spots in the show, with the rest of the bill made up of variety performers. These included a comedy double act, a girl who did foot juggling, a couple of roller-skaters and the Coppa Cousins, although Greta had left the duo by this time.

As the first week progressed, the audience seemed to get thinner and thinner on the ground. It soon became obvious that there was no way the show could run for eight weeks. There wasn't a black face to be seen either. To make matters worse, we discovered the Ghanaians couldn't even afford the ticket price, which is why our audience had been predominantly white.

'I reckon there are more people on stage than in the audience,' I remarked.

Although I'd been joking, we were all worried about what would happen and who would pay our wages.

Sensing our frustration, the major secured us another booking in Kumasi, where we entertained men working in the gold mine. The only problem was that the booking only lasted three days.

'But what will we do after that?' I said to the rest of the cast.

By now, we were all beginning to feel uneasy. With no crowd, we knew there'd be no spare cash to pay our wages.

'The show isn't doing well because the Ghanaians can't afford to pay the extortionate ticket prices,' I remarked as we all sat discussing the problem backstage one night after the show. 'Yes, the ex-pats came to see us but how many times will they want to watch the same show?'

As we pondered our predicament, the major loomed into view.

'I've had a little bit of a brainwave,' he began. We all looked up at him, waiting to see what it was.

The major glanced over at an empty chair to the side of us.

'May I?' he asked.

'Be our guest,' I replied with a wave of my hand.

'The thing is ticket sales. The show hasn't been, erm, selling quite as well as I thought it would.'

'Tell us something we don't know,' one of the performers muttered under his breath.

The major looked up, took out a handkerchief from his top pocket and wiped his nose.

'Yes, quite,' he agreed. 'Anyway, the thing is, I think we should take the show to Nigeria!' he exclaimed. He threw his hands into the air with excitement, as though he was the bearer of good news. 'What do you all think? It's just that I'm certain I'll be able to secure some work there.'

Suddenly, the group was a buzz of excitement.

'Nigeria?' someone repeated. 'Well, if you think you can get us more work, why not!'

Soon everyone was chattering away, ready to pack their bags at any moment.

'Hang on a minute,' I said, raising my hand to stop them.

The major turned around in his chair. He seemed a little crestfallen when he realised that I wasn't quite as enamoured by his brilliant plan.

'But Nigeria. It's not Ghana, is it?'

The major shook his head.

'Yes, but the thing is—'

I cut him off mid-sentence.

'But my contract – in fact, all our contracts – cover us from London to Ghana, not Ghana and Nigeria. In fact, Nigeria isn't mentioned anywhere.'

'And your point is what precisely, young lady?'

'My point is this. If you take us to Nigeria, we will no longer be in Ghana, which would relieve you of your duty and responsibility to get us all a safe passage back to London.'

A few of the other artistes had stopped chattering and had turned to listen. Some had nodded their heads but the majority had seemed angry with me. They didn't want me to scupper their chance of some profitable work. After all, if we didn't work, we didn't get paid.

'Are you saying you won't go?' one asked.

'Yes, that's exactly what I'm saying.'

Some of the cast became cross because the show had included us all and, without one, you couldn't have the other.

'You're going to ruin this for the rest of us, Pat.'

But I didn't care. My main priority was to get us all back to London, as agreed.

I walked over towards Nick.

'Are you mad at me?'

'Not mad. I'm just disappointed,' he replied. 'But I understand where you're coming from. I'm just worried what we're going to do for money.'

After much discussion, it was eventually agreed that we would all stay in Accra and, more importantly, in Ghana.

Deep down, Nick and the others knew I was right. Our contract with the major had been issued by Equity, the performers union, so we knew it was watertight. We also knew we'd get back to England eventually. The issue right now was where would we live and how would we feed ourselves.

With no audience to fill the theatre, the show was eventually cancelled and the major stopped paying our wages, just as I had feared. Thankfully, some ex-pats took pity on us and offered us a place to stay until we could get something more permanent sorted. I'd only taken £10 to Africa. My plan was to receive a percentage of my wage with the rest being paid directly into my bank account back home. But with no income and my spending money all gone, I was brassy broke and unsure what to do. One of the ex-pat families – a couple from Liverpool – had offered to put a few of us up in their home. The couple had a young daughter, so I offered to babysit because I wanted to try to repay their kind hospitality.

'Are you sure, Pat?' the mother asked me.

'Absolutely. It's the least I can do after everything you've done for us.'

By now, we were pretty desperate and wondered how we'd survive the coming weeks without pay.

One day, I was sat at home, moping around, when I had a brainwave. I called the variety troupe together and explained my plan. A journalist called Derrick Webster, who worked for a news agency called Reuters, had heard about us and had tracked us down. He wanted to do an exclusive interview so that's exactly what we did.

'Is it true that you're all stranded out here?' he asked, taking out his notebook and pen.

'Yes,' I replied.

Derrick asked how we'd ended up in such a dire situation, so I explained about the show and why it'd been cancelled.

'So you've had absolutely no wages?' he said, writing it down.

'We did to start with but, once the show was cancelled, the money stopped. All we have left is our plane tickets home but that's weeks away.'

'So what will you do?'

'I haven't a clue,' I said, throwing my hands up in despair.

It was true: no one knew quite how we would manage to survive the coming weeks. But I did know that, no matter how generous the ex-pats had been, we couldn't expect to live off their goodwill forever.

Derrick wished us well. He explained that he'd write up our story and, hopefully, manage to place it in a newspaper. To our astonishment, the story appeared in the *Daily Mirror*. The entertainments manager of a hotel at Accra airport had read about our stranded troupe and called us to a meeting. He had a proposal.

'So, what you're saying is you'd like us to perform here, free of charge, but you will give us a free roof over our heads. Is that right?' I said as we all crowded into his office.

'We'd also provide all your meals too,' he insisted. 'After all, you've got to eat!'

'All right,' I said with a smile, looking around the room at my fellow performers, who all nodded in agreement. 'In that case, we'd love to take you up on your offer. Thank you!'

'You've got yourself a deal,' one of the other performers said, stepping forward. He took the manager's hand and gave it a grateful shake and, one by one, we all shook on the deal.

'Great. When can you start?'

'Tomorrow?'

The following evening we played to a packed out hotel. It

had seemed everyone had read our story and had all turned up to show their support. The floor show was a great success. We decided to work out a variation to the programme so that the audience wouldn't see the same show every time. Thankfully, our plan not only worked but it kept bums on seats. We continued to change the show until the date of our return flight grew closer.

A few days later, I was lounging around the hotel pool when I spotted Derrick heading towards me.

'Hello, Pat,' he said, shaking my hand. 'Mind if I sit down next to you?'

'No, Derrick, please do,' I said, waving my hand towards an empty chair.

'Hey, I didn't know you were engaged,' he said, spying my engagement ring.

I glanced down at the diamond ring on my wedding finger. Both England and my fiancé seemed a million miles away.

'Yes, I became engaged just before I came to Africa,' I explained.

'So who's the lucky man?'

I told him all about Phil and our whirlwind romance.

'So he quite literally swept you up off your feet?'

I laughed.

'Yes, I suppose you could say that.'

'I bet you can't wait to get back to England to see him? I mean, you must miss him, being so far away from home.'

I nodded my head and looked down.

'I do, yes. But as long as we continue to sing and dance for our supper, we'll be all right.'

Derrick chuckled, but he was determined he wasn't leaving

without a good story. I also realised how powerful publicity could be, especially when you were a performer. Getting your face in the paper was like gold dust because there was no such thing as bad publicity in the show business world.

'So,' Derrick said, pointing at my engagement ring, 'would you sell your engagement ring to catch a flight back home?'

I looked at the ring and thought of Mam and Dad waiting for me back in Featherstone.

'Yes, I think I would.'

He listened, thought for a moment, and asked if he could send a photographer later that morning to take a photograph of me.

'Whatever for?' I asked.

'Your story, of course.'

Hours later, I was standing showing off my engagement ring as the photographer took lots of pictures of me. My story, as Derrick had put it, was that I'd sell my ring to get safe passage home and back into the arms of my loving fiancé.

'Pat, could you look a bit sadder?' the photographer suddenly chipped in, breaking my thoughts. He shifted his head out from behind the lens. 'It's just that you're supposed to be stranded out here.'

'Yes, right. Sorry,' I said, pulling the saddest face I could muster.

Back home, I was painted as a waif and stray – an innocent Yorkshire lass lost on the other side of the world. In reality, I was actually rather enjoying my enforced holiday, sunbathing on a beautiful West African beach and enjoying a daily swim in the cool blue sea.

Unbeknown to me, thousands of miles away in rainy Yorkshire, my uncle Alfred, Mam's brother, was passing on his way to work for the local gas board when he spotted a poster advertising the day's newspaper.

YORKSHIRE DANCER STRANDED IN AFRICA, the headline screamed.

'Bloody hell, I 'ope that's not our Pat,' he mumbled as he nipped inside quickly to buy a copy.

To his horror, he spotted a photograph of my sad face staring out at him from the front page. Alf drew a sharp intake of breath and hotfooted it straight round to my house.

''Ere, Sarah. Your Pat's on front of t'newspaper,' he said, showing her a copy.

Mam let out a shriek of horror and promptly fell back down into her chair.

'Go and get our George. He's just down t' road,' she sobbed as she read the story of her daughter, stranded thousands of miles away in Africa.

Mam and Dad couldn't afford a telephone, but I'd written to them telling them not to worry if they read a story in the newspaper. Unfortunately, the post was slow and my letter hadn't reached Featherstone. With no letter, Mam was absolutely frantic. By the end of the day, it'd seemed the whole of Featherstone had read the paper and my story. Concerned neighbours and friends flooded into the family home to check what the latest news was.

'Come 'ere,' Aunt Alice had said, taking Mam in her arms and trying to soothe her. 'Yer know Pat. She'll be fine. She's a survivor, Sarah, just like you and George.'

But Aunt Alice's words had fallen on deaf ears because my mother was convinced she'd never see me again. Soon the whole of Yorkshire was rooting for me. The Featherstone pensioners had called an emergency meeting at the local church so they could hold special prayers. Meanwhile, the children at my old grammar school had held an assembly so that they could pray for my safe and swift return.

Back home, the newspapers, not wanting to miss out on the scoop, approached my fiancé, Phil, to ask for a comment.

'If Pat has to sell the ring, yes, I think she should,' he insisted as photographers jostled around him, trying to take his picture. 'All I want is for her to be back home, safe and sound.'

At the end of what should have been a simple showbiz tour, by the time our plane touched down on the tarmac in London, we were greeted by what can only be described as a media scrum. Everyone, it seemed, wanted my story – the poor Yorkshire girl, stranded thousands of miles from home.

Of course, Phil was also waiting in the arrivals lounge, along with his parents.

'Give her a kiss, Phil. Go on,' the photographers called out, trying to get a front-page picture of the reunited sweethearts.

With reporters waiting to speak to me, I gave my story freely. After that, things settled down and suddenly I became yesterday's news.

With no money and nowhere else to go, I stayed with Phil's parents. Once I'd managed to scrape enough spare cash together, I caught a train home to see Mam and Dad.

'Come 'ere, our Pat,' she said, hugging me for all I was worth.

'My little lass,' Dad said, unpeeling Mam's arms so he could have a hug.

'You 'ad us all worried. Yer mam's been sick wi' worry.'

Mam dabbed tears from her eyes.

'I nearly died when our Alf brought t'paper round,' she said, filling me in on what had happened. 'Then I got yer letter, so I knew yer were all right. But yer almost frightened me to death. Never, ever do that to me again!' She scolded, wagging her finger at me as though I were still a child.

'I won't, Mam. Promise.'

Moments later, there was a knock at the door. It was Aunt Alice.

'I've come to see t'adventurer. Is she in?' she said, running over to give me a hug.

'Here, let's see this famous engagement ring then,' she asked, grabbing my hand in hers. 'Oh, int it lovely? Well, yer had me, yer dad and yer poor mam scared to death. But it's good to 'ave yer back home, Pat.'

For the rest of the day, the kettle remained on permanent boil as neighbours and friends called round to hear about my African adventure. Suddenly, I'd become a local celebrity, although not for the right reasons.

After a week, it was time to return to London to look for work.

'Promise me no more daft trips,' Mam insisted as she held me tight and kissed me goodbye at Featherstone train station.

'Promise,' I said.

I meant it.

With no income, I remained living at Phil's parents' house. In the meantime, I signed on the dole and tried to look for work.

One day, I spotted an advert for a local beauty-queen competition. I entered and, to my delight, I won not only the crown but the £20 cash prize. The money kept me afloat as I waited for my next big break.

In the end, I was offered two jobs. One was a contract to dance at the prestigious Pigalle – a top London nightclub – but the contract was for me alone and not Nick. It didn't feel right, so I accepted the second gig – a summer season in Weymouth as choreographer and principal dancer. Although I'd been tempted by Pigalle, I chose the latter because I was loyal to Nick and the act we'd worked so hard to perfect. It turned out to be the best decision of my life because, unbeknown to me, I was about to meet the love of my life.

CHAPTER 12

GET ME TO THE CHURCH ON TIME

With the Weymouth job pending, I returned to Miss Bell and the Theatre Girls Club for a couple of weeks so that I could rehearse.

'Nice to see you back, Patricia,' Miss Bell smiled as soon as I opened the door. 'So, how long do you intend to stay this time?'

'Oh, only a couple of weeks,' I said, putting my case on the floor. I walked over to the reception desk and signed my name in the book. 'It's just until I start my next show.'

Miss Bell nodded and showed me to my dormitory.

The following day, we started rehearsals at a theatre in London. I was told we'd be helping out with the choreography for the show, mainly working with the chorus-line girls. The cast were lovely and I couldn't wait to sort out the routines. That same morning, we were introduced to some of the other principals for the big production numbers. Top of the bill was a Welsh comedian called Johnny Stewart. Johnny had just come fresh from performing in *Sunday Night at the London Palladium*. The new line-up for Weymouth had also included stars such as Jack Douglas, Joe Baker and a Scottish female comedienne and impressionist called Janet Brown. Janet later went on to become famous for her impressions of Margaret Thatcher, England's first female prime minister.

'Hello, I'm Johnny. Johnny Stewart,' a dark-haired man with a Welsh lilt in his voice said. He stepped forward, took my hand and shook it. 'Do you remember me?'

I was a little confused until he explained that we'd met once before, while I was staying at digs in Hackney.

'The face looks familiar,' I remarked, 'and not just from the television.'

'Aunty Ada's house,' he said, trying to jog my memory.

Then I remembered. Before I'd left for Africa, I'd briefly stayed over at a boarding house in London. The landlady had been a lovely, warm Jewish lady. She was an eccentric and the theatricals had loved her, giving her the nickname Aunty Ada.

'Ah, yes, that's it! I remember now,' I replied. 'I think we met over dinner.'

'Yes, we did,' Johnny said, smiling straight back at me. It made me blush.

I momentarily scolded myself. It was obvious he was a terrible flirt and a real charmer.

Pat Wilson, you are an engaged woman! I thought.

As if reading my mind, Johnny's hand came to a halt as he felt the engagement ring on my finger.

'Ah, I see you're already taken,' he remarked. 'Shucks, I guess I'm too late!'

I was a little taken aback, but I couldn't be sure if he was being honest or just playing for a laugh. He was, after all, a comedian.

'Now then, about this routine,' I said, trying to change the subject.

Nick and I helped Johnny with a scene called the Viennese, where he sang the 'Drinking Song' in a beautiful tenor voice. I could tell that he loved this particular routine because swathes of girls would swirl around the stage in front of him as he sang.

Soon it was time to leave for Weymouth. Nick and I, and three chorus girls, had booked to stay in a boarding house close to the theatre, which was situated on the seafront. Once in Weymouth, we continued with rehearsals. Each morning, as soon as I arrived at the theatre, Johnny would be waiting for me to try to charm his way into my affections.

'So,' he said, standing by the entrance as I walked through the door one morning. 'When are you going to let me take you out, Pat?'

I put a hand to my mouth and pretended to think about it.

'Hmm, now, let me see. Never?' I quipped, walking away.

'Aww, don't be like that.'

It made me smile. Secretly, I was sweet on Johnny Stewart, but I was still only twenty-two and he was nine years older. They say that with age comes confidence and Johnny certainly had that – by the bucket load. Many found it endearing, but I felt completely intimidated and out of my depth. In spite of my stage persona, I was still a shy Yorkshire lass trying to find herself in the big, wide world. Still, if I wasn't going to go out with him, I'd make sure no one else would either.

'If Johnny Stewart asks any of you out, you are to say no,' I instructed the chorus girls. 'This is a professional show and we can't have people flirting on stage.'

The dancers nodded their heads. I was not only the show's chorographer; I was also the principal dancer. It was typical female logic on my part. For some reason, I didn't want to see any of the other dancers on his arm either. In spite of my own advice, I soon found myself falling for the charms of Johnny Stewart.

'Go on, let me take you out, Pat,' Johnny asked whenever we danced together.

'Not a chance, buster,' I would say, laughing and pretending to bop him on the nose as we practised together on stage.

'Why not? What's wrong with me?' he asked on one occasion.

In truth, there was nothing wrong with him. Absolutely nothing – that was the problem.

'You're a married man,' I declared.

I remembered overhearing someone say that Johnny had once been married.

'Divorced,' he corrected, pointing down at his ringless finger. 'Besides, it was an awful long time ago.'

'Yes, but I'm engaged,' I added, pointing towards the ring on my own finger.

And so the pattern continued until, in the end, Johnny decided to change tactics.

One day, I was in the dressing room when I heard the chorus girls giggling.

'Yes, he asked me out too but I said no,' one girl whispered to another.

'Who?' I said, immediately turning around in my chair. 'Who asked you out?'

'Johnny Stewart,' the dancer replied. 'But don't worry, we both said no.'

I felt my heart sink to my knees and that's when I realised – I was in love with Johnny.

'I can't understand it,' he said one night as he waited in the wings, ready to go on stage.

'Understand what?' I said.

'No one will go out to dinner with me. I keep getting the cold shoulder from all the girls. What's wrong with me, Pat?'

I stifled a smile.

'Oh, nothing, I'm sure.'

'So what about you? Won't you let me take you out to dinner? Go on, it'll be fun – just the two of us.'

I realised I'd been a complete fool and had denied my feelings for Johnny.

'Go on then,' I said, giving him a nudge with my elbow.

Johnny shook his head in surprise.

'Was that a yes?'

I nodded.

'Yes, it was a yes.'

Although I'd agreed to a dinner the following evening, Johnny's confidence still frightened me to death. I'd felt so intimidated by him that, by the following evening, I knew I had to get out of it. Standing in the stage wings, I began to yawn. It was enough for him to notice.

'Tired?' Johnny asked as he came off stage.

'Yes. I'm exhausted. Listen, do you mind if I cancel for tonight?'

'No, that's fine,' said Johnny, although he looked disappointed.

'It's just that I think I'd like an early night.'

'No, I quite understand,' he replied.

But I immediately regretted my decision.

A few nights later, Johnny and I had performed on stage together. It was a simple routine, where Johnny played my stage lover, with Jack Douglas taking the part of my husband. At the end of the sketch, Johnny had to lean forward and kiss me. Up until that point, it had always been a 'stage' kiss. However, that evening, instead of pretending, Johnny grabbed hold of me and kissed me full on the mouth – in front of a packed theatre! The kiss had left me breathless.

'That was a bit sly,' I whispered from the corner of my mouth as we bowed to rapturous applause.

'I know, but a fella's got to take his chances when he can,' he said, still facing towards the crowd.

As we exited the stage, Johnny asked me out to dinner again. This time I accepted. I'd decided that I didn't want to fight my feelings for him any longer. Of course, the other girls laughed when they realised I'd been in love with Johnny all along. Everyone could see that we were completely right together. It had just been me who had needed a little extra persuasion.

I was still engaged to Phil but, deep down, I knew I'd never marry him. A week or so later, Phil had travelled down to Weymouth to see me. Unfortunately, as he stood there waiting at the stage door, I pulled up outside in Johnny's car. Phil looked over at Johnny and Johnny looked over at Phil. I knew in my heart of hearts what I had to do, so I stepped out of the car, pulled the engagement ring from my wedding finger and went over to speak to him.

'I'm so sorry, Phil, but I can't marry you. Here,' I said placing the ring in the palm of his hand. 'I'm so sorry.'

'But, Patty...' Phil began as I turned to walk away.

I stopped in my tracks and turned back towards him. 'I'm sorry, Phil, but I don't love you.'

'But, Patty,' he cried and it made me cringe.

'And please don't call me Patty. I've always hated it.'

I felt like a complete cow, but I knew I had to break his heart in order for him to move on. I'd already decided that I wanted to spend the rest of my life with Johnny, and I knew that Phil, or anyone else for that matter, couldn't do anything to change that.

A few weeks later, Johnny was reading the newspaper when he stumbled across a story written about an old friend of his – an Irish singer called Ruby Murray. Johnny told me that Ruby had got married to one of her fellow performers, who she'd been starring in a show with.

'Maybe we should do the same,' I remarked, raising a quizzical eyebrow.

Johnny looked down at the newspaper, closed it and folded it up in his hands. He looked up at me, a smile playing across his lips.

'All right then, let's get married!'

My head spun around to face his.

'Was that a marriage proposal, Johnny Stewart?' I shrieked.

Johnny shrugged his shoulders. 'I suppose it was.'

We went down to the register office on Monday afternoon and arranged to be married just two days later, on the Wednesday. But there was a problem. The registrar had seemed concerned when Johnny explained he'd been married.

'But I'm divorced now,' he explained.

'Can I see your decree nisi?' the registrar asked him.

Johnny and I looked at him blankly.

'Er, I don't think I have one,' Johnny replied. 'Even if I did have, I wouldn't have a clue where to find it.'

'But you're definitely divorced?' the registrar asked.

'Definitely.'

'In that case, I'll need to see your decree nisi before your wedding day.'

I was confused. I didn't understand what a decree nisi was and why we needed one.

'But what if we haven't got it?' I asked.

The registrar sat back in his chair and tapped his finger against a pile of papers on his desk.

'If I don't have Mr Stewart's decree nisi on my desk before Wednesday, I'm afraid you can't get married.'

I put a hand to my mouth and gasped.

'What, you mean it'll stop the wedding?'

The registrar nodded grimly.

'I need it to prove that Mr Stewart is divorced and not about to commit bigamy.'

Johnny slumped back in his chair. He looked totally defeated. But I wasn't.

'All right, so where can we get a copy of it?' I said.

'Somerset House,' the registrar said. He sifted through a pile of papers. 'If you wait a moment, I should be able to find an address for you.'

We left his office with a provisional wedding date for the coming Wednesday. I crossed my fingers that the relevant paperwork would arrive in time and on Wednesday morning, Johnny and I dashed over to the theatre to see if there was a letter for us.

'It's very important,' I insisted, as the front-of-house manager flicked through the morning's post.

'This one says it's for a Johnny Stewart,' he finally said.

'That's me,' Johnny replied, taking the envelope from the manager's hand.

'I feel sick,' I remarked, holding a hand against my throat. 'I hope this is it.'

I watched as Johnny ripped open the brown paper envelope and pulled out the letter. My eyes scoured his face, waiting for a reaction as he read and re-read it.

'What is it, Johnny? Have they sent it through?' I asked. My heart beat furiously as I waited for him to speak.

'This is it!' he said, holding the letter aloft. 'It's my decree nisi, Pat!'

With that, he scooped me up in his arms and twirled me around as I threw my head back and laughed.

'Pat Wilson, will you marry me today?' Johnny asked, planting my feet back down on the ground.

Tears of relief flooded my eyes and then it dawned on me.

THE GIRL IN THE SPOTTY DRESS

'I'll need to go into town first. We're getting married at two o'clock and I haven't got a thing to wear!' I grinned as tears of happiness streamed down my face.

Johnny took the decree nisi to the registry office to confirm the wedding, while I washed my hair in the theatre's dressing room. I then nipped into town, where I bought myself a beautiful blue corduroy dress. It was hardly a wedding dress but, with its nipped-in waist, as soon as I pulled it on, I felt a million dollars. I didn't care that it wasn't a white dress or that we weren't getting married in a church – all that mattered was I was about to marry the love of my life.

At 2pm Johnny and I walked into the register office and a little while later we emerged as Mr and Mrs Stewart. It was 3 September 1956. We'd needed two independent witnesses, so Johnny had popped outside and dragged in a poor unsuspecting couple off the street. Three hours later, we were back at the theatre in time for the afternoon matinee. We hadn't told a soul what we'd just done, but someone must have spotted my wedding ring because, after the show ended, Jack Douglas, my 'on-stage' husband, had an announcement to make.

Jack stepped forward from the line as the three of us took our bow. Johnny and I glanced at one another because we knew it wasn't in the script and, for a moment, we thought he'd gone quite mad.

'What's he doing?' I whispered to Johnny.

'Search me.'

Jack raised his hands and waved them down in a bid to quieten the audience and the applause.

'Ladies and gentlemen,' he began as a hush descended across the theatre. 'You've been a fantastic audience. Thank you so much for coming along to tonight's performance. We really hope that you've enjoyed it. Now, if it's all right with you, I have an announcement to make. We've just discovered that Johnny has just married the lovely Pat this afternoon. They thought we didn't know but we all noticed the ring on her finger. Now I'm sure you would all like to join me in wishing the happy couple all our love and success for the future.'

The Gardens Pavilion in Weymouth erupted as members of the audience began to stand, cheer and whistle in celebration. Soon, everyone was on their feet, clapping wildly. Johnny and I stepped forward into the spotlight to take another bow. It's rare that I'm ever lost for words but, at that moment, I was speechless. Remarkably, and for the first time ever, so was Johnny.

CHAPTER 13

THE BEVERLEY SISTERS AND THE FAR EAST

The following day, I sat down and wrote a letter to my parents. 'Dear Mam and Dad,' I began, the pen poised in my hand as Johnny sat by my side.

I turned to him.

'How on earth am I going break it to them that their only daughter has gone off and got married without a word?'

'Here, give me the pen,' he said and sighed. 'What do you want me to write?'

'I just think I need to tell them that I'm absolutely certain we've done the right thing and that I hope they'll feel as happy as I do right now.'

Johnny passed the pen back to me.

'I think this is something you need to do, Pat.'

He was right, of course. In the end, I explained that it would have been pointless for Johnny and I to wait because we were always so busy performing. Also, we'd never be able to plan a big, white wedding because we never knew where we would be.

'Do you think it's all right?' I asked, handing him the letter.

Johnny read it and nodded.

'I think it's perfect. It says all it needs to say.'

If I had thought my parents would be upset, I was wrong. Instead, they jumped on a train and travelled all the way down to Weymouth to meet their new son-in-law. Thankfully, they got on with him like a house on fire and welcomed Johnny with open arms.

'Come on, lad.' Dad said, giving him a friendly slap on the back. 'Let me buy yer a pint t'welcome you t'family properly.'

Mam and Dad stayed for a week or so before catching the train back home.

'Yer better look after her!' Mam said, wagging her finger at Johnny before they left.

Johnny circled an arm around my waist and smiled back at her.

'I will. I promise!'

Sadly, I'd decided that, now I was a married woman, my dancing career with Nick had to come to an end. I knew I couldn't continue to chase jobs up and down the country because I wanted to be with Johnny.

'I'm sorry Nick,' I said. 'The last thing I expected when I came to Weymouth was to end up a married woman.'

Nick was disappointed but very understanding.

'It's all right, Pat. You and Johnny are made for one another – anyone can see that. I wish you all the best for the future.'

'But what will you do?' I asked, feeling guilty that our duo would be over once the show had come to an end.

'I'll just audition for another girl.'

So that's what he did. When the season had finally ended, I hugged Nick and wished him well. It felt sad to be saying goodbye, but I knew in my heart of hearts this part of my dancing career was over for good.

A few weeks later, I received a letter with an offer for me to star in pantomime. A lady called Gladys Laidler, who was a very famous principal boy at the time, had sent it. Gladys was married to Francis Laidler, who was well respected for his pantomime productions. I'd actually worked for him many years before when I'd been a chorus girl in my first show at Leeds.

'Where's the pantomime?' Johnny asked when I told him about the job offer.

'It's at the Bradford Alhambra.'

'It's a good theatre, Pat,' he replied, although I could tell he didn't want us to be parted any more than I did. 'What's the part?' he asked, breaking my thoughts.

'She wants to offer me the part of the cat,' I said glancing down at the letter. 'It's for *Puss in Boots*.'

Johnny nodded his head grimly.

'That's a good part too,' he agreed.

'I know,' I said, resting the letter down on the table in my dressing room. 'It's a part I've always wanted to play,' I sighed.

I jokingly slapped my thigh in a puss-in-boots style. It made Johnny laugh.

'But I can't take it,' I decided.

'Why ever not?'

I held him close and planted a kiss on his lips.

'Because I've got a new role – here with you. I'm your wife, Johnny, and I can't think of a part I'd rather play.'

After we'd married, Johnny and I had discussed working and living apart. We both knew the only way our marriage would survive the tough world of show business would be if we worked together as a team. I could have been offered the best spot at the London Palladium, but I wouldn't have been tempted because wild horses couldn't drag me from Johnny's side. Instead, I decided to become Johnny's personal assistant. I made phone calls, chased agents and dealt with all his business enquiries. He even asked me to help write comedy scripts for him.

'But I don't have a clue how to write a script,' I gasped, thinking he'd lost the plot.

'It doesn't matter, Pat. You've been in pantomimes all your life and they are the most heavily scripted pieces of theatre out there.'

A writer for a proposed show would send over a basic script to us, and we would write in all of Johnny's entrances. He'd come up with the gags, while I helped with the choreography and his movements on stage.

'No, you need to be more over to the left when you say that line,' I'd say, directing him from the stalls.

Johnny also tried out all his new gags on me first.

'You can help me fine-tune them,' he explained.

After the season at Weymouth, Johnny was called to perform in a show out in Cyprus for the troops. He'd signed the contract long before we'd married, so he had to honour it. Johnny would be working for Combined Services Entertainment (CSE for short). The CSE was the modern equivalent of ENSA (Entertainments National Service Association) and rehearsals would take place in the War Office. The office was based in a large baroque-type building, which was on Horse Guards Avenue at its junction with Whitehall, in central London.

The building was oddly shaped, with four distinctive domes that contained over 1,000 rooms across seven floors. It was in one of these rooms that the cast practised, and I helped with the choreography. After a few weeks, the cast flew out to Cyprus. I felt at a loose end, so I decided to return home to see my parents in Featherstone. Johnny was away for six weeks and I missed him dreadfully. It was the first time we'd been apart and I felt as though my right arm had been ripped off.

'Don't worry, love. He'll soon be back,' Mam said, trying her best to lift my spirits.

But nothing could. I was lovesick and counting down the days until Johnny came home.

Finally, he landed at a military airport and we met up in London.

'I've got a surprise. Shut your eyes, Pat,' Johnny said.

I did as I was told.

'Right, you can open them,' he said, dangling a key in front of my face.

'But what's it for?' I asked, taking the large silver key from his hand.

'Our first home – just me and you. It's not much – just a bedsit in Kilburn – but it'll suit us just fine.

The bedsit had belonged to one of the old theatricals, who had rented it out to supplement his retirement fund. It was basic by today's standards and situated at the top of an old Victorian building. We rented our own television but, other than that, the room was almost empty, with only a chest of drawers, a wardrobe, a cooker and a bed. It also had a vacuum cleaner but that blew out more dirt than it ever picked up. Still, at last we had somewhere we could call home.

The War Office and CSE offered Johnny another gig, but this time I was given the job of show choreographer. Although there was no dancing involved, management wanted movement both on and off stage to be as fluid as possible. The tour would take us to the Far East – a land I'd only ever dreamed of. At last, I was working for ENSA. I thought back to all those times as a child when I'd sit and tune into the shows on the radio. I'd hoped one day I'd be able to work for ENSA and now I finally could. It felt like a dream come true.

Johnny and I flew out to Singapore from a military airport just outside London a week before Christmas, in 1956. There were no long-haul flights, so we stopped off in Spain before continuing our journey to the Far East. The tour was booked to run for eight weeks, which meant we got to spend New Year's Eve in Malaya. The shows weren't quite as frequent as we would have liked because the troops were out on manoeuvres, so Johnny suggested we all go to watch an Australian singer, who was performing in a cabaret at one of the city's five-star hotels.

'She's supposed to be very good,' he said.

The cast agreed, gathered their things and we all headed over there.

The singer had a beautiful voice, just as Johnny had said. Back then, I didn't drink alcohol at all. However, I'd decided I was looking a little on the thin side and someone had told me Guinness was a quick way to put a bit of weight on. With this in mind, I ordered half a pint. I gulped it down quickly but it had soon gone to my head. The singer took her place behind the microphone and sang something I knew. It had a good beat, so I jumped up on the table and began to dance along. I don't remember much else about it, but Johnny later told me I'd gone down a storm.

'Please tell me I didn't do it,' I whined the following morning.

I rubbed my head. I had the mother of all hangovers.

'All right, you didn't do it.' Johnny laughed.

It took all the effort I had, but I lifted my head from the pillow and looked up at him through squinted eyes.

'Didn't I?'

Johnny smirked.

'Yes, of course you did. But everyone loved you, Pat!'

I threw a pillow at him. Sadly, I missed.

I'd been as drunk as a skunk and everyone had seen. I felt absolutely mortified and vowed never to touch the black stuff ever again.

We were performing in Singapore when someone asked if Johnny and I would like to go and visit families living in the poorer areas. It was explained that a visit by a TV star like Johnny would not only highlight their plight but would also bring more funds and aid to the country. We were walking around meeting the families when a friendly journalist approached me. After Derrick Webster had kindly helped rescue me and the rest of the troupe in Africa, I considered all journalists to be my friends. However, this one was different. Within minutes, he'd struck up a conversation and we started to chat away. Later that day, Johnny and I were introduced to a family who were struggling because they had triplets. The three baby girls were absolutely gorgeous, but their parents were desperately poor.

'It's so sad,' I said to Johnny, cradling one of the poor little mites in my arms.

The reporter had overheard and came over towards me.

'They're lovely, aren't they, Pat?' he remarked.

I nodded. Each girl was identical, from their tiny toes to their cute button noses.

'Would you adopt them, if you could?' the reporter asked as I cradled one of the babies in my arms.

I thought of the hardship and poverty they faced. Suddenly, I felt gripped by a maternal instinct to protect.

'Yes,' I said, holding the baby tight. 'Of course I would.'

'Any chance we could get a picture of you and Johnny holding the babies?' The reporter asked as a photographer zoomed forward from the shadows to take it.

Within days, the journalist had written the story up for the *Daily Sketch*. Once again, I appeared on the front page, announcing that I'd like to adopt the poor triplets. Of course, it had been an off-the-cuff remark I'd made in the heat of the moment. There was no way I wanted to take three babies away from their mother, but the reporter didn't let the facts get in the way of a good story.

COMEDIAN AND HIS WIFE VOW TO ADOPT POOR TRIPLETS AND BRING THEM HOME! the headline screamed, but I was still thousands of miles from home, so I didn't have a clue about my part in the breaking story.

A few weeks later, just before we flew home, we were browsing around the shops when we came to a halt outside one that sold portable camera equipment.

'Let's go inside and have a look,' I suggested, glancing over at the cameras in the window.

'What for?' Johnny asked.

'That,' I said, pointing over at the portable camera. 'Imagine if we were able to film our own shows. Wouldn't that be marvellous?'

Back in England, home filming had only just begun to take off, but it had already been widely available for a number of years in the Far East. In England, portable cameras cost a small fortune but were only a fraction of the price in Singapore. After a bit of bartering with the shopkeeper, we left the store with a portable camera, lens and a screen.

'But how will we get all this stuff home?' Johnny asked, looking at all the bags in our hands.

I tapped the side of my nose.

'Don't worry, I've got a plan.'

Back at the hotel, I packed the electronic equipment inside the padding of my stage costumes.

'But what if we get caught going through customs?' Johnny said, beginning to panic.

'Don't be daft. We won't.'

We landed back in England and sailed through customs with nothing to declare. But I could've killed Johnny. He had such a guilty face that he'd almost given the game away. Once we'd cleared customs, we boarded the coach along with the rest of the troupe. We were just about to set off when we heard a voice over the airport's loudspeaker.

'Could a Mr and Mrs Stewart please return to customs,' the voice announced.

Johnny's head spun to face me.

'Bloody hell, Pat, we've been rumbled! I knew we shouldn't have brought all that stuff home.'

The rest of the cast looked worried too. They were all in on the secret and knew all about my stowed-away portable camera.

'Oh, my God!' I said, my heart pounding ten to the dozen. 'We've been discovered!'

Johnny and I warily approached the customs man. To be truthful, we were half-expecting to be handcuffed at any moment. Instead, he handed us a note.

'What does it say?' I said, trying to read over Johnny's shoulder.

He looked up at me and, without warning, began to laugh out loud.

'It says, "Please could you not leave the airport because there are press men wanting to speak to you."'

I looked up at the customs man.

'But what is it about? What do they want with us?' I asked.

'The triplets,' he replied.

I pulled a puzzled face.

'The triplets out in Singapore. The ones you said you wanted to adopt. It's been in all the papers. Why, haven't you seen it?'

Suddenly, the penny dropped. I looked up at Johnny and we both dissolved into a fit of laughter.

The customs man looked at us as though we were completely mad.

'Well, thank god for that!' Johnny said, clutching at his heart.

We gave a full and frank interview to the waiting press and told them that we had absolutely no desire to adopt someone else's triplets.

'We haven't even had children of our own yet,' I said, winking at Johnny.

After we'd returned home, Johnny was offered more work through his agent Keith Devon. Although he was part of a larger agency, Keith was the sole agent to Johnny, a comedian called Ted Rogers, who later went on to present a popular show on TV called *3-2-1*, and the Beverley Sisters. Keith had offered Johnny some work in a variety show, performing at Finsbury Park, and other London theatres alongside the Beverley Sisters.

The eldest sister was Joy and she was, as her name had suggested, a joy to be around. We hit it off immediately and soon became very good friends. Joy had married a footballer called Billy Wright, who was the team captain for England. Billy also played for Wolverhampton Wanderers, so we ended up doing a show with the Sisters at the town's theatre. Billy and Joy were always together and theirs was a match made in heaven. The Bevs also included the twins Barbette (or Babs for short) and Teddie. All three were lovely to work with.

THE GIRL IN THE SPOTTY DRESS

The theatrical circuit was a community within a community. Most of the big names had come from working-class backgrounds just like mine. Although they were rich and famous on stage, off it they were the most down-to-earth, honest folk you could ever hope to meet. And that's precisely what the Bevs were. In all the years that Johnny worked alongside them, they never once let fame or fortune go to their heads. Instead, they remained friendly and approachable, particularly to the younger performers trying to get a foot on the showbiz ladder. I always thought that this marked out who the true stars really were.

CHAPTER 14

SHOW ON
THE ROAD

A few months after the shows with the Beverley Sisters, I
started being sick at home.

'Still not feeling right?' Johnny said, holding me gently as my
head hung over the toilet bowl.

I groaned.

'No, I reckon I must have picked up a flu bug or something.
I'm going to call in at the doctor's surgery later today.'

A few hours later, I walked into the GP's surgery, where I took
a seat and waited to be seen. There were a few people in front
of me, but back then doctors operated a first-come, first-served
service, so you had to sit and wait your turn.

Johnny and I were living back at Auntie Ada's house in
Hackney, so I didn't know the doctor at all – he just happened to
be the nearest one. When it was my turn, I stood up, knocked on
his door and entered the room.

'So, what seems to be the problem Mrs...'

'Stewart,' I replied. 'I've recently got married,' I said, showing him my wedding ring.

'Congratulations. So, tell me, what is it that I can do for you today?'

My shoulders slumped as I began to explain all about my awful sickness.

'I don't know what it is, Doctor. I just can't stop throwing up.'

He leaned back in his chair and listened to me reel off my symptoms. Then he told me to get undressed behind the curtain.

'Why? Do you think it's something serious?' I asked, disappearing off behind the curtain. I was naïve, and I didn't have a clue what was going on.

What the doctor said next almost knocked me for six.

'Do you think you might be pregnant, Mrs Stewart?'

'Pregnant! Me? Good Lord, I don't think so!'

But the doctor wasn't convinced.

'Well, why don't you let me examine you and I'll be able to tell.'

After a thorough examination, during which he palpated my stomach, the GP concluded, 'I'd say you were about four months.'

I left the surgery completely numb and returned home to Johnny in floods of tears. During the examination, the doctor had given me an internal. But I was still so young that I felt I'd been unfaithful to my new husband.

'It was horrible,' I said, shuddering in Johnny's arms.

'But he's a doctor, Pat. That's what they do.'

'I don't care,' I sobbed. I used the cuff of my jumper to soak up my angry tears. 'It's just not right. It's not decent!'

In spite of my reservations and lack of knowledge, my pregnancy progressed as it should. One day, my midwife handed me a list of things to buy in preparation for the baby. One of the things on the list was a vest, so I went out and bought two.

'Er, why have you bought a vest?' Johnny asked, picking it up from the top of the side cabinet.

'Because it's on the list, and I need one if I'm going to have this baby!' I snapped.

I was pregnant and hormonal and Johnny knew better than to try to argue with me. I was still wet behind the ears, so I truly believed I couldn't give birth without buying a vest first.

Towards the end of my pregnancy, I decided I would return home to Yorkshire, where I planned to give birth.

'Oh, let me get me hands on that grandchild of mine,' Mam said, laying her hands flat against my belly.

'She can't wait, Pat,' Dad remarked as we all joked about her building excitement.

'Just wait till I get that baby in me arms...' she said, her eyes misting over with happiness. 'So... 'ave you thought about names, you two? Yer know, one for a girl and one for a boy?'

I glanced up at her, my hands cradling my swollen pregnant belly.

'We were thinking Victoria for a girl and Peter for a boy.'

Mam nodded in approval.

'Lovely. Aren't they both lovely names, George?'

But by now, with all the talk of babies, Dad had sat down and buried his head behind a newspaper.

'Aye, lovely,' he mumbled.

Mam and I shared a secret smile as she rolled her eyes in mock annoyance.

'Well, all yer need to know is you must never miss a feed because a baby that's well fed through t'day is less likely to wake up through t'night.'

I had no idea how to look after a baby, so I soaked up my mother's advice. Johnny and I stayed with my parents over the festive season. My cousin was throwing a party on New Year's Eve and I was determined not to miss it. Everyone came to the party and I soon found myself surrounded by family. Even though I was nine months' pregnant, I was having a great time. That was until my labour pains started. As the first contraction soared through my body, I doubled up with pain.

'Are you all right, our Pat?' Mam asked, dashing across the room to check on me.

'Yes, it's nothing,' I lied. 'Must be the rich food or something.'

But it wasn't and I knew it. I was a dancer and a control freak to boot. I was convinced that, if I told my body not to have the baby before midnight, it wouldn't. I didn't want the baby to arrive just yet because I didn't want to spoil a good party! Instead, I gritted my teeth and suffered through my contractions without telling a soul. I continued to sing, dance and party away because I was determined I'd stick it out until midnight and see in the New Year. Eventually, after what had seemed like hours, the hands of the clock ticked onto midnight and everyone cheered and hugged one another.

'Happy New Year, Pat,' Johnny said, pulling me to one side to kiss me gently.

'Johnny,' I whispered. 'Can you take me home now? I don't feel very well.'

After saying our goodbyes, Johnny walked me back to my mother's house, where I promptly fell into bed. I'd hoped sleep would somehow help ease the pain.

I can do this. I can control these labour pains, I convinced myself. *I'm a dancer: I should be able to control the pain.*

But of course, it was all nonsense – no one can control the birth of a baby, dancer or no dancer. I didn't sleep a wink that night. Eventually, I gave up trying and climbed out of bed around 6am.

'Johnny, can you take me to the hospital now. I think the baby's on its way.'

After going into a bit of a blind panic, Johnny jumped into the car and drove me to Southmoor hospital, in Hemsworth, West Yorkshire. At 8pm that evening I gave birth to a beautiful baby boy. We called our New Year's Day baby Peter. Back then, husbands weren't allowed in for the birth, so Johnny sat outside anxiously, waiting for news. When the nurse finally called him in, Johnny came bursting through the door.

'Oh, Pat,' he sniffed, trying to keep his emotions in check as he held our newborn son for the first time. 'He's absolutely beautiful.'

I looked down at Peter, happily slumbering in Johnny's arms.

'He is, isn't he?' I said, wiping away tears of relief.

The following morning, Johnny called in to see us. He immediately went straight over to Peter's cot. He dipped his head in to take a look, straightened up and let out a sigh of relief.

'Well, thank God his head's all right!' He'd said it so loud that the whole ward turned to look at him.

'What do you mean, his head's all right? There's nothing wrong with his head, Johnny Stewart!'

Johnny realised I was annoyed so he tried to explain. 'No, I didn't mean that,' he said, holding both hands up in peace. 'It's just that, erm, when I came in yesterday, well, erm, it looked kind of funny.'

'What do you mean, funny?' I huffed, crossing my arms angrily across my chest.

I was a doting new mum, so I was protective of our son but furious with Johnny.

My husband stood in front of me and held both hands apart by four or five inches, as though he was clutching an imaginary ball.

'I don't know. It just looked, well, it looked kind of... elongated, er, like a rugby ball.'

'A rugby ball!'

'Yes, a rugby ball.'

'I can tell you're bloody Welsh!' I shouted. 'I'll elongate you in a minute!'

I picked up the bunch of flowers he'd bought me and threw them straight at him.

'Sorry, sorry,' he said, cowering by the end of my bed.

'A rugby ball, indeed!'

Looking back, Peter's head probably had been elongated,

due to all the pushing and shoving, but, in my eyes, he was my beautiful boy.

I remained in hospital for ten days, until it was time for me to be allowed home. The hospital kept first-time mothers in until their babies had reached a decent weight. The midwife also wanted to be sure the new mother knew how to bathe her baby too. Johnny had fetched in some of the baby clothes that we'd bought for Peter. They seemed to swamp his little body but I didn't care – I was taking my lovely boy home where we could all be a family.

A few weeks after Peter had been born, Johnny decided to buy a 22-ft long touring caravan.

'It'll be our new home,' he said, beaming as he wrapped his arm around my shoulder. 'Just you, me and little Peter.'

The caravan came in handy because it meant we'd always have digs wherever we were. It also meant baby Peter would never have to sleep in a separate room to us. We'd tow our new home from town to town and park it up in whichever town Johnny was appearing in that week. When the show was at an end, we'd hook the mobile home up to the car and move on to the next show. When Johnny wasn't touring, we'd tow the caravan to my parents. Dad had a huge garden, so Johnny would back up the caravan as far as he could before half the village turned out to help them push it into the garden. We lived inside Mam's house, but the caravan was always there waiting for us. If Johnny had another booking, we'd simply hook it up and off we'd set.

Later that year, Johnny was given a gig doing a summer season for a man called Harold Fielding. Harold was Tommy

Steele's agent and he'd booked up a load of acts for a summer tour he was putting on. Harold was a well-known and respected agent but he was also very superstitious. His superstition was so irrational that he forbade his performers from wearing the colour green.

'Green,' Johnny said, shaking his head when he told me later.

'Why has he banned green?' I asked, a little baffled.

'Because he says it's unlucky.'

'But what if you have a really expensive costume but it's green?'

Johnny shrugged his shoulders.

'Doesn't matter. You still wouldn't be allowed to wear it, not in his show.'

I shook my head. It sounded ridiculous, but then show business was full of eccentrics, all with odd little habits. Another common superstition was about sneezing in the dressing room. If someone sneezed, they'd have to turn three times afterwards to try and undo all the 'bad luck'. Another superstition was no knitting in the stage wings. I never found out why but then I didn't knit. The colour green was just another thing to add to an already bizarre list.

Johnny began the tour, so I packed up the caravan and we headed out on the open road once more. I was thrilled when I realised that Dickie Valentine would be appearing on the same bill. By this time, Dickie had left the band and was now doing a solo act.

'Pat!' Dickie said, throwing his arms around me as soon as he saw us all heading through the door.

Above left: Bonny Baby – Pat's modelling career began at the age of three.

Above right: Dancing Queen – Starting out in the world of show business.

Below left: Beautiful Ballerina – Performing at the age of seven.

Below right: Gala Queen – Pat opened Purston Park in Featherstone, West Yorkshire, in 1949.

Above: Queen for the Day – Opening Purston Park.

Below left: Bikini Babe – Pictured in Pat's first season at Blackpool aged just seventeen.

Below right: Some Like it Hot – In a promotional shot.

Right: Chorus Girl – Pat (*standing centre*) in her first pantomime in Leeds.

Left: All that Jazz – Pat (*second left*) in her second season with the Tiller Girls at Blackpool.

Right: Let's Face the Music and Dance – Pictured at Blackpool's North Pier (*second left*).

Beach Babes – The photographic contact sheet from Pat and Wendy's photo shoot with Bert Hardy on Blackpool beach, in 1951.

Above left: Blonde Bombshell – One of the many promotional shots Pat has been in over the years.

Above right: Hi de Hi – Pat performing in the summer season at Butlin's in Clacton.

Below left: Stranded – On the beach in Africa, Pat with the other performers after they were left dancing for their supper.

Below right: Bohemian – Pat in her outlandish raffia shoes in a shot taken in Blackpool in 1950.

Above: The Good Old Days – With Barney Colehan at Yorkshire Television Studios on the set of *The Good Old Days*.

Below left: Career Girl – Pat pictured in Glasgow during the 1950s.

Below right: Dynamite Duo – Nick and Pat Lundon in a promotional shot.

Above left: Whirlwind Romance – Pat and Johnny pictured on their wedding day.

Above right: Land of Song – A newspaper cutting featuring Pat and Johnny, dated 21st July 1961.

Below left: Ooh La La – Pat in a promotional shot taken in London.

Below right: Laying the Foundations – Pat and Johnny in a 1960s promotional shot.

Above left: Blast from the Past – A letter from Lord Lofthouse written to Pat.

Above right: Older and Wiser – Wendy and Pat with photographer Bert Hardy on London's River Thames in 1987, re-enacting Bert's famous photograph from the *Picture Post*.

Below: Blackpool Tiller Belles – Pat (*left, end of line*) and the Tillers pictured on Blackpool's North Pier.

© *Popperfoto*

Dickie looked down at Peter, whom I was cradling in my arms, and stroked a finger gently against his cheek.

'Is he yours?' he asked.

I nodded proudly. 'And this is my husband, Johnny.'

Johnny stepped forward and shook Dickie's hand warmly.

'So where are you on the bill?' Johnny asked.

'I believe I'm top of it.'

'Well, in that case, I'm supporting you. I'm the next act down.'

It didn't matter one jot that Dickie and I had once dated because I was now married with a son. If anything, the fact they'd both dated the same woman seemed to bring them closer together because Johnny and Dickie became great friends.

A few months later, Johnny and I discovered that I was expecting another baby.

'I'll take on all the work I can,' insisted Johnny, holding my hand. 'I just want to support you and our boy.'

Eventually, the show came to an end. Thankfully, Johnny had been asked to appear on a television show, which was going to be screened live from the Prince of Wales Theatre in London. He was working front cloth – a theatrical saying for performing in front of the closed curtain – with Dickie appearing later in the same show.

Johnny was only performing a five- or six-minute spot, singing the classic Welsh song 'We'll Keep a Welcome in the Hillside'.

'Far away a voice is calling, Bells of memory chime,' he began to sing.

Without warning and totally off script, Dickie stuck his head through the curtain and called, ''Ello, my darling,' in his best Charlie Drake voice.

The audience howled with laughter. It had been totally off the hoof, so Johnny had been as surprised as everyone else.

A week or so later, Johnny was appearing up at a theatre in Glasgow to do the exact same routine. Although Dickie wasn't in this particular show, Johnny had almost died when his friend stuck his head through the curtain and did exactly the same gag. Dickie, who was supposed to be down in London, had paid out of his own pocket to travel all the way up to Scotland to pull the prank on Johnny. It had certainly worked and the two men laughed about it for days afterwards.

With Christmas fast approaching, Johnny was asked to appear in pantomime in Peterborough. I was heavily pregnant and exhausted from looking after Peter, who was a boisterous thirteen-month-old toddler.

'I think I'm going to go back to Yorkshire to stay with Mam,' I decided.

Johnny nodded. It was all very well being on tour with Johnny but now that we had another baby on the way, I knew we needed to put down some roots.

Back in Yorkshire, I tried to keep myself busy and get out as much as I could. With Johnny performing miles away, I felt lonely. To occupy my time, I'd take Peter out for a walk in his pram to Purston park – the place where I'd cut the ribbon all those years before – so that we could both get some fresh air.

One morning, as I was helping Peter into his coat, I felt a telltale contraction stab at the side of my stomach. I didn't want

Peter to miss his trip to the park, so I ignored it. I sat on a park bench as contractions soared through my body but, once again, I refused to give in. Taking short breaths, I walked all the way home, where I stood and did a pile of ironing. A couple of hours later, I walked along the street to Auntie Alice's house to ask if my cousin Ron could collect me at 9pm prompt.

'What for?' Ron asked, scratching his head.

'It's just that I think I'm in labour,' I replied, my voice both steady and calm. 'But I don't want to go in just yet because I don't think I'm quite ready.'

Ron looked at me as though I was nuts and so did Auntie Alice but no one dared say a word. I turned on my heels as their mouths hung open and headed back to Mam's house to continue with my ironing. Sure enough, Ron pulled up outside in his car on the dot of nine.

I was admitted to hospital that evening and gave birth to a baby boy at 6am the following day. Unfortunately, there had been a vomiting bug sweeping through the hospital. As a result, all the patients were only allowed one visitor each to try to stop it from spreading. Johnny was still stuck in pantomime, but I wanted him to be the first person to see our baby, so I refused all visitors until Johnny came home a week later.

'He's gorgeous, Pat,' Johnny said, gently taking him from my arms.

'What about his head?' I asked, a mischievous grin spreading across my face.

'His head is perfect too,' Johnny said, smiling and holding him close.

THE GIRL IN THE SPOTTY DRESS

We named our second son Stephen. Fortunately, Johnny never mentioned the shape of Stephen's head or uttered a word about rugby balls ever again!

CHAPTER 15

BRING ME
SUNSHINE

After Stephen had been born, I stayed at my mother's with the children until Johnny landed another job. He'd had been given a contract to do a summer season at Llandudno, in Wales. Ironically, it was with the Issy Bonn agency, even though I was trying to sue the same agency through Equity for non-payment of wages from my disastrous stint in Africa. This proved to me that there was no ill feeling and that, actually, people respect you more if you fight for what is rightfully yours.

We packed up the caravan and, with the help of neighbours, managed to pull it out of Dad's garden and back onto the road.

'Thanks, everyone!' Johnny called through the open car window as we waved goodbye.

The street was lined with children, friends and neighbours, who all wished us well on our travels.

'I'm going to miss Yorkshire,' I said with a sigh as the car towed the caravan through the narrow streets and we began our long journey to Wales.

The Welsh show turned out to be a great success but, instead of sitting home alone at night, I'd pop a coat on Peter, wrap Stephen up in a blanket and push the pram towards the theatre. I'd take both boys into Johnny's dressing room backstage, where I'd make up a little bed for Peter. I'd leave them both slumbering while I nipped to the side of the stage to watch the rest of the show. Back then, people left their children sleeping in prams at the bottom of the garden. There wasn't the same worry over child safety as there is today.

Every Sunday we'd go out to lunch. Even though he was still a baby, Stephen was much bigger than Peter. There had only been two ounces between them at birth, not that you would have guessed. As they grew, Stephen not only became larger but the taller of the two, until soon he towered over his elder brother. With Peter digging his heels in and refusing to walk, I bought a double pushchair. Sunday was the only day Johnny didn't work so, one day, I fed the boys, and set off to a nearby restaurant. I asked if we could have a table by the window and placed the pushchair outside, where I kept my children in full view. I did this week after week until one Sunday, when I decided to buy Peter a lollipop.

'You've been such a good boy that Mummy's bought you something,' I said, holding out the sticky lolly.

I hadn't bought Stephen one because he was still only five months old.

'Here you go,' I said, handing the lollipop over to Peter.

His little fingers stretched out like a starfish to grab it.

'Ta,' I said, mouthing the word.

'Ta,' Peter mimicked, taking the lolly from my hand.

I was sat inside tucking into some Sunday lunch with Johnny when we heard a God-almighty scream. Fearing something awful had happened. I looked up to see Peter's face purple with anger as he screamed his lungs out. I dashed out of the door and over towards the pram.

'Peter, whatever is it?' I asked, checking him over.

'Lolly, lolly,' he wailed. His little hand pointed angrily over at Stephen. My five-month-old baby was quite happily sucking away on it.

Seconds later, Johnny ran up behind me.

'What is it, Pat?' His voice was in state of panic but I could barely talk for laughing.

'It's Stephen,' I gasped, in between breaths. 'He's stolen Peter's lollipop!'

'What the...' Johnny shook his head.

We'd seen it all.

The fact I'd had two boys just thirteen months apart seemed to make Stephen grow up quicker. If anything, as he grew, most folk assumed they were twins, rather than brothers. Peter put on eight ounces a week, whereas Stephen was piling on at least a pound a week. I loved taking them both to the baby clinic because I'd always get a pat on the back from the nurse, particularly when she weighed Stephen.

'I don't know what you're feeding this little man, Mrs

Stewart, but he's a bruiser!' she said, placing him down on the baby scales and watching the needle spin around the dial.

After the summer season ended, we hooked up the caravan and headed back down to London. We parked it up in Haringey, where we lived behind a garage while Johnny performed in panto. A few months later, he was offered a gig over in West Germany. He'd be performing in the same tour I'd done for the American troops all those years before.

'I almost broke my bloody neck out there!' I sniffed, as I began to explain all about the highly polished floor in the Enlisted Men's Club.

'I swore I'd never set foot in one of the places ever again and I didn't!'

Johnny smirked, but he could still see how angry I was.

'Well, I doubt I'll be doing much dancing, Pat, so I reckon I'll be safe.'

Suddenly, I remembered something.

'Oh no.' I sighed.

'What? What is it, Pat?'

'Comedians,' I said, recalling what had happened all those years before. 'The comedians always die on their feet because the American soldiers just don't understand our dry sense of humour.'

Johnny scoffed. 'Rubbish!'

'It's true, Johnny. What you need to do is include some Irish songs because every American claims to have an Irish connection somewhere along the way.'

'Really?' he said, sitting up in his chair.

'Absolutely! It's foolproof.'

Johnny planned out his act and left for the American base camps in West Germany. Sure enough, with the songs included, every time one of his jokes fell flat on its face, he'd turn on the Irish charm, even though he was actually Welsh.

'You should have seen them, Pat,' he said once he'd returned home. 'These big, butch Americans crying into their beers like babies as soon as I broke into Danny Boy.'

The tour had been a complete success. Even better, Equity had successfully sued the Issy Bonn agency as a result of my African tour and I was given £300 – a small fortune back then. Some of the other members of the cast had warned me not to go ahead with legal action.

'You'll never work again if you sue, Pat,' they'd insisted.

But they were wrong because not only did Issy Bonn keep booking Johnny up for shows, but the three of us remained good friends over the years that followed.

With summer approaching, we did another season down in Weymouth, where we'd got married. We staged our own show at the open-air pier theatre with a double-singing act from Wales: a soprano and an organist called Oliver. There were already two other big shows on at the time but, thankfully, we seemed to pull in the crowds. On some of the quieter days, I was trying to think of different ways to put bums on seats when I recalled our last time in Weymouth. Jack Douglas and Joe Baker had run *Crackerjack* – a stage version of the popular children's television show – during the morning. At the time, Jack had asked if I could help out, so I did. I couldn't believe how many children turned up to take part. More so, I couldn't believe how many parents and grandparents had turned up to watch.

'I think we should put on a kid's talent show,' I said to Johnny one morning. 'When I helped Jack out with that children's show, you should have seen how many people turned up.'

'You think it'll work?' he asked.

'Yes, I do.'

Soon it had been decided. We'd hold children's talent shows on the pier every morning. On Fridays we held the 'talent finals', handing out vouchers to the winners. I soon realised that the more children I took through to the final show, the bigger the audience would be. All the proud parents, grandparents, aunties and uncles would turn up to see if their own little star would win the show.

Thursdays were also quiet, so I staged Bonny Baby competitions, which were just another ruse to put bums on seats. I wrote letters to Cow and Gate and Farley's Rusks and, to my delight, both companies sent me loads of goodies to give out. It was a win-win situation because not only were they free, but they made the show seem well organised and professional. I even pulled in a nurse from Weymouth hospital and paid her a small fee to adjudicate 'the show'. We'd advertised the event in the hope that a few mums might turn up with their babies – anything to fill an empty theatre on a wet Thursday afternoon.

However, when we arrived at the theatre on the first Thursday, we were stunned by how many were there. Around 200 mums and dads held screaming babies in their arms, with prams blocking the foyer. It was absolutely packed!

Johnny took one look and turned around to face me.

'You're on your own,' he gasped.

He grabbed the boys' hands and scarpered off towards the beach.

I stood there not knowing quite what to do or where to start. Even the nurse looked a little startled. We had created a monster!

'Right,' I said, walking alongside the queue. 'Could you all please line up so that we can begin the judging process?'

Thankfully, my friend Wendy, who was a dancer in one of the other shows, had come along to help.

'Don't leave me, Wendy,' I whispered, grabbing her arm for moral support. 'I can't do this alone.'

Wendy looked at me, her face determined.

'Don't worry. I'm going nowhere, Pat,' she promised and she rolled up her sleeves and got stuck in.

All the babies were carried onto the stage – one by one – in the arms of their doting mother, while the nurse judged and Oliver played a light-music medley on the organ in the background. The afternoon had been going swimmingly, and I smiled and tried to keep the contestants flowing. Finally, after the last baby had been carried on, the nurse stood up and handed me the results on a piece of paper. I took it from her, sorted out a few things backstage to keep the tension going and then strode back out to take to the microphone.

'Ladies and Gentlemen,' I began. 'I have here the results of our Bonny Baby competition in my hand,' I said as a hush descended around the packed room.

I glanced down at the piece of paper. On it there were

hundreds of names, instead of just three, and that's when I realised – I'd picked the list of entrants by mistake. For the first time ever, I froze on stage. I was completely dumfounded. Wendy looked at me from the wings but I couldn't tell her what was wrong.

'Er, actually, we're not quite ready yet,' I said looking off to the side of the stage at Wendy. 'Just give us a few more moments, and I'll ask Oliver to play some music for us.'

Oliver looked a little puzzled, but did as he was told while I ran off the stage towards the wings and Wendy.

'Pat, what's wrong?' she asked.

'I've only gone and binned the bloody results by mistake!'

Wendy put her hand against her mouth and gasped.

'Quick,' I said, waving my hand over towards the dressing room. 'I think I've thrown them in the bin!'

We dashed back to look for the winners as puzzled mums nursed irritable babies. Backstage, Wendy and I were on our hands and knees searching through the bin when, after what had seemed like a lifetime, she triumphantly held up a piece of paper in her hand.

'Got it!'

I was so happy that I almost cried with relief.

'Wendy, I could bloody well kiss you!' I said, planting a lipsticked kiss on top of her head as we both ran back towards the stage.

Of course, no one had a clue of the chaos backstage. Instead, I serenely stepped back towards the microphone and announced the winner. Then I realised I had another problem – the list didn't say which baby had come first, second or third. With nothing else for it, I chose each one at random. The nurse looked up at me as though I'd gone mad. I thought the parents would lynch me because it was clear first prize wasn't better looking than second or, indeed, third. Needless to say, I never made the same mistake again.

'Tell me again,' Johnny said, clutching his sides with laughter as I recounted the whole sorry tale to him later that evening.

'Don't!' I scolded. 'Next time, Johnny Stewart, you're coming with me!'

The Bonny Baby competitions settled down into a routine and soon we were filling the theatre most days. A few weeks later, we decided to put on a late-night show down the road at a ballroom, to bring in a bit more income. We'd quite literally finish one show and head to another for a cabaret show. It did so well that we were booked to go back the following year, but one of the big agencies had felt threatened and tried to stop us. In short, we had become the victims of our own success. Our shows were not only cheaper than the other productions but they were good, with all the landladies recommending them to their guests.

Once the summer season was at an end, Johnny travelled to another pantomime, this time in Birmingham. Performing alongside him was a comedy duo called Morecambe and Wise, who had just exploded onto our TV screens with their hit BBC show.

Over that Christmas season, Eric and Johnny became great friends because they both shared the same sense of humour. Ernie had always played the straight man and he was, in more ways than one. Overshadowed by his wife, Ernie would keep himself to himself after the show. Meanwhile, Eric would always be first at the bar having a laugh and getting the rounds in. One particular evening, halfway through the run, Morecambe and Wise had the audience on their feet clapping and cheering. Moments later, it was Johnny's turn to follow them on.

'How the hell am I supposed to better that?' he asked as we stood waiting in the wings.

Johnny was usually so full of confidence that I'd never seen him falter before. For the first time in his life, he seemed really nervous. Suddenly, he began to undo his belt and then he unbuttoned his trousers.

'Johnny, what on earth are you doing?' I screeched, thinking he'd gone completely mad.

'I'm thinking on my feet,' he said and grinned. 'Watch this, Pat.'

Eric and Ernie had finished off their routine and had turned to wave to the crowd. They were just about to exit the stage when Johnny walked on behind them – his trousers falling straight to his ankles. Eric turned his head and spotted Johnny standing trouserless behind him.

'What's he doing, Ernie?' Eric asked, speaking into the microphone. His face was completely deadpan as he began to wiggle his trademark glasses around as though he couldn't quite believe his eyes.

Without another word, Eric nodded over to Ernie and winked. Ernie smiled, and the two of them undid their trousers and dropped them to the ground too. Soon, all three men were standing on stage waving at the audience with their hairy and puny little legs on show. The audience lapped it up and were rolling around in the aisles. Eric and Ernie were ultimate professionals. Even though Johnny had dropped his trousers behind them, they didn't break their stride. Sadly, the show came to an end, although Eric and Johnny vowed to keep in touch.

Just before he left panto in Birmingham, Johnny received a call from a friend who was also a BBC radio producer. He gave him the tip that Ivor Emanuel, who was appearing in *The Land of Song* – a Welsh religious TV programme – was planning to leave. On his advice, Johnny wrote to the producers and was offered an interview to be his replacement. In fact, the producer travelled all the way to Birmingham just to see Johnny.

The TV show was in Welsh and, although Johnny had been brought up in Llanelli, where Welsh had been his first language, he'd gone through the war speaking English, so he'd forgotten some of his native tongue. Undeterred, he was given a couple of English songs that had been translated into Welsh. The plan was that he'd learn them both so that the producer and director could judge his performance. But there was a problem – he only had a week to learn them. By the end of the week, he'd driven me mad singing 'Popo the Puppet' and bloody 'Sing a Song of Sunbeams'! However, he still didn't feel confident enough to travel over to Cardiff for the audition.

'But what will you do?' I asked.

'I'll have to make an excuse,' he said, picking up the phone in the theatre foyer.

Johnny dug out a piece of paper and dialled a number.

'I'm awfully sorry,' he began, 'but I've got a Sunday concert, so I won't be able to come. Could we make it another day?'

The studio bosses agreed, which gave him another week's grace. More importantly, it gave him more time to learn and perfect both songs. Johnny not only wowed them with his beautiful Welsh tenor voice, he also landed the job. When the pantomime finished, we simply packed up the caravan and headed off for our new adventure in Wales.

CHAPTER 16

KEEP A WELCOME IN THE HILLSIDE

We pulled the caravan into Wales and into a caravan park called Fontygary. It was a lovely holiday park, populated not only by weekly holidaymakers, but also people who had bought a caravan as a second home.

Once on site, Johnny began working on the *Land of Song* TV programme. He was earning around £400 a month so, for once, we had a regular and steady income.

We soon became very friendly with a couple called Eileen and Charlie. Charlie had been a successful businessman, so the couple were very wealthy. Charlie had made his fortune buying and selling things, but he was also a moneylender. The caravan park was only open in the summer because it closed throughout the winter months. By this time, Peter was almost five years old and due to start school after Christmas. Deep down, I knew we needed to settle instead of moving from one place to another because it wouldn't be good for the children to be constantly uprooted. Besides, now that Johnny was on TV, there was very little to stop us.

'I'm sick of all this travelling,' I complained one morning over breakfast. 'It's too cramped in here with us and two children. We need to buy a house, put down some roots and stay in one place, Johnny,' I said. 'We need to buy our own house.'

But he wasn't convinced.

'Houses cost a fortune, Pat, and what if the money stops coming in. What then?'

I huffed and got up to clear away the breakfast plates. But I wasn't prepared to give up.

Later that evening, we were sat having dinner with Charlie and Eileen when the same conversation started up again.

'But we know nothing about buying a house, Pat,' Johnny argued. 'Besides, how would we manage to pay a mortgage month after month?'

Charlie leaned forward, causing the ice cubes to chink together inside his glass of scotch.

'The thing is,' he said tapping his finger against his glass, 'when you've got a mortgage to pay, you'll always find the money.'

Charlie leaned back and looked over at his wife. 'Isn't that so, Eileen?'

Eileen nodded.

'It is. You see, everyone has hard times, Johnny. But somehow, you always manage to find the money for the mortgage because you need a roof over your heads. And not just *your* heads – what about the boys?'

I looked over at Johnny, who was listening intently.

'All right then. We'll go and have a look tomorrow morning,' he decided. 'But we'll just have a look. We're not rushing into anything.'

I took his head in my arms and kissed him full on the lips.

'I love you, Johnny Stewart. You are the best husband a wife could ever wish to have!'

Charlie and Eileen laughed, and we made plans to head over to the estate agents the following day.

In spite of his reservations, we put down a deposit on a detached house in St Mellons – a suburb on the outskirts of Cardiff. We sold our caravan for the princely sum of £100 and moved into our detached three-bedroom home. The property sat in the middle of so much land that it felt as though the house had its own grand gardens. After living in a caravan for so many years, it finally felt good to have so much space. The only problem was that, because the house had cost us £3,500 – a small fortune in those days – we didn't have any spare cash to buy furniture with. Undeterred, I spent what we did have on a set of net curtains to stop the neighbours from peering in.

'It doesn't matter,' I said to Johnny as we walked around the empty rooms. 'We'll soon earn enough money to buy furniture.'

But our world came crashing down only a few months later when Equity – the actors and performers union – called all its members out on strike, including those working in TV.

'That's it,' Johnny said, flopping himself down on the bare floor. 'If there's no work, there'll be no money to pay the bills, especially not on a big place like this!'

Johnny threw his hands up in despair.

'It'll be all right,' I said, trying to calm him. 'Remember what Charlie said.'

'I know, but if I can't work, how can I earn money to pay for it?'

For a moment I was completely stumped and then I remembered.

'The northern clubs!' I gasped. 'You need to work the northern club circuit. They'd pay a fortune for a good comedian like you.'

Johnny wasn't convinced, so I picked up the telephone and called all the clubs I could think of in the Yorkshire area, asking for the names and phone numbers of the ones I didn't. Soon I not only had a list, but I'd managed to secure him lots of bookings.

'But where will I stay?'

'You can live with Mam and Dad.'

'But what about you and the boys?'

My heart sank because I knew it would mean we'd have to live apart. But tough times call for tough measures.

'We'll be fine here,' I said, trying to reassure him. 'But when the money starts to come in, could you please send some home so that I can buy a bed?'

So that's what he did.

Johnny was paid £60 a night by every club he played at. He started off in Sheffield and slowly worked his way around each working-man's club in Yorkshire. After an evening's work, he'd stuff his wages into an envelope and post the cash back home.

'Look, boys!' I said, opening up the first envelope. 'We've got enough to buy a bed!'

Later that day, I popped into Cardiff and bought a double bed. I shared it with the boys until I had enough to buy them a bed each. Once the boy's rooms had been fully furnished, I concentrated on the rest of the house, beginning with the carpets.

'I'll take you to the cash-and-carry warehouse if you like. They'll be much cheaper there,' Charlie suggested.

'Oh, would you?'

I was grateful to Charlie because he always seemed to know where he could lay his hands on a bargain. It was only when we walked around the cash-and-carry that I realised how cheap the goods were.

'Blimey! You can really pick up a deal in one of these places, can't you?' I remarked.

'You certainly can, Pat. How do you think I made my money? Buying and selling things – it's a sure way to making a fortune, as long as you buy the right thing.'

Soon Christmas was upon us. But with money still tight, Johnny decided we'd have to tighten our belts even more.

'We won't be able to afford to buy Christmas presents for the boys this year,' he said as he sat at the kitchen table counting up what little money we had.

'Why? How much money have we got left?'

Johnny sighed and looked down at the handful of notes.

'Once the mortgage is paid, all we'll have left is thirty pounds,' he said, holding the bank notes aloft. 'And that,' he said, shaking them, 'will have to see us all through Christmas.'

Johnny had a pantomime booking in Swansea the following month, so I knew we just had to keep going until then.

'Here,' I said, taking the money from his hand. 'I've got an idea that will give us a Christmas to remember.'

'But you can't do much with thirty quid.'

'Can't I?' I replied, tucking the money inside my purse. 'Just you wait and see.'

I telephoned Charlie to ask if he'd take me back to the cash-and-carry. The following day, we headed over there and I bought a hundred sheets and a hundred towels. But when I returned home clutching boxes of linen, Johnny thought I'd lost my marbles.

'You've spent it on what?' he gasped, opening one of the boxes to peer inside.

'Towels and sheets,' I replied, stacking one box on top of another.

'But what do we need with all these sheets and towels?' Johnny gestured at the empty room. 'We haven't even got furniture!'

'Johnny,' I said, dusting off my hands. 'You said we wouldn't be able to give the boys a Christmas. But there's no way on God's earth my boys will miss out on Christmas presents, and this linen,' I said, tapping the top of a box, 'will be our ticket out of poverty.'

Johnny looked at me, bewildered.

'You don't get it, do you? I'm going to sell it, make a profit and use the money to buy the kids some toys.'

He scratched his head.

'But where will you sell it?'

'Door to door.'

Johnny threw his head back and snorted with laughter.

'Wait. Let me get this straight.' He grinned. 'You plan to sell towels and sheets door to door, like a gypsy?'

I nodded.

'If I have to, yes. I'll do anything to make sure our boys don't do without this Christmas.'

Although he hadn't been entirely convinced by my plan, the following morning Johnny helped me load up the car with the boxes of towels and sheets.

'Of course, you'll have to drive me,' I said, finally slamming the boot of the car shut.

'But I'm on TV! What if someone recognises me?' he exclaimed.

'Tough! There's no way my boys are going without and that's that,' I said, climbing into the passenger seat.

Johnny wasn't very happy but he drove the towels, the sheets, our two boys and me from village to village and door to door.

'Who's that in that car?' a lady asked as I held out a towel to demonstrate the quality.

'They wash very well. All the stains...' I said, giving her my usual sales patter.

But she wasn't listening. Instead, she was craning her neck, trying to look behind me and into the car.

'That looks just like that man off the telly, Johnny whatshisname...' she said, desperately trying to remember his surname.

'Stewart?' I offered.

'Yes, that's him! The one who does that *Land of Song* show on the telly.'

I turned to see Johnny sliding down in the driver's seat. He was trying his best not to be spotted.

'No, it's not him,' I said, holding the towel aloft. 'It's just my husband, although he gets it all the time. Personally, I don't think he looks a bit like him. Anyway, about this towel...'

By the end of the week, I'd not only managed to shift the entire stock, I'd covered the £30 I'd spent on it and, to my delight, managed to turn a £60 profit.

'Well, I have to hand it to you, Pat, you could sell coals to Newcastle,' Johnny remarked as we threw the last of the empty boxes into the dustbin.

For once, we were cash rich. We packed the boys into the car and headed to Featherstone, so that we could spend Christmas with Mam and Dad. In spite of Johnny's initial reservations, we did indeed have a Christmas to remember. As for the boys, we bought them a swing and seesaw.

'This is great!' Peter said, dragging Stephen outside for a go on the swing. 'Mum, Mum,' he called. 'Can you push me higher?'

I'd had the swing and seesaw delivered to Mam's garden in time for Christmas Day. But as I was leaving the shop, I spotted a sideboard out of the corner of my eye. It was a bargain at just £12.

'I'll take that too,' I said, opening up my purse.

A week later, I paid for the swing, seesaw and sideboard to be delivered to our home in Wales on the back of a wagon.

Johnny had already signed a contract for a panto in Swansea, but by now I realised how easy it had been to approach the northern clubs and secure work. As long as you knew who to approach, you were halfway there. Before we left Yorkshire, I'd watched a programme on TV that had featured working-men's clubs in Wales. Although they were exactly the same as the ones Johnny had performed at in Yorkshire, they didn't feature professional acts. I had a brainwave.

'Johnny,' I said, looking up at him as the brilliant plan formed inside my head. 'When we go back to Wales, I'm going to set myself up as a theatrical agent.'

Johnny folded his newspaper and glanced over at me.

'Are you serious?'

'Deadly.'

And I was. Wales didn't have a clue what was about to hit it.

CHAPTER 17

AGENT EXTRAORDINAIRE

Once I had an idea in my head, there was no stopping me. As soon as we had returned to Wales, I telephoned HTV (ITV Wales and West England) to inform them that I was going to bring professional club entertainment to Welsh working-men's clubs. The producers loved the story, and I appeared on the evening-news programme a few days later.

It took me two weeks to obtain a theatrical-agency licence from the local council but, once I had it, I was ready to start taking my first bookings. I began with a week's worth of bookings. I did it mainly because I wanted to get work for Johnny, so that he could be back home with me and the boys, where he belonged.

Johnny was still busy in panto, which had a twelve-week run, so he didn't finish until March. With Johnny already performing, I booked a couple of singers and a pianist. I promised every club that the show would bring the house down and it did. My only problem was that I was managing the same artistes at seven clubs at the same time. This meant one club would always have to have the dud end of the booking, namely putting the act on a Monday or Tuesday night. Each club had wanted the artists to perform at the weekends because it was their busiest time. To try to solve the problem, I devised a system where the acts would alternate between the clubs. It meant each club would all get a booking for Saturday and Sunday night. Soon I was swamped with work and started to represent up to thirty or forty acts a week. I was not only securing bookings and keeping old friends and acquaintances in work; I was also getting paid 10 per cent of every commission. I became so busy that I opened up an office in Llanelli, in West Wales, run by a concert secretary I'd met over there.

With Christmas over and done with, we decided to move. Peter was ready to start school, so I dressed him up for his first day and walked him there. The headteacher stood at the front of the room and read out all the children's names off a list. The room had slowly emptied, leaving only Peter and two other little boys standing there. I couldn't understand it because I'd put Peter's name down months before.

'I'm afraid there isn't any room for your sons at this school,' the headmistress informed us all.

I was annoyed and so were the other mothers, but the headmistress refused to budge.

'I'm afraid you'll have to take them back home. They won't be able to start school until after Easter,' she decided.

With no school to go to, I packed up Peter and Stephen on the train and travelled to Swansea to watch Johnny perform in the show. He seemed baffled when he saw us arrive at the stage door, so I told him all about the school having no room.

'But he's five. He needs to be in school,' Johnny reasoned.

'I know, but she was adamant she wouldn't take him, so there's nothing we can do or say that will change her mind.'

Later that evening, following the performance, Johnny and I returned to his hotel. As we walked into the reception area, we bumped into an old friend of ours who had risen through the ranks to become an MP for Swansea.

'Pat!' he said, holding his arms out in greeting. 'How lovely to see you and you're with your boys too!'

He bent down a little so that he could shake Peter's hand.

'So tell me, young man. How old are you these days?'

Peter blinked up at him.

'I'm five,' he replied.

The MP straightened up and looked over at me a little baffled.

'If he's five years old, he really should be in school.'

I wrapped an arm around Peter.

'I know,' I said, and I explained my predicament with the school and the headmistress.

'But that's outrageous!' he exclaimed.

'I'll tell you what,' he suggested. 'I could raise it in the House of Commons if you'd like.'

My face broke into a huge smile.

'Oh, would you? That would be wonderful!'

A few days later, he did indeed raise the question in the House of Commons. The press heard about it, and soon we had the *Western Mail* knocking on our door wanting a photograph of Johnny and Peter. A journalist asked us some questions and Peter and Johnny made the paper. I didn't think much more about it, but it turned out our timing had been impeccable. I hadn't realised, but there was a general election coming up. A week or so after the story had run, I was elbow deep in washing some clothes in the sink when I heard a knock at the door. I answered it to find James Callaghan standing on my doorstep. At that time, Callaghan was the MP for Cardiff.

'Can I come in, Mrs Stewart?' he asked politely.

I was a little taken aback but I invited him in all the same. I offered him tea or whisky. He accepted a glass of whisky, so I cracked open Johnny's best bottle.

'It's about your son, Peter, and the school's refusal to take him,' he began.

I nodded and poured him a large glass.

'Yes. My son is awfully upset about it,' I replied as I explained what the headmistress had said.

'Well, I hope that I may be able to help you there.'

After Jim Callaghan had left, I realised it was an opportunity for free publicity, so I rang up the *Western Mail* journalist, who'd called at our house the week before.

'You'll never guess who knocked at my door today,' I said, telling him all about Jim Callaghan's promise to sort out Peter's education.

Of course, the reporter was all ears and the newspaper ran the story in full. Less than a week later, a letter landed on the doormat at home. I smiled as I opened it up. It was from the headmistress. She'd written to tell me she'd changed her mind about how full her school was. There was space for Peter and the two other children after all.

'Great!' Johnny said as I relayed the good news.

'Well, it is and it isn't,' I remarked.

'Eh?' Johnny said shaking his head.

'The thing is, because I've kicked up such a big stink, I'm worried the headmistress will see us and Peter as troublemakers. And I don't want Peter Stewart to be the name on every teacher's lips for the wrong reason.'

'So you don't think we should send him to school?' Johnny said, settling back down in his chair.

'No, it's not that. I think he should definitely go to school — just not that one.'

In the end, we decided to enrol Peter at a Welsh-speaking school in Cardiff.

'I'd like my boys to be able to speak Welsh, just like their father. Besides, if they end up on the stage, they'll have another string to their bow.'

Peter's new school was the other side of Cardiff, so he boarded a bus every day. It was a private school, but the bus had been laid on by the council to transport pupils to the only Welsh-speaking school in the city. As he climbed on board, I couldn't help but smile. Seeing him reminded me of all the bus journeys I'd made to Leeds with Mam so I could become a dancer. She'd done everything to give me a better start in life, and now it was my turn to do the same for my son.

However, Stephen wasn't quite as keen to go or even spend a day at his Welsh-speaking nursery. Instead, he'd kick up an almighty fuss every time I tried to leave the room. In the end, the nursery decided it would be best if it gave me a temporary job as 'orange juice lady', at least until he'd settled.

I decided that, if my boys were going to learn to speak Welsh, so should I. I began by taking a twelve-week course with a private tutor, who brought me up to O-Level standard. I wanted to be able to understand enough of the language that I could help my sons read the books they brought home.

With my orange-juice-lady role finally at an end and both boys in school, my agency continued to flourish.

The following summer, Johnny was asked to go to Clacton to do a season at Butlin's. The local council had decided to put on a gala, with decorated floats to raise money for the town's chosen charities, and Butlin's had wanted to get involved. It was the summer holidays, so the boys and I travelled down to spend time with Johnny. As usual, he'd thrown himself into proceedings and had helped organise a float for the parade.

'I thought Stephen and Peter could stand on it. We could dress them up,' Johnny suggested.

'But we don't have any costumes. What will we dress them up as?'

He thought for a moment and remembered a pair of old boxing gloves he'd spotted backstage.

'Boxers! They can go as boxers. Peter could be Cassius Clay (Muhammad Ali) and Stephen could be Brian London, the heavyweight British boxing champion.'

I knew that, once Johnny had a good idea in his head, there was very little I could do to change his mind. He dressed both boys up in shorts before tying a 16-oz boxing glove onto each of their hands. The gloves looked absolutely huge on their four- and five-year-old arms. I stifled a laugh as soon as I saw them.

'Those gloves look enormous on them!' I said, smirking.

Johnny explained that was the point.

'It'll make people laugh.'

An hour or so later, the floats had lined up to sail through streets packed with the good people of Clacton. They'd turned out in their droves just to cheer them on, throwing coins onto each float as they passed by.

Mam had come to stay, so together we rented a bungalow just outside the town centre. After the parade had finished, Mam and I took the boys home so that we could bath them and put them to bed.

'You sort Peter out while I see to Stephen,' I called from the front room.

'All right. Come 'ere, sunshine,' Mam said, grabbing Peter by the boxing glove. She led him through into the bathroom and started to run a bath.

Moments later, I heard a shriek and then Mam called out, 'Pat, come 'ere quick!'

Panicked by her voice, I flew into the bathroom, where I found her kneeling down next to a red-faced Peter. Both of them were surrounded by hundreds of copper pennies scattered across tiles on the bathroom floor.

'What the—' I gasped.

'It's 'im,' Mam said, pointing a disapproving finger at Peter. 'I've just taken his glove off and this is what came flying out,' she said, looking down at the coins on the floor. 'He must 'ave had it hidden in there the whole time,' she said, holding up an empty boxing glove.

'But where's it all from?'

I walked over to Peter, knelt down and held his shoulders in both hands to try to make him look at me. 'Peter, you must tell me where you got all this money from, otherwise I will be very cross.'

Peter shrugged his shoulders and cast his eyes downwards.

'The float,' he finally whispered. 'I picked it up from the float.'

Mam put a hand to her heart as though she'd been struck by lightning.

'Oh, my Lord,' she gasped, as though Peter was one of the Great Train Robbers!

'Right!' I snapped, 'that's it! What you've done is wrong, Peter. Do you understand? That money was meant for charity, not for you. We will have to gather it all up, put it in a bag and take it back to where it belongs.'

Peter looked up at me, desperately trying to blink back tears.

'You won't tell Dad, will you?' he begged.

'Of course I will! You'll have to take it back to the manager at Butlin's and you'll have to say sorry.'

Peter's body slumped as he absorbed the enormity of the situation.

'He's done what?' Johnny exclaimed when I rang him up to tell him.

'I know. But the worst thing is he must have had some help

because he couldn't pick up all those coins himself. He had a bloody big boxing glove on his right hand, so Stephen must have helped.'

'But he's only four!' Johnny gasped.

'I know, but you know what he's like. They're as thick as thieves, those two. Stephen just does what Peter tells him to.'

I heard Johnny sigh on the other end of the line.

'Right, that's it! Put him in the car and bring him over. He'll have to apologise and explain himself to the manager.'

Within the hour, we were standing in the manager's office as Peter tried to explain what he'd done.

'I'm really, really sorry,' he said as he wept, with Johnny and I stood behind him.

But then I noticed the manager's face. He was trying his best not to laugh.

'What you've done is very naughty indeed,' he said, scolding Peter, who bowed his head in shame.

With his head dipped down, the manager looked up and gave us a sly wink. He thought the whole thing had been bloody hilarious. So did we after we'd got over the shock.

The money was duly returned, along with a note of apology, and was then sent to Clacton Council, where it ended up in the charity funds along with the other money.

A few weeks later, I was sat at home working when the phone rang. It was a club in Gloucester.

'Is that Pat Stewart?' a gruff voice asked on the other end of the line.

'Yes.'

'Do you put on wrestling?'

For a moment I was speechless.

'Wrestling?'

'Yes, wrestling. You know, like the stuff you see on television on Saturday afternoon.'

I didn't have the first clue about wrestling, but I knew my mother was an avid fan.

'Oh, that sort of wrestling. Yes, of course I do,' I lied. 'Here, give me your number and I'll get back to you.'

I didn't have any idea what to do or where to start, but I also didn't want to turn work down. I called up Mam, who told me who was and who wasn't big in wrestling. The following Saturday, I sat down in front of the TV so that I could watch it

'What are you doing?' Johnny asked as I sat down with a pen and notepad.

'I'm waiting for the TV credits to roll so I can write down all the wrestling promoters' names.'

Johnny looked at me oddly.

'Why would you want to do that?' he asked.

'Because I'm going to book up some wrestling acts for a club in Gloucester,' I replied.

I waved my hand to try to get him to move out of the way of the television.

'Er, I see,' he said.

By now, he'd come to expect the unexpected from me.

Once I had all the names, I looked through the phonebook and dialled them up.

'I'd like to book up some wrestlers, please.'

The man on the other end of the phone asked me if I wanted ring lights.

'Yes,' I said, trying to sound as though I knew what I was talking about.

'And seconds?' he added.

I didn't have a clue what they were, so I asked him to explain. When he told me it was the man who worked the corner and waved the towel up and down, I refused.

'No, we have our own seconders,' I told him.

I booked the wrestlers, called up the club and secured the booking and, more importantly, my commission.

A week or so later, Johnny, Mam, Dad, the boys and I were sunning ourselves on a beach in Spain when I remembered something.

'What day is it?' I asked, suddenly sitting up straight on my sun bed.

'It's Saturday, why?' Johnny replied.

'Is it?' I said, leaning back against the sun lounger. 'I hope the wrestling's going down all right in Gloucester.'

Mam and Dad looked over at me as though I'd lost my marbles!

'As long as you don't expect me to go down there to collect your ten per cent commission!' Johnny quipped.

With that I began to laugh and so did Johnny. My work as an agent had taken my life on a strange and sudden turn, but I loved every single moment of it.

CHAPTER 18

ABERFAN DISASTER

With agency work flooding in, we sold our first house and made £200 profit in the process. We used the money to put down the deposit on a three-storey house in a nice area of Cardiff. It cost us £4,000, which seemed like a small fortune, but business was booming, so I decided it was worth the risk.

'I don't know what we'll do with all this space, Pat,' Johnny said, surveying the large empty rooms.

'Don't worry, I've already earmarked the bottom floor as an office.'

Johnny paused for a moment to consider it.

'It sounds like a plan. We could live on the two upper floors but the bathroom needs a bit of work.'

He was certainly right about the bathroom. It was extremely old-fashioned and in desperate need of a makeover. I knew

Johnny wouldn't be able to tackle it alone, so I called up Dad, who travelled down from Featherstone to lend a hand.

One sunny October morning, Johnny and Dad were up in the bathroom doing some tiling, while I worked downstairs. I picked up the phone and spoke to Bing, a concert secretary, about some acts for an upcoming show at his local club. Bing was a miner and had taken the call underground on the pit bottom.

'Let's talk about these acts, Bing.' I began.

I was greeted by silence on the other end of the line. It was obvious that he wasn't listening. Something or someone had distracted him. Then I heard panicked voices as someone relayed news to him in the background.

'Pat, I've got to go,' Bing said urgently. 'There's been a coal slip in Aberfan, near Merthyr Tydfil.'

'No!' I gasped. A hand shot up to my mouth in horror.

'Pat,' Bing said, 'it's serious. I've just been told that it has fallen in on a school.'

My blood ran cold as I absorbed the news.

'Listen, I can't speak. I'll have to go. Call you later,' he said, blurting out the words before the line went dead.

I felt sick. I regularly booked artistes over in Merthyr Tydfil, so I knew the area well. One of my acts – a comedian called Lennie Leighton – lived there. I knew it was a close-knit community and a disaster like this would devastate the whole area and the people living in it.

'Johnny, Dad!' I called upstairs. 'Come quick! There's been a coal slip on a school.'

I heard a clatter as Johnny and Dad dropped what they were doing and came tearing down the stairs. We sat in the kitchen and switched on the radio, waiting for news. Suddenly, a newsflash came on. The newsreader's voice was solemn as he announced that a landslide had engulfed an entire school and some houses close to it.

I dashed through to the front room and turned on the television. Grainy black-and-white images appeared. They showed miners – hundreds of them – armed with picks and shovels, trying to dig out children trapped inside Pantglas Junior School. Eyewitnesses had described how the landslide had flowed like liquid, demolishing everything in its path.

A local man told a reporter that once the landslide had stopped, everything fell silent.

'In that silence, you couldn't hear a bird or a child.'

We watched in horror as the news went from bad to worse. The entire school had been engulfed along with eighteen nearby houses. The children had been looking forward to their school holiday only a few hours earlier. But now they were trapped, believed to be dead, along with their teachers.

'That's it!' Johnny said, clearly emotional. He wiped the tears from his eyes and stood up. 'I'm going over there to help.'

But as he grabbed his coat and headed towards the door, Dad stopped him.

'Johnny, those men are miners,' he said, pointing at the television screen. 'They know what they're doing. You don't.'

But Johnny was adamant and shrugged him off. He held up his hands.

'I'll dig with these if I have to. There must be something I can do to help.'

'Johnny, it don't matter. With all t'will in t'world, yer'll be more of a hindrance than a help. They know what they're doing,' my father explained. 'They're experienced at this sort of thing. They're trained for emergencies like this. If they can't rescue those poor souls, no one can.'

Dad was right, of course, but we, along with the rest of the nation, felt helpless as we sat there, watching and waiting for news.

The rescue had continued throughout the day and long into the night. My heart sank every time a stretcher was brought out covered with a blanket because you knew another life had been lost.

That evening, when the boys came in from school, I hugged them just that little bit tighter.

'Those poor, poor parents,' I said as I wept, holding Stephen in my arms.

'I can't even begin to imagine how they are feeling,' Johnny said and sighed sadly.

As the rescuers battled in vain, news emerged that 144 people had died in the mudslide, including 116 children. The majority of those youngsters – 109 of them – had been aged between just seven and ten years old: the same age as Peter. The last living victim had been found just before 11am – less than two hours after the landslide. Over 40,000 cubic meters of debris, which was 12 meters deep in places, had covered the village in a matter of minutes. They didn't stand a chance.

Witnesses had described hearing a noise similar to a jet engine passing overhead as the spoil tip slid down and ran over the top of the school. Those that hadn't died of suffocation were killed by the impact of falling debris.

Tragically, if the disaster had struck only a few moments earlier, the children wouldn't have been in their classrooms; if it had struck a few hours later, the school would have broken up for half-term. Parents had lost their children, and older brothers and sisters would grow up without siblings. Youngsters who'd missed school that day lost all their friends in one fell swoop.

As Wales and the rest of the country began to mourn the dead, more news filtered through. Lennie, one of my artistes and a dear friend, had lost both his sons in the disaster. As soon as we heard, Johnny and I drove over to see Lennie and his wife. It'd only been a few days but I can still remember the silence. It hung heavily in the air as we parked up the car. Everything felt still – as though the clock had stopped the moment the disaster had struck. It was obvious Lennie was absolutely devastated. As soon as he answered the door, his grief was clear for all to see, etched deeply into his face. We'd wanted to call by, to let him know that we were there for him. His wife sat still and silent in a corner of the room, numb with shock that both her boys would never be coming home.

'If there's anything we can do, Lennie. Just let us know,' I said, giving him a hug.

But no one or nothing could take away their pain.

Within days, a fund had been set up to help families who had lost children and relatives in the disaster. Naturally, performers from the showbiz world stepped up and offered to do whatever they could to help. As a theatrical agent based in Wales, I found myself in the thick of things, and I organised one charity fundraiser after another. This continued for months. I worked tirelessly for free, more than happy to help where I could, until one day when I received a telephone call from a club.

'We'd like to book a show to raise funds for people affected by the Aberfan disaster,' the voice on the other end of the line explained.

'And when is it you'd like them to perform?' I asked, looking down my list of available artistes.

'Sunday lunchtime.'

I stopped what I was doing because that's when it hit me. Some clubs were no longer holding these charity fundraisers out of the goodness of their hearts; they were using it as a way to boost takings behind the bar. Sunday lunchtime drew in a good crowd but no ladies were allowed in the clubs on Sunday lunchtime, so it was quite clear that this particular club was just looking for a spot of free entertainment. I was absolutely furious.

'Listen, I'm not getting paid a penny for this,' I told him, with clear disgust in my voice. 'And neither are the artistes, who have given all their time for free. But you are just using us to boost your bar takings.'

He realised that I'd sussed him out.

'Erm...' he mumbled.

I threw down the phone in a temper just as Johnny strolled through in through the door.

'What's up?' he said, spotting the look on my face.

'This has got to stop. Little shows here and there,' I said. 'What we need to do is one big, final show – something that'll raise a fortune. We need to bring all the big stars to Wales for a one-off show at the New Theatre. It'll raise a heap of cash, and put an end to people trying to make money off the back of such a horrible disaster.'

Johnny nodded.

'If anyone can do it, you can.'

A few weeks later, the Cardiff Committee for Aid to Aberfan was formed. We held a meeting in Caerphilly, and I began pulling in favours from all the contacts I'd built up over the years. I managed to get Shirley Bassey to donate one of her glamorous evening dresses to put up for auction. I also helped book The Clarke Brothers – two fabulous tap dancers from America – Victor Spinetti, and Eddie Thomas – Howard Winston's boxing manager. I tried to book George Raft, an American actor who'd performed alongside Marilyn Monroe in the film *Some Like It Hot*. George had starred in lots of great films and had played many roles, including that of a gangster. It'd mirrored his own life because George had grown up in virtual poverty in Hell's Kitchen – a poor neighbourhood in Manhattan, New York. As a young man, he'd been surrounded by real-life gangsters and petty villains. The problem was that he'd continued to count them among his friends. Unfortunately, he was denied entry into the United Kingdom 'due to his underworld associations'.

After that, the Aberfan Aid Committee seemed to hit one brick wall after another, particularly when it came to booking acts.

'It's as though people want us to fail!' I complained.

I was baffled as to why people didn't want the show to be anything other than a huge success.

'I just wonder if the big agencies are somehow blocking us,' I voiced out loud to the rest of the committee.

Just then, a voice piped up from the back of the room, breaking the silence. It belonged to one of the performers. He was a lovely man, who was also a practising homosexual. It was something that was still considered a taboo at the time although thankfully times were slowly changing.

'I know someone who might be able to help. I can have a word with the boys if you like?' he offered.

I figured any help would be better than none.

'Yes, all right,' I said, looking up from my list of performers. 'If you think it'll help, please go ahead and speak to them although I doubt they'll be able to do anything.'

But the theatrical smiled and nodded his head knowingly.

'Oh, I'm sure they will.'

CHAPTER 19

THE KRAY TWINS

A charity football match was held between TV personalities and Welsh internationals during the day and, later that evening, our all-star gala at Cardiff's New Theatre began. The place was absolutely packed out as Johnny closed the first half of the show to rapturous applause.

'They seemed to like it,' he gasped as he came running off the stage.

'They loved you, Johnny. You knocked them out!'

I felt proud of Johnny and the other entertainers; proud to be part of such a fantastic fundraising show. Afterwards, still on a high of adrenalin, the cast decided to head across the road to the Park Hotel for a drink. Glasses were raised as we chinked them together in celebration of a job well done.

'You were great, Johnny. You were the hit of the show!' one of the other performers remarked.

Johnny bowed his head and blushed. He was a natural comedian but he was also a very modest man. We took our drinks and went over to sit with Eddie Thomas and his wife Kay. Eddie had taken part in the show, although he was a boxing promoter, not a performer. The four of us were good friends and we got on famously even though our professional paths very rarely crossed.

Eddie organised boxing in a West End club and he'd often invite Johnny along as his guest. Heartbreakingly, Eddie had also been one of the first people on the scene of the Aberfan disaster. He'd once been a miner, so he used his expertise to help organise the rescue attempts. He'd brought some of the children's bodies up himself along with the miners from Merthyr Vale, carrying them to a temporary mortuary set up inside Bethania chapel. Although he was a former boxer and an all-round tough guy, Eddie was also a very sensitive man. He didn't like to talk about what had happened that day, but everyone knew what he'd done and the whole community never ever forgot his efforts.

As the two boys started chatting about the evening, I took a seat next to Kay and sipped slowly at my gin and tonic. I'd only taken one or two sips when Kay's face changed expression from one of happiness to one of complete horror. The colour had drained from her face and she began to slide down in her chair, cursing and muttering away to herself. She held her glass up in front of her mouth to try to disguise her words, but I was close enough to hear.

'Fucking hell!' she gasped. 'What on earth are they doing here?'

'Who?' I said, following her gaze and about to turn in my chair.

'No, Pat! Don't!' she hissed, tapping me on the arm. 'They might see you looking!' she panicked.

But I couldn't help myself. I had to see who on earth she was talking about and what she was so afraid of.

As I turned my head, I spotted a group of very suave young men coming in through the door. They were all suited and booted with Brylcreemed hair and sharp suits. Their suits were grey and extremely well-tailored and expensive looking. Two of the men, in particular, seemed almost identical, as though they were brothers. I noticed that, although their suits were well cut, they also seemed to be bulging forward around the inside breast pockets. I presumed they must have something stuffed in them – possibly a bunched up handkerchief.

'But who are they?' I asked, completely clueless as to why Kay was cursing away.

'It's the Kray twins,' she hissed through gritted teeth. Her face was as white as a sheet.

I looked over towards Eddie, but he didn't say a word. Johnny was also strangely silent. It was as though everyone had heard of these twins – everyone apart from me.

'But who are the Kray twins?' I demanded to know.

Kay looked up at me through her long eyelashes as though I'd gone completely mad.

'What, do you really mean you've never heard of the Krays before?'

I shook my head.

'Nope, I've never heard of them. Why? Should I have? Are they famous?' I asked, thinking they must be actors or something.

Kay snorted. It was clear she didn't think what I'd just said was funny at all. I watched as the twins and their friends sat down in some chairs opposite us. I looked back at Kay and asked her to enlighten me.

'It's the Kray twins, Pat. They're bloody murderers! That's what they are,' she said in her soft Welsh lilt.

I looked at Kay, then at the brothers and back again.

'Murderers!' I exclaimed. 'Why, who do they murder?'

Kay put her finger against her mouth as her eyes widened with fear.

'Shush, Pat. They might hear you!'

I presumed that, because Kay was married to Eddie, the Krays must be involved in the boxing world.

'Are they boxers then?'

Kay, who had just sat back up, was about to answer me when she began to slide down in her chair once more.

'Jesus!' she gasped, almost crossing herself. 'Don't look now but they're coming over!'

I turned to see a man, who wasn't one of the brothers, walk over towards our table. My eyes darted back towards Kay. She looked as though she was going to die of fright.

'Excuse me,' the man said, tapping Johnny lightly on the shoulder.

I noticed his body stiffen underneath the man's touch.

'Yes,' Johnny replied, looking at him with a polite smile.

The man dipped down and whispered something in Johnny's ear. I craned my neck towards them so that I could hear.

'The boys wondered if you could just come over for a minute because they want to have a word.'

My heart beat furiously inside my chest as I watched my husband stand up and walk across the bar towards the Kray twins.

I turned to face Kay. By now, her eyes were on stalks.

'What do you think they want with Johnny?' She gasped, her mouth hanging open.

I shrugged.

'I haven't a clue. Why? Do you think I should be worried?'

Eddie and Kay looked each other and then back at me.

'They are murderers, Pat!' Kay hissed. 'East End gangsters. They're well known for it. I can't believe you don't know who they are.'

'But what do they want with Johnny? He's not a gangster. He's a comedian!'

Kay put down her drink on the table with such force that the alcohol rose up and spilt over the edge of the glass, soaking her beer mat.

'I don't know,' She replied looking up. 'But I think we're about to find out. Here comes Johnny now.'

As Johnny returned, I noticed his face was clouded over with worry. It made me nervous but, at the same time, I needed to know what the Krays wanted with him.

'Is everything all right?' I asked, resting my hand on his arm gently. He slumped down into his chair as though the stuffing had been knocked from him.

'Yes, yes,' he muttered. Johnny picked up his pint of bitter and took a nervous gulp. 'Everything's fine.'

Kay leaned forward, her eyes burning with curiosity.

'But what did they want, the Kray twins?'

Johnny looked at his pint and placed it back down on the table.

'I don't know,' he said. 'It was all a bit strange.'

'Strange. Why?' Kay asked. It was clear she was dying to know – we all were.

'Well,' Johnny said, looking over one shoulder to check that no one could hear him. 'The boys wanted to know how I could do a performance like the one I did tonight and not be a bigger star.'

I nodded because I agreed with the Krays.

'And what did you say when they asked you that?' Kay asked, leaning forward in her chair.

'I said I didn't know.'

'And then what happened?'

'Well, that was it, you see. They asked if anyone was holding me back.'

I was puzzled.

'But why did they ask you that?'

Johnny shrugged.

'I don't know. But maybe it's got something to do with that man on the committee – you know, the camp fella.'

And that's when it hit me. I recalled the moment when the old theatrical had promised to 'have a word with the boys'. But I'd been worried one of the agents had been 'blocking' the show, not Johnny's career. I gasped because, suddenly, it all fell into place.

Kay turned away from Johnny for the first time to look at me.

'What is it, Pat?'

I explained all about the trouble we'd had booking the acts, and why I thought the Krays had come to the show.

'So they know one of the organisers?' Kay gasped.

'Yeah, I think so. That must be why they turned up here for tonight's show.'

Kay exhaled and fell back in her chair.

'Talk about friends in high places!'

But Johnny hadn't finished.

'That's not all,' he said, picking up the beer mat and twiddling it around nervously in between his fingers.

'Why, what else did they say?'

'Erm, the boys asked if they could represent me.'

Kay rolled her eyes and exhaled a deep breath.

'Johnny,' she said, grabbing his hand in hers. Her face was deadly serious. 'Tell me you said no. Promise me you won't have anything to do with them.'

'Why not?' I asked, sensing a good business opportunity. 'If they want to represent him, why not?'

Kay looked at me as though I'd just lost the plot.

'Because they are murderers, Pat!'

'To be honest, Kay, I don't think I have any say in the matter anyway,' Johnny butted in. 'I've given them our home telephone number. I'm sorry, Pat, but I couldn't say no – not to the Krays.'

'Its fine, Johnny,' I replied, patting his hand in reassurance. 'It'll be all right. Everything will work out fine, just you mark my words.'

And it did. But we never did receive the call.

One day, I was pottering around at home when Johnny shouted at me to come into the kitchen.

'Pat, here!' he called.

I ran through to the other room, where I found him crouched over the radio, listening intently.

'It's the Krays,' he said, pointing at the radio. 'They've just been arrested.'

That evening we watched a news report. Detectives from Scotland Yard had arrested the brothers, along with fifteen other members of their 'firm'. With the twins safely locked inside their cells, their reign of intimidation was finally over. This had helped bring more witnesses forward. Following a subsequent trial at the Old Bailey, the Krays, along with fourteen others, were convicted. Both brothers were sentenced to life imprisonment, with a non-parole period of thirty years, for the murders of George Cornell – an associate of a rival gang – and Jack 'the hat' McVitie, whose body was never found. Their sentences were the longest ones ever passed down at the time.

'Oh, well,' I said, standing up to switch off the television set. 'That's another boat we've missed.'

Years later, I discovered that Reggie Kray had given the largest single amount to the Aberfan Aid fund by an individual. He'd donated £100 from himself and his brother, Ronnie, and had handed it over on the night of the show. The £100 donation may not sound much but, back in the day, it was worth the equivalent of £3,000 in today's money. It was a time when a pint of beer cost 8p and a loaf of bread only 5p. In spite of their reputation, protection rackets, murder and long-term frauds, when it came to charity, it seemed the Krays were more generous than most.

CHAPTER 20

WAITING IN THE WINGS

A year or so later, I discovered that I was expecting my third child. Johnny was working all hours at the New Theatre in Cardiff. He was performing in the pantomime *Cinderella* when I'd fallen pregnant. We'd joked it had been an immaculate conception because we were both so busy – me with the agency and Johnny with the panto.

One day, when I was around three months pregnant, I gave Johnny a lift over to the theatre for the matinee performance. It was very difficult to find a parking spot, so we drove around a bit until I could find a space. I parked up my Mini and headed inside. I was only supposed to park in the space for an hour but I'd overstayed my time. When I finally dashed back to the car, I found a grim-looking traffic warden placing a ticket on the front of my windscreen.

'I'm awfully sorry,' I gasped. 'I'm pregnant. I was feeling quite ill,' I fibbed, clutching my stomach. 'I had to sit inside until the sickness went. For safety's sake, I didn't want to come out and start driving until I felt well enough.'

The traffic warden cast his eyes down to my flat stomach and scoffed, as though he didn't believe a word of it.

'Well, you can tell that to the magistrate,' he grumbled, like the true jobs-worth he was.

I was furious even though I'd been caught bang to rights; I was annoyed that he hadn't believed I was pregnant!

I later recounted the story to Johnny, but he was annoyed when I insisted that I planned to appeal the ticket.

'Just pay the bloody fine and be finished with it!' he barked.

But I was adamant. My hormones were all over the place, and to me it had become a matter of principle.

'No, because I am pregnant! Besides, he didn't know if I was feeling sick or not.'

Johnny looked at me aghast.

'But you weren't sick.'

'Well, that's true,' I agreed. 'You know that and so do I but he didn't. And what if I had been? No, I'm going to fight this for pregnant ladies everywhere,' I announced dramatically.

Once my mind was made up, there was no way I was backing down. The traffic warden had been rude and I didn't want him treating other ladies the same way.

Johnny shook his head as though he'd completely given up on me.

By the time the case had reached magistrates' court, I was

heavily pregnant. In fact, my stomach entered the room before I did. Thankfully, the magistrate was a lady and so she was entirely sympathetic to my cause. She also made the traffic warden, who I decided to christen 'Bulldog', look like a damned idiot for bringing the case to court in the first place.

'I think, given Mrs Stewart's condition,' she said, gesturing over towards my heavily swollen belly, 'that there is no case to answer. Why it was ever brought in the first place is beyond me,' she remarked, shooting the Bulldog a stern look before dismissing both the case and me.

I left the magistrates court feeling very pleased with myself. Although after that day, I was wary of the Bulldog. I envisaged him and his mates prowling the streets of Cardiff, hunting for me to seek revenge against my little red Mini.

I continued to run my agency right up until the last moment of my pregnancy. The final act I booked was Ronnie Hilton, who just missed out on being the UK's first representative in the *Eurovision Song Contest*.

I'd already decided I'd give up my agency office in South Wales. In the end, I handed it all over to Len, a former concert secretary, who was based at my Llanelli office, because I realised just how much time and effort it took. Sadly, once I'd let go of the reins and had walked away, the agency folded within a matter of months.

Our daughter, Rachel, was born a few weeks later, in September 1968. Unfortunately, and in true form, Johnny had missed the birth because he was away performing at a show in Morecambe. The months passed, and I happily settled down into my new role as full-time mum to our three children. One day the following summer, I was sat at home feeding Rachel when Peter and Stephen raced into the kitchen looking for me.

'Mum, Mum!' Peter yelled. 'Can we do *Junior Showtime*?'

Junior Showtime was a popular children's television programme on ITV, which was screened every Tuesday.

I took the spoon from Rachel's mouth and looked over at the boys. They were both standing there begging for permission.

'But *Junior Showtime* is filmed in Leeds,' I told them.

'Yeah,' Stephen chipped in, 'but they're going to do auditions in Cardiff this Saturday.'

I considered it and shook my head.

'But how can you do it?' I asked. 'You only know Welsh songs and it's a British show. You don't even know any English songs.'

Peter refused to give up.

'Please, Mum. We can learn. We'll work hard, won't we?' he said, turning to look at his brother who was nodding his head furiously in agreement.

'I just don't think it'll work.'

The boys groaned, but they wouldn't let the matter drop because they were both as headstrong as me.

'Well,' Peter declared confidently, 'I bet our dad will give us something.'

Although I had my doubts, Johnny had seemed more than happy to indulge them.

'Our boys on the stage!' he said, beaming proudly. 'It'll be like history repeating itself.'

For the next few days, it certainly felt like it. Johnny helped the boys rehearse an old military pantomime sketch. Stephen took on the role of the comic, while Peter played the straight man.

'That's it, now you hand the rifle to Stephen,' Johnny said, directing them from an armchair in the front room.

The sketch was simple enough. Peter would tell Stephen to put his rifle where he had his, and Stephen would go and place it on Peter's shoulder. It was silly pantomime nonsense but the boys loved it. With a comedian as a father, they practised it over and over again until their timing was just perfect. Days later, we arrived for the audition at the Royal Hotel in Cardiff. The foyer was packed with children dressed in ballet frocks, bridesmaid's costumes – in fact, every type of costume you could imagine. They were all dolled up to the nines and hungry for fame.

'Here, give Rachel to me,' Johnny said, taking her pushchair from me.

I smelled a rat.

'Why?' I asked as I watched him turn and head straight for the hotel door.

'It's like that bloody Bonny Baby Show in Weymouth,' he remarked, looking at all the junior wannabes in the foyer. 'I'm not staying here. You're on your own!' he called as he ran towards the door.

'Johnny Stewart, you come back here now!' I shouted after him.

But Johnny wasn't listening; he was too busy making an escape.

'Don't worry,' he called. 'I'll look after Rachel. See you all later!'

With that, he was gone. I cursed him silently.

'Where's Dad gone?' Stephen asked, looking up at me.

'He's gone for a walk,' I huffed.

Despite Johnny's sudden disappearing act, the boys' audition went well. The executive producer of *Junior Showtime* was Jess Yates who I'd worked with years earlier. Jess was the ultimate professional and, if he recognised me, he didn't let on. Then again, neither did I. The boys left me in the corridor and disappeared off into a room, where they performed their comedy sketch and finished on a song. Suddenly, the door opened and an assistant popped his head around the corner, looking for me.

'Could you come in, please? Jess would like a word.'

I smiled as I sat down in front of Jess.

'They're good,' he said, 'but they need a lot of work. Can you give it to them?'

I cleared my throat.

'Yes, I think I can. They've pulled this routine together in less than a week. Four days, to be precise.'

Jess sat behind his makeshift desk and listened to what I had to say.

'Well, in that case – and if you can bring them up to standard – I'll put them through for the show.'

A few weeks later, we travelled to Leeds so that they could perform on *Junior Showtime*. Of course, Johnny was delighted his sons were following in his footsteps.

'Look at them,' he said proudly.

'Yes, it's just a shame you didn't stick around for the audition,' I sniped, giving him a hard nudge with my elbow.

The boys were a great success. They performed four times

on the TV show and even bagged themselves a write-up in the theatrical newspaper *The Stage*.

'The Stewart Brothers have just made their TV debut,' Johnny said, reading the review aloud, '...so Mike and Bernie Winters had better watch out because the Stewart Brothers are here!'

'Hey,' he gasped, placing the newspaper down in his lap. 'Maybe we ought to send them to stage school?'

But the boys didn't seem keen and neither was I. Once they'd gone upstairs to bed, I decided to speak to Johnny.

'It's true. Both boys were good on the show, but have you noticed something?' I began.

Johnny looked away from the TV.

'Noticed what?' he replied.

I sighed. I didn't want to put a damper on their dreams but, at the same time, I wasn't sure quite how to say it.

'Yes, they were good on the show, but they never want to practice.'

Johnny shrugged his shoulders.

'Yeah, I suppose you're right.'

'So I don't think we should push them if they don't want to do it. If they really wanted to, they'd be begging us to stay up and practice all night long.'

Johnny looked back at the TV screen.

'Yes, I suppose you've got a point.'

A few weeks later, the phone rang at home. I picked it up to a lady from Yorkshire Television.

'We wondered if Peter and Stephen would like to come and perform on the show again?' she asked.

Both boys were at home that day because it was St David's day, so all Welsh pupils had the day off from school.

'Could I ring you back?'

'Yes, of course. Just let me know,' she replied as I replaced the receiver.

I walked into the lounge. Peter and Stephen were lounging around on the sofa, engrossed in a programme on TV.

'Do you want to do another *Junior Showtime*?' I asked, standing in front of the TV set to get their full attention.

'Oh, yes please!' they chorused.

I was surprised. Maybe I'd misjudged them.

'It's just that I've had Yorkshire Television on the phone.'

Both boys smiled. I knew something wasn't quite right, but I couldn't put my finger on it. My mother's instinct told me that they were both up to something.

'Just answer me one question,' I said, crouching down so that I could look them both in the eye. 'Why don't you ever want to rehearse between shows?'

Peter looked guilty as Stephen shot him a sideways glance. Neither of them replied.

'Because you're not going to get better,' I continued. 'You're not going to get better if you don't practise. You'll both stay exactly the same. That's why you need to rehearse in between shows.'

They both looked down guiltily until Stephen suddenly dropped them both in it by piping up, 'We do it so we can have a day off school.'

Peter's eyes bored into Stephen to try and shut him up.

'Right, I see,' I said, straightening up. 'Well, in that case, neither of you will do the show.'

The boys groaned. Peter turned and gave his brother a frosty stare.

Armed with the truth, I went back into the hallway, picked up the phone and returned the call.

'I'm sorry, but Peter and Stephen won't be able to do any more shows,' I explained. 'They're retiring as of today.'

The lady sounded a little surprised until I explained.

'They only do it to get time off school.'

'Ahh, I see.'

After that, the boys' show-business career came to an abrupt end.

'It's bloody hard work,' I told Johnny later that evening. 'And if their hearts aren't in it, they'll never get on.'

Johnny agreed.

'It's true. It's one of the greatest jobs in the world. In fact, it's the only job that'll pay you a wage and give you a round of applause. But when times are tough, it can be one of the hardest jobs in the world.'

Although they never set foot on a stage again, both boys went on to carve out extremely successful careers for themselves. So I like to think the decision I made that day was the right one.

CHAPTER 21

PRISON SHOW AND SEX OFFENDERS

Unlike the boys, Rachel was a fussy child who would scream blue murder if a stranger came to talk to her. One day, when she was about four years old, Johnny and I were standing outside a theatre in Ryde – a seaside town on the Isle of Wight – when a man came over to speak to us. Johnny was holding Rachel in his arms as the man approached.

''Ere,' he said. 'Aren't you a beautiful little thing. Let's have a cuddle,' he grinned as he tried to take Rachel from Johnny's arms.

Rachel was a typical blonde-haired, blue-eyed, adorable little girl but she didn't much care for the man. As soon as he went to grab hold of her, instead of screaming, she balled up her tiny fist and planted a right hook clean on his mouth.

'No!' she bawled.

Unfortunately, the man in question happened to be a gangster from the East End of London. He was one of many criminal types who regularly travelled over to visit friends and associates locked up inside two prisons on the island, Albany and Parkhurst. He wasn't used to being told no either, especially by a little girl. As Rachel punched him, the villain reeled back in shock. He ran his fingertips along the edge of his mouth, feeling for blood, and looked back in horror at her.

''Ere, you seen what she just did to me?' he gasped.

I took a deep breath.

'I'm terribly sorry,' I said, stepping forward to offer him a tissue. 'It's just that Rachel's frightened of strangers, so I think you must have shocked her.'

Johnny apologised too. Meanwhile, Rachel sat there, indignant in his arms, annoyed he'd encroached on her personal space. Thankfully, although he was a hardened crook, he also had a sense of humour; however, he never asked Rachel for a cuddle again.

Our daughter's feisty nature didn't stop there. Once Johnny had finished the summer season at Ryde, we travelled back home. One afternoon, a friend had popped around for coffee but, as she got up to leave, she realised her car keys were missing.

'That's strange,' she said, scouring her handbag. 'I could have sworn I'd put them in here.'

But the keys weren't in her bag or anywhere else in the room. After an hour, we'd turned the house upside down looking for them.

'I'm so sorry, Di, but I can't find them anywhere,' I sighed, holding my hands up in defeat.

Di had also given up the search.

'Never mind, Pat. Thanks for looking. I must have misplaced them somewhere,' she said, picking up her bag.

'Yes, but you drove over here, so they must be here somewhere. Only where they are, I do not know.'

I checked beneath the cushions on the sofa one last time.

'I'll tell you what,' I said, throwing the last one down. 'I'll drive you back home.'

'But what about the kids?'

'Oh, Johnny can put them to bed.'

But Di was adamant she didn't want to put me out.

'No, I'll be fine, honestly.'

I held up my hand to silence her.

'Nonsense! Your keys must be somewhere in this house, and I'm determined to find them. Now, the least I can do is run you home until I do.'

Johnny put all three children to bed while I took Di home.

The following morning, I was just about to resume the search for the missing car keys when Rachel approached me. She had something in her hand.

'Mummy, here are that lady's car keys,' she said, holding them up as though butter wouldn't melt.

'Oh, Rachel. That's wonderful!' I said, giving her a hug. 'But where did you find them?'

She looked a little guilty. Her face blushed as she turned in her shoes and stared down hard at them.

'I took them,' she whispered.

I was furious.

'Rachel! That's naughty. Why on earth would you do such a thing? We spent ages looking for them last night. Listen,' I said, bending down to her level, 'you must never take something that doesn't belong to you, do you understand?' I held her arm so that she'd have to look at me.

'Sorry,' she replied, her eyes brimming with tears.

'But why, Rachel? Why did you take them?'

Rachel lifted her little face and looked at me properly for the first time.

'Because I like Di and I didn't want her to leave.'

Although I was cross with her for taking the keys, a part of me couldn't stop laughing. She'd hidden them to keep Di a prisoner in our house!

With her keys safely in my hand, I picked up the phone and rang Di to tell her the good news. When I explained why Rachel had taken them, Di burst out laughing.

'Oh, bless her little heart,' she said with a chuckle.

'Bless her, indeed! What on earth am I going to do with her?'

Johnny had overheard as he passed me in the hallway. After I'd put the receiver back down, I noticed that he was smirking.

'What's so funny?'

'It's Rachel,' he said and chortled, giving me a nudge with his elbow. 'She's a chip off the old block, eh?'

Although I'd forgiven her, a month or so later Rachel was back to her usual tricks. Only this time she pushed a friend's handbag down the toilet!

'Rachel,' I said, calling her into the front room. 'Where's the handbag?'

He face clouded over because she was annoyed she'd been rumbled. She led both me and my friend into the bathroom. I was puzzled until Rachel stepped over towards the toilet and lifted up the seat.

'What? It's in there?' I gasped, looking at her in disbelief.

'But it's not wet. It got stuck!' Rachel insisted.

She gave the straps a sharp tug and the bag popped out.

Although my friend thought it was all highly amusing, I failed to see the funny side. Thankfully, after another telling off, Rachel decided to end her days as a prankster.

Shortly afterwards, laughter left the house when I received a phone call from my Dad one Sunday morning as I was preparing dinner.

'Pat, its yer Mam,' he began, his voice crumbling as he spoke.

I knew in an instant that something terrible was wrong.

'What's the matter, Dad? What's wrong with Mam?'

'I'm sorry, love, but yer mam passed away in her sleep last night.'

Although I was devastated, I immediately switched onto auto-pilot.

'I'll drive straight up,' I insisted. 'I don't know how long it'll take me but I'm on my way.'

I almost dropped the phone in shock before grabbing my car keys and handbag. Johnny heard the commotion and came to find me.

'Pat, what's wrong?' he asked as soon as he saw the look on my face.

'It's Mam,' I said numbly. 'She's dead.'

I was utterly devastated, but I couldn't cry because the shock had numbed me.

'Here, give me the keys,' Johnny said, holding out his hand. 'I'll drive.'

I refused.

'No, please let me. It'll keep me busy.'

There were no motorways linking Wales to Yorkshire then, so we packed the kids in the car and took the back roads. The journey took hours. When we arrived, Dad was waiting in a state of shock. I hadn't cried up until that moment but, as soon as I saw him, I broke down.

I was a married mother of three in my late thirties, but my own mother had been the driving force behind me and my career. She'd simply made me the woman I'd become and, without her, I felt utterly lost. I helped sort out the funeral and even suggested that Dad come to live with us. He tried it but only lasted a few weeks before he wanted to go back home.

'It's where I've lived all me life,' he explained. 'I need to go home, Pat.'

Life was tough without Mam on the end of the phone. Whenever I had a problem, I'd walk to the telephone to call her. That's when it would hit me – she had gone. Suddenly, the world felt an empty place without her, but I picked myself back up for Johnny and the sake of our children.

A few months later, in the summer of 1974, Johnny was offered a show down south, in Babbacombe, near Torquay. He'd been asked to take top billing in the *Fol de Rols* – a show Bruce Forsyth had done the year before. Like Bruce, Johnny had been asked to be the lead comedian. It was a review show, and it included a series of sketches and chorus girls. In short, it was a typical, good old-fashioned seaside show. The *Fol de Rols* was set to run for twenty weeks so, during the summer holidays, I travelled down with the children so that they could spend time with their father. By this time, Peter was fifteen, Stephen fourteen and Rachel just five years old.

One night, after the show had finished, I was with the children in Johnny's dressing room when a man knocked at the door. He had a favour to ask. The man, who went by the nickname 'the Arab', worked as a senior prison warden at a nearby jail.

'I just wondered if you and the rest of the cast would be interested in coming to the prison to do a show for the inmates,' he asked Johnny. 'It's just that I reckon the men would love you and it would really help lift morale.'

Johnny turned to me.

'What do you think, Pat?'

'Do it,' I replied. 'A show is a show. Besides, it'd be good for them to experience a little bit of Johnny Stewart humour.'

The Arab smiled warmly. He seemed utterly delighted that we'd agreed to do it.

'So I can book you then? I mean, you'll all come?' he asked.

Johnny nodded.

'It'll be a pleasure.'

Both men shook on it, and the Arab promised to be in touch to sort out the necessary arrangements. On the day, the Arab picked us up in his car and drove us out to lunch at a nearby pub. The rest of the cast had agreed to meet us there.

'Where's the prison then?' Johnny piped up from the back seat.

'Oh, it's Dartmoor prison. They're a bit isolated up there. That's why I thought the men would love to have some visitors.'

The Governor's wife had offered to look after our children in her living quarters so that I could accompany Johnny and the Arab into the prison grounds. The prison was situated inside a large, grey, imposing building in Princetown, positioned high on Dartmoor. The main gate had been built with the same dreary grey brick used for the rest of the prison. The whole place felt foreboding. It was an entirely depressing place to look at and to be. As soon as we'd passed through clearance and various prison gates, the Arab led us all through into a huge open space, which was the prison's main hall. On the opposite wall someone had painted an amazing mural of the last supper in intricate detail.

'Why,' I said, my breath stolen away by its sheer magnificence, 'that is beautiful. Who painted it?'

The Arab looked up at it dismissively, as though he'd seen it one too many times.

'Oh, that,' he replied. 'It was painted by one of our previous prisoners.'

I was astounded that the prison had once housed such a talented artist and wondered what his crime had been. I glanced around, taking in the rest of the room. At one end there was a stage but, other than that, there was very little else. However, the room was busy with around thirty young men milling about. The men were clean shaven, wore grey trousers and smart blue-striped shirts. Initially, I assumed they were social workers. It didn't, for one minute, cross my mind that they were actual prisoners.

The cast began to discuss the position of the stage and the show, so I wandered off towards the side. Within minutes, one of the prisoners approached me and struck up a conversation. I explained that my husband would be the main act in the show that afternoon. He smiled warmly and explained that he was a musician.

'Oh,' I said. 'What do you play?'

'The trombone,' he replied in a strong West Country accent.

'Oh, I love the trombone, especially when it's played well.'

The man nodded and looked down bashfully.

'Well, I'm not that good but I try my best.'

'So what is it you do here?' I asked, changing the conversation.

He continued to stare at his feet.

'I committed murder.'

I was gobsmacked. I was so shocked that, for the next minute, I stumbled over my words, wondering how to reply.

'Er, so, erm, what did you do?' I asked, cringing as soon as the words had left my mouth.

'Well, I was drunk. I hit someone with a house brick and it killed him,' he replied bluntly.

'Oh.'

I didn't have a clue what to say, so an uneasy silence hung in the air.

'But while I've been in here, I've become a reformed character,' he said, suddenly breaking the silence. 'I used to drink back then but I'm better now. I used to have a very bad temper but I don't anymore. That's when I decided to learn to play an instrument, so I chose the trombone.'

'Ah, I see,' I answered, nodding my head. 'So it's been good for you then – the trombone?'

The man looked up and smiled.

'So how are you getting on with it? Do you play regularly?' I said, pressing him further.

He sighed and shrugged his big heavy shoulders.

'That's my problem, you see. I don't have the trombone anymore.'

I felt a little sorry for him; it was obvious he'd loved his brass instrument.

'Why? Did they take it off you?'

'Nah, nothing like that,' he said shaking his head.

I was confused, so he decided to elaborate.

'One day, I was practising in my cell, but I couldn't get the tune quite right. I practised and practised but it just wouldn't come.'

'So what happened?' I asked.

'Well, I lost my temper. That's when I smashed the bloody thing against my cell wall. Couldn't play it after that because it was bent out of shape – it wasn't any use.'

I gasped. It was quite clear that his temper was no better now than when he'd committed the murder!

Although all the warning signs were there, ringing loudly inside my head, I was so taken back by this revelation that I found myself babbling. As usual, I said the first thing that came into my head.

'Well look, when you get out of here, do look us up. We're in the phonebook,' I insisted. 'We're listed as Mr J. Stewart.'

Johnny, who'd been standing next to me chatting to the Arab, overheard. He stepped forward and grabbed my arm.

'Sorry to interrupt,' he said, smiling at the prisoner, 'but can I just borrow my wife for a moment?'

Once we were out of earshot, Johnny asked me what on earth I was doing.

'I'm just trying to be friendly.'

'Well, don't! These men are prisoners. They're not in here for the good of their health. The Arab overheard you just now and told me to get you away before you caused a bloody riot!'

I apologised because I knew he was right.

'Sorry, Johnny,' I whispered.

'Well, you will be if he knocks on our door in a year or so's time!'

Just then, the Arab walked over.

'Pat, you're going to have to leave here because they'll be letting the others in. You'll have to go up on the balcony up there,' he said, pointing up towards the back of the hall.

'But why? I've already been down here mixing with the prisoners and I didn't even realise.'

Despite the trombonist's violent temper, the Arab explained that he and the other men in the room were considered 'good-behaviour' prisoners.

'But the ones coming in now, well, they're the big boys. No ifs and buts – you'll have to go upstairs.'

I looked over to where he was pointing. There was a balcony across the back of the room, but it was already full with around a hundred other prisoners sitting in the seats.

'But there are prisoners up there,' I remarked. 'What's the difference?'

But the Arab didn't mince his words.

'Yes, but they wouldn't be interested in you.'

'Why, what's wrong with me?'

'Nothing. It's just that lot,' he said, pointing back at them, 'are all child sex offenders.'

My mouth fell open. I was still in shock as I made my way up the stairs to the balcony to take my seat alongside some of Britain's worst sex offenders. Within moments, the hall was flooded with another 300 men, who took their seats for the performance. The show began to a rapturous applause. It was clear the men appreciated the cast putting on a performance to break up what I suppose must have been a mundane existence. The prisoners laughed like drains when Johnny acted out a particular sketch with one of the female artistes. He played the part of a married man who was having an affair. The man's mother-in-law found out and sniped back, saying she wanted to kill him.

As quick as a flash, Johnny retorted, 'Well, that could be arranged.'

We'd left the line in the sketch without even thinking although past experience had taught us it hadn't always got a laugh. However, that day, among murderers and thieves, it'd raised the biggest laugh of all. In fact, it stopped the show! Looking back, I suspect that many of those men had wanted to kill someone, even if they hadn't already. Johnny ended on it as he took a series of bows to his appreciative, if not captured, audience.

'The ones sitting next to me on the balcony all looked so normal,' I remarked after the show.

'That's the problem. They do,' the Arab chipped in.

He led the way and took us on a guided tour of the cells. We passed one cell that belonged to an accountant who'd been jailed for fraud. I'd expected to see a messy cell with nude pictures of women plastered against the walls. Instead, apart from the bars and the small window, it was so spotless that it looked like a hotel room. On his wall, there wasn't a nude in sight, only a beautiful painting of an English landscape, which he'd cut out from a magazine. He obviously stared at it while he whiled away the hours, months and years of his sentence.

At the end of the summer holiday, the children and I caught the train back to Wales, leaving Johnny to finish off the rest of the season.

As the train had pulled away from the station, the children began to compare the gifts that had been given to them by the Dartmoor prisoners. I'd been presented with a set of iron figures, made from old nails that had been welded together. They were quite beautiful, and I planned to put them on my fireplace when I returned home. The prisoners had sewn Rachel a few small soft animal toys to play with and had given our boys miniature mailbags with their names printed on the front. They read, 'HMP Dartmoor – Peter Stewart' and 'HMP Dartmoor – Stephen Stewart'.

A man sitting opposite us noticed the mailbags and commented on them.

'They're nice bags,' he said, pointing over at Peter's.

Peter nodded and pulled his mailbag closer to him as the train rumbled on.

'So,' the man's wife said, trying to strike up conversation, 'what have you all been doing for the summer?'

Peter looked at the man and his wife. He pointed down at his mailbag bag and announced something. He said it so loud that the whole train carriage heard.

'We've been to Dartmoor Prison because that's where my dad is.'

Passengers turned to look at us as an awkward silence hung in the air.

Up until that moment, I'd been sitting there all prim and posh. I was dressed in my finest clothes surrounded by my three beautiful children, but Peter had destroyed my image in one second flat.

'Oh, right. I see,' the woman mumbled, turning away from us.

Her husband shot me an odd look before disappearing back behind his newspaper. He stayed there for the rest of the journey.

I looked down at Peter who smiled back up at me. He had the face of an angel. I'd wanted the earth to swallow me whole right there and then, but it was no good because Peter hadn't even realised he'd said anything wrong.

CHAPTER 22

TAP SHOES
AND TUPPERWARE

'He said what?' Johnny chortled as soon as I rang him to tell him what Peter had done.

'Don't! It's not funny. You should have seen the way everyone looked at me. No one spoke a word to us after it.'

'Oh, don't. I think I'm going to die laughing,' Johnny howled, begging for mercy.

I imagined him wiping tears of mirth from his eyes.

'Listen love,' he said after he'd managed to compose himself. 'It won't be long before I'm home. I've only another month to go.'

I couldn't wait, even though Johnny's wages had come in handy. Now that I'd given my agency up, and with an extra mouth to feed, things had begun to feel a little tight. In fact, I was so strapped for cash that I decided to sell my beloved Mini. I loved my car but keeping a roof over our heads was more important than having a nice runaround, so I mentioned it to a friend of mine, called Kay.

'I think my manager's looking for a new car, Pat. I could ask her, if you like?'

'Yes, please do.'

A few days later, Kay and her manager – a lady called Myrna – arrived at my door.

'Hello, Pat,' Myrna said with a smile. 'Kay says you might have a car you're looking to sell.'

'Yes, that's right,' I said. 'It's just around here,' I gestured, pulling on my coat. 'Are you looking to buy it for yourself?'

'No,' Myrna replied. 'I'm looking to buy it for my husband. He works at the hospital.'

Just then, I spotted a smart blue Hillman car parked in the drive.

'But whose car is that?' I asked.

'Oh that,' Myrna said, turning around. 'That's mine. It's a company car. It comes with my job.'

I was flummoxed. Her car was absolutely gorgeous.

'Why, what job do you do?'

'I'm a Tupperware manager and they give you a car.'

I looked at Kay and then back at Myrna.

'But Kay works for Tupperware and she hasn't got a car?'

Myrna nodded.

'No, that's because Kay's an agent. I get one because Kay's in the group I manage.'

Suddenly, a light bulb flashed inside my head. I needed to sell my car, but I also needed a job to make ends meet.

'What are the chances of me becoming a Tupperware manager?' I asked.

'There's every possibility. I'll tell you what, why don't you come along on Monday, and I'll introduce you to the distributors.'

Sure enough, after I'd sold her the car, I turned up on the Monday morning and explained that I wanted to be a Tupperware manager.

'My husband is about to go into pantomime in Porthcawl and, now that I've sold mine, I won't have a car. So, you see, I'm afraid I won't be able to work for you unless you make me a manager,' I said cheekily.

After a bit of deliberation, it was decided that they'd make me a manager, even though I had no one to manage. However, I did have one thing going for me and that was a good diary of contacts. Before the meeting, I'd booked up a number of potential Tupperware parties, so they realised I had an inkling for selling, if nothing else.

To my delight, I was also given a car. Back on four wheels, I drove myself around Wales, hosting numerous parties. I was thirty-six years old, but I'd just bagged myself a new career, swapping my tap shoes for Tupperware. I loved my new life and sold those plastic bowls with a passion. At one point, I became so busy that I was hosting up to ten parties a day. My sales were so successful that I was given prizes. I won cut glass, a couple of bikes for my boys and even managed to bag us a free holiday in Spain. Over the three years that I worked for Tupperware, I rose up through the ranks to become one of their most successful managers, earning £300 to £400 a week.

THE GIRL IN THE SPOTTY DRESS

One afternoon, I'd taken Rachel, who by this time was six years old, along to one of my parties.

'Just sit there and be a good girl and don't speak to Mummy before Mummy speaks to you.'

It sounded harsh, but I knew any slight distraction could lose me a booking. My bookings not only helped to pay the mortgage; they kept the family afloat whenever Johnny found himself in between jobs.

'I won't,' Rachel said, crossing her heart with her finger.

She was a good girl, and I knew that I could rely on her. I sat her down with her dolls in a corner of the room and I got on with the business of hosting the party. By the end of the afternoon, I had a queue of ladies all eager to put their names down for their own Tupperware party.

'I'll be with you all soon,' I said as I rummaged around in my bag for my diary.

I looked up to see Rachel sitting with her arms angrily folded across her chest.

'Rachel, are you all right?' I asked.

'Yes, but I don't think much to this party,' she replied in a loud voice.

The ladies in the queue gasped and all turned to look at her. For a split second, I didn't know what to say, so I decided to humour her.

'Why, Rachel? What's wrong with the party?'

I dreaded what her answer might be.

Rachel huffed and held out her hand as she counted off the faults one by one against each finger.

'Well, there's no jelly, no ice cream, there are no party games... and there's not even a blancmange!' she complained.

Suddenly, the room erupted with laughter.

'Well, thank goodness for that,' the hostess said with a hand against her chest. 'For a moment, I wondered what she was going to say.'

Still, it had been a lesson learned. After that, I never took Rachel to a Tupperware party again.

After three years working for the company, I decided I'd had enough. It was the early 1970s and there was a new product on the market called Portmerion pottery, so I became an agent. It turned out to be a good move because the pottery proved very popular. In fact, it sold so well that I went out and bought myself a van to transport it to parties. After a particularly good sales run, I decided I needed to stop selling for other companies and sell goods myself.

'I think I'm going to buy and sell my own stock,' I said to Johnny one morning over breakfast. 'What do you think?'

He glanced up from the kitchen table.

'What, you mean stop all the parties?'

'Yes.'

Johnny thought for a moment. 'Well, you've spent years making a fortune for everyone else, so maybe now it's time to do it for yourself.'

With Johnny on board, we travelled up to Stoke, where I sourced and bought the best pottery I could find. I also ordered some cut glass from Czechoslovakia. It was so good that it rivalled the items sold in H.Samuels jewellers. I even brought in a couple of agents to sell the goods at parties because I reasoned three agents were better than one. Soon I had a warehouse full of stock and both Peter and Stephen working for me. The boys would pack the party orders up, and Johnny would drive around delivering them. With sales going well, I decided to set up my own market stall in Cardiff on Sunday, where I sold pottery and other fancy goods.

Soon the summer season was upon us. Johnny had landed a gig down in Weston-super-Mare. I decided to travel down to spend some time with him. By now, Rachel was nine years old and horse mad. She'd found a riding school nearby, where she volunteered to help out on a daily basis. It'd kept her busy and it also meant I had time on my hands. One day, I was wandering around when I passed a market near Brean sands. I spoke to the Toby – the man who ran the market – who also happened to be the Toby at the market in Cardiff, where I had a stall.

'Hello, Pat,' he said, smiling warmly as I approached. 'What are you doing here?'

'Oh, Johnny's doing a summer season down here,' I explained. 'But listen, I'd really like to sell pottery and other fancy goods here. What are my chances of hiring a space?'

The Toby nodded.

'Not a problem. I'll sort you one out.'

With my new stall in place, I brought down a van full of goods from my warehouse in Cardiff. With nowhere safe to store it, I loaded it into Johnny's dressing room.

'Hang on! Where on earth am I going to sit?' he complained, looking around the packed-out dressing room.

I picked up a box off his chair and popped it on top of an enormous pile in the corner of the room. I went back to his chair and tapped it with my hand.

'There. Look, you've plenty of room now!'

Johnny rolled his eyes, huffed and clicked on the lights around his dressing-room mirror.

'It's beginning to look like a bloody warehouse in here,' he moaned as he applied his stage makeup.

With my stock scattered from Cardiff down to Weston-Super-Mare, I decided to open more market stalls. I roped in friends and Peter and Stephen to help me. Between us, we sold at markets in Chepstow, Cardiff, Pontypridd, Newport and Port Talbot. Within the year, I'd built up the business so much that I had to buy another van. I also got Rachel to help me out on Sunday mornings in Cardiff.

With theatres becoming less fashionable and cinemas taking over, Johnny's bookings began to dry up. Instead, he'd spend hours travelling to the wholesalers to source more goods to sell on the market stalls.

A few years later, when Peter and Stephen were in the sixth form, they mentioned they were going out that night to a party.

'Is it in Cardiff?' I asked.

'Yes,' Peter replied. 'But it's not in a pub, it's at someone's house around the corner.'

I was just relieved that my boys weren't going out drinking in the busy city centre.

'Well, just be careful and look after each other, won't you?'

'Yes, Mum,' Peter promised as he closed the door and they headed off into the night.

Around 10pm, I was thoroughly shattered, so I left Johnny watching TV and headed upstairs to bed. I was awoken a few hours later by voices in the hallway. I pulled on my dressing gown and ran downstairs, where I found Stephen standing with a policeman, who was talking to Johnny.

'Whatever's the matter?' I gasped, wondering what the police were doing in my house. I looked behind them and that's when I realised Peter was missing.

'Where's your brother?' I asked Stephen.

'That's why I'm here,' the officer told me. 'Peter's at the hospital. There was an altercation at the party. I'm afraid he's sustained a nasty cut to his face.'

'Oh, my God!' I gasped. 'Is he going to be all right?'

The policeman looked up at me and nodded.

'Yes, although I'd like to take you to the hospital to see him.'

'I'll get changed now,' I gasped and ran upstairs to get dressed.

Over the next few hours, a picture began to emerge. Peter and Stephen had been at the party when a few men had turned up drunk. They knew the householder so, when they'd become rowdy, she hadn't called the police. Peter stepped in to try to calm the situation down and a fight had broken out. At some point, one of the men had smashed a plastic glass into Peter's face. Although it hadn't been glass, it was sharp enough to cut open his face. In fact, the doctor told me my son had been lucky not to lose his eye. Frightened and unsure what to do, Stephen and his friend ran to their headmaster's house nearby and he'd called the police.

The police eventually charged one of the men with assault. I was told it was so serious that the case would be transferred from magistrates to crown court, where a tougher sentence could be passed if the accused was found guilty. We waited months for the case to go to court but, eventually, the day arrived. I sat and listened as one teenager after another gave evidence for the prosecution. I was thoroughly disgusted by the men, particularly the one who'd almost blinded my son because he'd pleaded not guilty. A week or so later, the jury retired to consider its verdict. I was stressed out because the case had taken its toll not only on my boys but on the whole family. One day, I was outside speaking to one of the court clerks. I asked him how long it usually took a jury to reach a decision.

'That depends,' he replied. 'Sometimes it can be straight away, sometimes it can take ages. But you'll know they're back if you see the defendants walk past us and out of the court.'

Just as he'd said the words, the door of the court swung open and out stepped the defendants. They laughed out loud as they ran past me and towards the exit.

'Tara, love!' They shouted and smirked, trying to goad me.

I turned back towards the court clerk.

'Does that mean...'

He nodded his head.

'Sorry but it looks as though they've been found not guilty.'

A fury had boiled up inside me. I marched back into the courtroom, where the jury were standing up to leave. I stood in the middle of the court and began to shout.

'I hope you never have a child come home with his face cut like that!' I hollered.

The court clerk had run in after me and told me to be quiet, but by now I couldn't help myself.

'How can you let them go?' I screamed at the jury. 'Just look at what one of them has done to my son. How dare you do this?'

I felt someone grab my arm on either side. I turned to see two police officers who were trying to restrain me. They'd heard the commotion and had come running up from the court cells below. They thought I was a defendant on the loose! Johnny, Stephen and Peter jumped to their feet and ran over to try to rescue me.

'Let her go. She hasn't done anything wrong!' Johnny protested. 'Can't you see she's upset?'

It didn't matter; I was still ejected from the court. I sat outside on the steps and cried my eyes out. I was furious because, in my mind, they'd got away with it. For months afterwards I simmered with anger, keeping my eyes open, looking for the man who'd been found not guilty of almost blinding my eldest boy. I scoured crowds, looking at every face I passed, but I never saw him.

One day, almost a year later, I was working on one of my market stalls. It was a particularly cold Sunday morning, but I knew I had to carry on and work to pay the bills. Peter and Stephen were busy manning a stall at different market some miles away, so Rachel was helping me out. Johnny and I had bought her a couple of ponies, so it was her way of paying us back.

I was sipping a hot cup of tea, stamping my feet against the cold ground to stop them from going numb, when I spotted a familiar face in the crowd – the man who'd been found not guilty of attacking Peter. He was walking along without a care in the world with his wife and baby. I felt my stomach clench with anger. I knew it was wrong, but I couldn't help myself. My eyes scanned my stall, looking for a small but expensive item. Within seconds, I'd found one: a pile of silver-plated coasters. I picked them up and was delighted when I realised they fitted perfectly in the palm of my hand. I closed my fingers and encased them. Rachel looked over at me, wondering what on earth I was doing.

'Whatever you do, don't say a word!' I hissed, putting a finger against my lips.

Rachel's gaze followed me as I strode straight up to the man. As he passed by my stall, I plunged a hand inside his coat pocket, withdrew it and held up the coasters.

'Thief!' I shouted, looking him directly in the eye.

Other market traders had heard the commotion and came running over to try to restrain him. The market lads held him down as he tried to protest his innocence.

'But I haven't done anything!' he shouted as his wife looked on in horror.

'Tell that to the police!' one of the other traders remarked.

The police were called and the man was arrested and taken away.

'Phone your dad,' I told Rachel, pushing some coins into her hand.

She took them and rushed off to use the nearest phone box.

Of course, the man continued to protest his innocence at the police station. At first, they didn't believe him, until he explained all about the case and the fact he'd been acquitted of attacking my son.

Ten minutes later, Johnny arrived at the market. As soon as I saw him, I fell into his arms, sobbing. I knew I'd done wrong but I couldn't help it – I'd just wanted justice for my boy.

'Pat, this is serious,' Johnny said when I explained what I'd done. 'You could get into trouble for this.'

'I don't care,' I said defiantly. 'I just hope he felt as scared as Peter did.'

The police eventually let the man go, but they never did come to see or question me. Even if they had, I would have taken my punishment. I didn't care – I just wanted justice for my son.

CHAPTER 23

MAKING ENDS MEET

Rachel's love of ponies continued and soon her two animals had increased to four. Pony livery didn't come cheap, especially living in a city centre. She was competing in show jumping and dressage events, so we decided to sell our house in Cardiff and find a smaller home with a bit of land attached. We bought a two-bedroom bungalow for £26,000 at auction. It was in a small village in mid-Glamorgan called Wick, with the property set in a couple of acres of land. We suddenly went from having a city house to a place in the country but, because we had people waiting to buy our Cardiff home, we had just two weeks to complete the sale and move. It happened so fast that our dining-room furniture spent the first night stacked on the driveway!

By now, the boys were older; both had got engaged and were close to buying properties of their own. As a temporary measure, we bought a caravan for them to sleep in, which we parked on land at the back. Stephen eventually left home to marry his wife, Claire, and then Peter moved in with his fiancée.

Although theatre work had begun to dry up, Johnny managed to secure a summer-season booking in Margate, followed by a pantomime in Walthamstow, London. By now, he was fifty-nine, so he was starting to slow down. Deep down, he realised theatre work, coupled with lots of travelling, was essentially a young man's game. Once his stint in panto had come to an end, Johnny travelled back home to Wales. At that time, there had been a general water shortage even though it was still the middle of winter. It was a cold day in late January. Johnny had been busy working in the field at the back of the house, trying to repair some fencing. A few hours later, the back door swung open and he walked inside with his hands covered in mud. He went over towards the sink to wash them.

'No, don't wash your hands just yet!' I said, remembering the water shortage. 'The cats need feeding. Do that first, then you'll only need to use one lot of water.'

'All right,' Johnny said as he went outside to feed the cats.

Rachel was busy in the field. She'd put water down for the ponies and had pulled on their night rugs before leading them, one by one, into the stable for the night.

'Dinner's almost ready,' I called out to her through the back door.

Rachel raised a hand to let me know she'd heard and was on her way.

As I turned around, I noticed that Johnny was standing there, watching her through the plate-glass window.

'Oh,' I remarked, pointing towards Rachel's pony as she led him across the field. 'Look at Lord Chester. Isn't he lovely?'

My husband turned and looked at me blankly.

'Who's Lord Chester?'

I waited for the punchline, only there wasn't one.

'Lord Chester. He's Rachel's horse, Johnny.' I smiled, thinking he was having me on.

But he continued to stare.

'Who's Rachel?'

Again, I waited for the punchline. Instead, I was greeted with silence.

'It's Rachel. She's your daughter.'

But by now, a sick feeling began to swell in the pit of my stomach. My instincts told me something was very wrong.

'Johnny,' I said, looking him directly in the eye, 'we have two other children. Who are they?'

But he seemed lost.

'I don't know,' he replied, honestly.

His answer came as such a shock that it felt like a punch to my stomach.

'We have Stephen. Now, who's the other boy?'

Johnny screwed up his face in concentration. After a moment or so, he suddenly remembered.

'It's Peter!' he said, waving a finger in the air.

I felt better.

'Yes! That's right,' I said, almost sobbing with relief. 'And who am I?'

'Why, you're Pat!'

I nodded my head gratefully but tears were streaming down my face. Although he knew who Peter and I were, it was clear something was seriously wrong.

Johnny looked towards the sink and then down at his filthy hands.

'Bugger your hands, Johnny,' I said. 'Come with me.'

I led him through into the front room and sat him down before running back into the kitchen to turn up the central heating. I knew I had to ring a doctor, so I ran into the hallway to make the call.

'Please come quickly,' I told him, my voice panicked and urgent. 'It's my husband. Something's wrong. He can't remember who his children are.'

The doctor said he was on his way, so I put down the phone and ran back in to Johnny. If this was a stroke and his brain was shutting down, I was bloody well determined I wouldn't let it.

I spotted a wedding photograph of Stephen and his wife Claire on the mantelpiece. I grabbed it in my hand and held it up in front of Johnny.

'Who's this?'

But Johnny looked blank. I could see he was totally clueless.

'I don't know.'

'It's Stephen and Claire,' I said, slamming the picture back down. 'They're married. It's your son, Stephen, and your daughter-in-law, Claire. Now repeat what I've just told you.'

'It's my son and my daughter-in-law,' Johnny replied, parrot-fashion.

'Yes!'

My eyes scoured the room. I saw a lighter resting on the side table, so I grabbed it.

'What's this, Johnny?' I asked, holding it up in front of him.

Johnny stared at it.

'I don't know,' he admitted.

'It's a lighter!' I said. I clicked against it so that the flame shot up out of the top. 'You use it for lighting your pipe. Now, tell me, what is it?'

'It's a lighter.'

I wasn't sure if I was doing the right thing or not, but I reasoned that if his brain was going to sleep, I'd poke it until I managed to wake it back up. I continued to hold up objects and ask Johnny to repeat what they were. I did this until the doctor arrived. For some reason, Rachel was nowhere to be seen.

The doctor wasn't our usual GP but one from the hospital. I explained what I'd been doing.

'I don't know if it was the right thing to do,' I panicked, trying to remember all the correct and incorrect answers that Johnny had given me.

The doctor nodded. 'It was. You've done exactly the right thing. Now,' he said, placing his bag on the floor, 'do you have any junior aspirin in the house?'

My youngest child was fifteen years old, so we hadn't had junior aspirin in the bathroom cabinet for a very long time.

'No, we don't, but my neighbour might.'

At the doctor's insistence, I ran three doors down to our neighbour Yvonne, who had young children. As soon as she answered the door and found me panicked and tear-stained, her face changed.

'Pat, whatever's the matter?'

'It's Johnny. The doctor is with him now, but we need some junior aspirin. Do you have any?' I asked, blurting out the words as quickly as I could.

Yvonne dashed over to a cupboard and pulled out a packet.

'Here, take them. Take them all. Just use what you need,' she said, pressing the packet into my hand.

'Thanks, Yvonne,' I called over my shoulder as I dashed back to Johnny and the doctor.

The doctor gave Johnny some junior aspirin and wrote out a prescription for some other medication.

'You need to stop smoking your pipe and your cigars immediately, Mr Stewart. Do you understand?' he warned.

Johnny nodded obediently.

Finally, Rachel reappeared. It'd transpired that she'd come into the house and had overheard. Fearing the worst, she'd run into her stables crying. She had then made her way to a neighbour's house and stayed until she was able to compose herself and return back home. I hadn't realised it then, but she was as heartbroken as I was to have witnessed Johnny in such a state.

Days later, we travelled to hospital so that he could be examined by a specialist doctor. It was the end of January 1983 and the wearing of seat belts had just been made law, but I had a job trying to convince Johnny to belt up.

'Why do I need this?' he asked, pulling the belt away from his body.

'Because it's the law, Johnny.' I explained.

'But I've never worn one before.'

'I know, but they've made it compulsory and, if you don't wear one, I'll get into trouble with the police. You know what they're like. They're always hanging around here trying to catch speeding motorists.'

It took some persuasion, but he eventually let me fasten one around him. By the time we'd reached Bridgend hospital, my nerves were completely frazzled.

'Come on,' I said, helping him out of the car.

It was a cold day, so Johnny was wearing a big leather coat. It'd made it even more difficult to move him.

We reached the specialist's office, and I sat down in front of the doctor.

'Now then, have you been smoking, Mr Stewart?' the consultant began, looking through Johnny's medical records.

Johnny looked him straight in the eye and shook his head.

'Nope!'

The doctor seemed satisfied.

'Good, good man. Now, take off your coat so that I can take your blood pressure.'

Johnny stood up and pulled his arms from his coat. It made his cardigan ruche up underneath. There was a bit of a clatter as something fell to the floor and landed by his feet. It was his pipe. The specialist looked down at the pipe and back up at Johnny, who was standing there with a guilty look on his face.

'Mr Stewart, if you don't stop smoking, it will kill you!'

Johnny just shrugged. Short of binning the bloody thing, I knew there was very little I could do to get him to break the habit of a lifetime. The doctor explained that he believed Johnny's memory loss had been caused by the main vein in his neck. It had become furred up from a lifetime's smoking habit. But, strangely at that time, no one mentioned the word stroke to me.

Thankfully, my husband seemed to improve on medication. But now and again, he'd forget certain words, which would frustrate him.

'It doesn't matter,' I coaxed.

But it mattered to Johnny. He'd spent his whole life being a comedian. He was the past master at the sharp one-liner, always delivering it with perfect timing, yet now he'd forget even the simplest word.

As the months passed, so summer season loomed. I realised Johnny would want to go and tread the boards again but, with his memory fading, I knew it'd be impossible for him to remember the routines.

'I'll tell you what,' I said one day as we sat outside in the sunshine. 'It's going to be such a lovely summer this year, so why don't we enjoy it for a change? Why don't you leave summer season?'

Johnny turned his head and looked at me, a little startled.

'But I always do summer season.'

'I know, but panto will be here before you know it, so let's get you well, then we can concentrate on pantomime.'

Johnny thought for a moment.

'It's just a little break. I think the rest will do you good,' I insisted.

'All right,' he agreed.

Although money was tight, the last thing I wanted to do was let him sign on the dole because I didn't want him to realise how ill he was or how redundant his career had become.

The summer season came and went.

'Let's leave pantomime, Johnny,' I suggested, as the autumn nights began to draw in. 'You can do summer season next year.'

A week or so later, I was speaking to my cousin, who worked for the department of health. I told her all about Johnny and how tight our finances had become.

'Pat, Johnny will be entitled to sick benefit,' she explained.

'Really?' I said, surprised.

'Yes, he should get sick benefit. You should go in and ask about it.'

By this time we were pretty much broke, with all our savings gone, so I did as she said. Although Johnny had been ill for the best part of the year, he had to be 'sick' for another month before we could receive payment.

One day, just before Christmas, Johnny had been working in the field, when he came in through the back door. At first, he'd seemed perfectly OK. He sat down as I made us a couple of hot drinks.

'Why don't you have a rest Johnny?' I suggested, pouring boiling water into two mugs. 'There's a good war film on in a minute. We could sit and watch it.'

'Yes, all right,' he said, standing up to take off his jacket.

I turned on the television, and we settled down to watch the film. Before it'd started, I turned to say something to Johnny about Stephen's wife, Claire, who was about to give birth to her second baby.

'I wonder what Claire will have this time: a boy or a girl?' I remarked.

Johnny looked at me blankly.

'Who's Claire?'

My heart sank because I realised whatever had happened before had happened again.

I immediately ran into the hallway and called the hospital. A nurse transferred me through to the specialist, who asked if Johnny had been taking his medication.

'As far as I know, yes.'

With the doctor still on the line, I popped my head around the door of the front room and asked Johnny if he was still taking his aspirin.

'No, I stopped,' he admitted. 'The blokes in the pub said it can cause internal bleeding.'

I went back and relayed the information to the doctor.

'Get him back on aspirin straight away!'

I felt terrible because I hadn't checked if Johnny had been taking his medication. I just assumed he had been.

In the meantime, with very little money coming in, I got myself a job working with the elderly. I'd never had a proper job in my life, because I'd always been self-employed in the theatre. But now, with Johnny too sick to work, I knew I had to.

The job involved making sure old folk who'd been discharged from hospital were returning home to adequate facilities. By this time, I was fifty years old and I thought my age would count against me. In a bit of a panic, before my interview, I changed my year of birth from 1933 to 1938, which would make me forty-five years old. To my delight, I got the job! I loved it and would often argue with the doctors to ensure my clients were kept in hospital until their homes had been made safe enough for their discharge. Eventually, though, my own age caught me up. It'd reached a point where, although I was being paid, the taxman couldn't find me. I'd been doing the job efficiently for quite a few months, so I knew I was safe.

'Here, let's have a look at that paperwork,' I told my manager. 'Oh,' I said, feigning surprise, 'I can see the problem straight away. Someone must have mistyped my date of birth wrong. I was born in 1933, not 1938!'

The error was accepted and I kept my job, which was a good thing because, by now, we were broke. To make ends meet, I took on an afternoon job cold-calling for an insurance company. But we were still struggling, so I got a third job, working in the evening, behind the till at Tesco.

Johnny's health had continued to worsen. Rachel was studying hard for her A-levels and had her heart set on university, so I didn't care what it took to keep us afloat as long as it did, even if it meant juggling three jobs. If life had taught me one thing, it was that I was a survivor.

A year later to the exact date of Johnny's first health scare, my father died of a heart attack. By this time, he'd remarried a woman called Rhoda whom I hated with a passion. Dad and Rhoda had got married only eighteen months after my mother had died, but we never saw eye to eye. I remember once they'd come to visit us at our house in Wick. Dad had been so delighted to see his only granddaughter that he'd given Rachel £15, which was quite a bit of money then.

Rhoda was sat at our kitchen table, but she made it clear she didn't approve of my father's generosity. As soon as he'd handed Rachel the banknotes, she sniffed, leaned in close and whispered in my ear, 'That's the only reason you want him, isn't it, love – because of what yer can get out of 'im?'

Dad overheard and had tried to silence her, but she refused to be told. She simply couldn't hold her tongue. I hated her from that moment on. So on 26 January 1984, when she rang me to say my father had been taken ill, my senses were on full alert. I immediately caught a train and travelled up to Yorkshire to see him. I didn't want to stay with Rhoda, only Dad, so I bedded down at the hospital for the night. I was glad I did because it meant I was by his side when he died just hours later. After Dad's funeral, there was an almighty wrangle over his estate. I spoke to a solicitor, who advised me to put a block on the will because I was the executor. Everything had been left to Rhoda, with no guarantee she wouldn't leave the lot to her own spouse when she died. I realised that, with a daughter planning to go to university and a sick husband at home, I needed to fight for what was truly mine. So I did. After months of argument, I travelled up to Yorkshire to try to reason with her.

'You know my father wouldn't have wanted this,' I argued.

To my surprise, Rhoda agreed with me.

'No he wouldn't,' she replied. 'But I don't care – tha's getting nowt.'

Johnny had also tried to speak to her, but Rhoda refused to budge, so I went back to my solicitor. It took a while but, eventually, we reached a settlement and I received £18,000 from my father's estate. It was a good job because I needed it to put Rachel through university when she later won a place at Bristol to study law.

CHAPTER 24

BLAST FROM
THE PAST

I was still working, looking after the elderly, when someone decided to put on a charity event to raise money for stroke victims. It was due to take place one afternoon at a nightclub in Cardiff, called the Ocean Club. They asked if Johnny could perform but I was wary.

'As long as it's for no longer than fifteen minutes,' I insisted. 'His health comes first.'

After we'd agreed, the press agent contacted the local paper, which ran a piece on Johnny Stewart. The article explained Johnny was a stroke victim, but that he'd be heading up the entertainment for the show. Before we knew it, a researcher from *BBC Breakfast* with Anne Diamond had picked up the story, so Johnny's performance was filmed for TV. Of course, Johnny was in his element but his fifteen-minute slot had soon turned into an hour. He loved it so much that we couldn't get him off! Not that I cared. In many ways, it felt good to see my husband regain his spark. I'd watched him deteriorate for so long that it was wonderful to catch a rare glimpse of the old Johnny Stewart.

As I looked on from the sidelines with my granddaughter, Rebecca, in my arms, a woman sidled over to me.

'Isn't he marvellous?' she remarked, pointing over towards Johnny.

'Yes,' I agreed and grinned. 'He's all right, isn't he?'

It was obvious this woman had no idea who I was.

'He's had a stroke, you know?' she remarked.

I turned to face her.

'Has he?'

'Yes. You know, he couldn't even speak when he'd had the stroke?'

'Really,' I replied, wondering what she'd say next.

'It's true. But his wife has taught him how to speak again and now look at him,' she said, gesturing over towards Johnny. 'He's up there doing an hour's patter!'

I didn't say another word, but I felt proud of my husband. By now, Johnny had suffered a series of small strokes, which had brought on a condition known as vascular dementia. It's a particularly cruel disease, which was slowly robbing my husband of his memory and razor-sharp wit. It was also taking him from me, piece by piece.

Johnny was still buzzing as he wrapped up his half of the show. His eyes were on fire as he left the stage.

'You were brilliant, darling,' I said, giving him a kiss.

I choked back my emotion because I knew it would probably be the last time I ever saw him perform... and it was.

The following day, Johnny had another, bigger stroke, this time more debilitating than ever before. It had put an end to his show-business career in a heartbeat, and it was one stroke from which he never fully recovered.

The years passed by. One Sunday morning, Stephen, his wife, Claire and their daughter Rebecca were over at my house when the phone rang.

'Won't be a mo,' I said and I left them chatting to Johnny.

I headed out into the hallway to answer the call.

'Pat,' a voice said as soon as I picked up the receiver. 'It's Paula, Claire's sister.'

'Hello,' I replied, half-expecting her to ask me to put Claire on the phone.

'No,' she said, realising my confusion. 'It's you I want.'

'Me? Why?'

'Listen, did you ever work at Blackpool when you danced with the Tiller Girls?'

I was a little taken back by her odd and unexpected question, but I answered her truthfully.

'Yes, I did. I danced on the North Pier. Paula, why are you asking me this?'

Paula was younger than Claire and, although I'd met her, I didn't know her very well. Paula, like Rachel, was a student, so my first thought was that maybe she was doing some research for a project.

'Pat, you're in a Sunday paper,' Paula said suddenly. 'I've got it here in front of me now. I knew it was you the moment I saw it!'

'Are you sure?' I asked, a little flummoxed.

'Absolutely! I'm looking at a photograph of you right now. You're sat on some railings but there are other photos of you in the paper too.'

'OK,' I said, recalling the Blackpool Belles photograph over thirty-seven years before. 'Tell me: what am I wearing?'

I heard the rustle of newspaper as Paula turned the page to have another look.

'A black-and-white spotted dress.'

'No,' I replied. 'It's not me, Paula. I've never had a black-and-white spotted...'

But as the words left my mouth, I realised the photograph had been taken in black and white. I put a hand to my chest and gasped, '...but I had on a cream-and-brown spotted dress.'

'Pat, you need to go out and buy this paper now. I'm certain it's you,' Paula insisted.

I almost dropped the phone in shock as I shouted to Stephen and Claire.

'Quick!' I said, grabbing my coat. 'I need to get to the shops before they shut!'

Stephen jumped in his car and drove me into Bridgend to buy a newspaper.

I handed over the money, wet a finger and flicked through the paper, with butterflies rising inside my stomach. Halfway through, I stopped turning and froze.

'My God!' I gasped, holding the paper open to show my son. 'It is me. It's me and Wendy Clarke!'

Stephen peered over my shoulder and grinned. 'Look at that,' he said and laughed. 'You're famous, Mum!'

I was still in shock. My hands trembled as I read the story printed at the side of the photograph.

'What is it? What do they want?' Stephen asked.

'It's an appeal. The BBC wants to recreate the shot for a new calendar. Only this time, we'll have our picture taken with Bert Hardy, the photographer.' I looked up at Stephen and gasped. 'My God, everyone's looking for us!'

As soon as we arrived home, I dialled the number printed at the bottom of the article. But it was a Sunday so no one was there. Instead, I left a message with my name and contact details.

Later that day, the phone rang and it didn't stop until late at night. Everyone had called to tell me the BBC was looking for me and Wendy. The newspaper had used different shots from the day, not just the side profile of me on the railings, so they'd all recognised me, from an ageing aunt in a care home to school friends I'd not seen for years. The following morning, the phone rang again. This time it was someone from the BBC, who asked if I could come to London.

I thought of my three jobs and sighed. I didn't have time to travel to Cardiff, never mind London.

'I can't,' I explained, my heart sinking.

'Why not?'

'Because I'm working.'

'Can't you get time off work?' the man at the BBC asked.

'I wouldn't have thought so,' I replied, thinking I'd have to run it past three bosses, not one.

'Look,' he said, 'if we send a helicopter for you, would you come then?'

I was astonished.

'A helicopter?' I repeated, as though I'd misheard him.

'Yes, that's right. A helicopter.'

Bloody hell, I thought. *There might be some money in this!*

'OK, let me find out. I'll ask at work and ring you back.'

To my delight, all three bosses agreed that I should go. Although the suggested helicopter ride never materialised, later that same day, I booked train tickets for me and Johnny to travel to London. I told the BBC that I'd paid for first-class seats. It'd been years since I'd been pampered, so I asked if they would pay for my hair and nails to be done too. I also billed for new clothes and taxis even though I drove my own car to the station. I reasoned that I'd never made a penny out of the Blackpool Belles photo, so now it was time to milk it for all it was worth. In total, my 'expenses' came to just under £500.

Once we arrived in London, we caught a cab to the Hilton, where Wendy was already waiting.

'I can't believe it! Wendy Clarke, as I live and breathe!' I squealed with excitement, holding out my arms.

'Pat!' Wendy shrieked and ran over to me.

'My God, it's been almost forty years but you haven't changed a bit!' I remarked, holding her at arm's length to look at her.

'Neither have you!'

Unlike me, Wendy had never married and didn't have children, yet the years just peeled away as we caught up on each other's news.

A few hours later, we boarded a boat on the Thames and enjoyed a champagne breakfast that had been laid on by the BBC.

'So do you still dance?' I asked Wendy.

'No,' she laughed. 'I work in a shop. How about you, Pat?'

I shook my head.

'No, Johnny's not been well, so I'm holding down three jobs as well as looking after him.'

Our lives had suddenly felt a far cry from our glamorous days as Tiller Girls, dancing on stage in Blackpool.

'Never mind,' I said, patting Wendy's hand with mine. 'They were good times, and I wouldn't swap them for the world.'

'Me neither,' she said and grinned.

'Besides, look at us now!'

Later that day, we were reunited with Bert Hardy, the *Picture Post* photographer.

'Hello, ladies!' Bert said, beaming from ear to ear. 'If it isn't my two Blackpool Belles. How are you?'

It was good to see Bert and catch up on that memorable day.

'I was mortified when the wind blew my dress up but not as horrified as I was when you published it, because I looked as though I wasn't wearing any knickers!'

The three of us began to chuckle during the photo shoot, only this time Bert wasn't the man behind the camera.

'Bert if you could just grab the hem of Pat's coat and lift it up slightly,' the photographer called as we started to laugh once more.

The photographer asked Wendy and me to sit on the railings of the boat, with Big Ben in the background, and we recreated the Blackpool Belles picture for the new calendar. It'd felt like a lifetime since we'd last met and, in many ways, it was. Back then, I'd been a giggling seventeen-year-old girl without a care in the world and her whole life in front of her. But with age comes responsibility, and now I had a sick husband to care for and my dancing career was a thing of the past.

The BBC picture library used the up-to-date photograph inside the calendar, with the old Blackpool Belles image featured prominently on the front.

Afterwards, we were asked to do a series of newspaper, radio and TV interviews, including BBC's *Pebble Mill* show, which was filmed in Birmingham. Sadly, Wendy wasn't on *Pebble Mill*, because she couldn't get time off work, but Bert and I went on.

For a brief moment, it felt as though I was there, back on stage, performing for the public. I realised just how much I missed my old way of life and also how much Johnny's illness had affected me. Before, I'd been surviving on a day-to-day basis, scratching around for money, but now I was sick of it. I had to do something positive, so I put our bungalow up for sale. Remarkably, I sold it three times over because I had numerous buyers interested. In the end, it went for £99,000, leaving us with a healthy profit. It was a good job because I knew we'd need it in the months and years ahead.

I decided to use the money to buy a new house off plan. It cost me £40,000, but I knew it would provide us with a secure future. There was a housing boom at the time. Property prices were going through the roof, and I couldn't afford to be gazumped by another buyer. With the extra money, I booked a holiday for us to Corfu. We hadn't had a proper holiday for years, so I thought it would be just the tonic.

Once we were in our new home, we settled down to the quiet life. Stephen and Claire had had a fourth child, so we became doting grandparents to Rebecca, Sally, Kate and Matthew. It wasn't long before I grew accustomed to my new role in life.

CHAPTER 25

LOSING JOHNNY

One day, Rachel telephoned me at home. By this time, she had finished her law degree at Bristol University.

'Mum,' she began, 'I've decided something – I don't want to be a lawyer.'

I was worried she was going to tell me that she wanted to become a perpetual student but Rachel laughed and explained: 'No, Mum. I don't want to go back to university; I want to go into advertising.'

A short time later, she landed herself a job in London, working for one of the big advertising agencies. It wasn't long before she was head hunted by an American firm that offered her the chance to go and work in Holland for a couple of years. Once over there, she met someone and her two-year stay turned into something more permanent.

'Why don't you and Dad come out to see me?' she asked one day.

So we did. Rachel lived in a beautiful flat that was situated on the border of the notorious red-light district in Amsterdam, and the bar around the corner had become her local. At that time, Rachel travelled all over the world with her job so, one afternoon, after she'd jetted off to America, we decided to nip around the corner to her local pub for a drink. Johnny and I soon got chatting to two men who served with the U.S. Air Force. They were based in Holland but were due to leave to carry out peace missions to Rwanda, flying over vital aid. Despite his doctor's advice, Johnny still smoked a pipe. He was puffing away on it quite happily as we all sat together in a corner of the bar, laughing and joking. One of Rachel's clients had shown her how to do the statue of liberty – a bar trick – which she'd taught me. It involved wetting your finger, setting it on fire and knocking back a drink, which sounds more dangerous than it actually was. It was a great party trick, so I decided to show the Americans how to do it.

'You wet your finger like this,' I said, dipping it in the alcohol. 'Johnny,' I said, gesturing over at him, 'Give me your lighter a minute.'

Johnny passed it over. I lit my finger and promptly knocked back my drink. It made the two American pilots fall about with laughter.

We were still laughing when the owner of the bar walked over to our table.

'I'm sorry,' he began, 'but I'm afraid I'm going to have to ask you all to leave.'

I glanced over at the Americans, at Johnny and then down at my unlit finger.

'But it was only a party trick,' I protested, thinking he'd objected to the flame.

The owner shook his head.

'No, it isn't that.'

'But what have we done wrong?' I asked, turning around in my chair to face him.

The owner looked at me as though it should be obvious.

'I'm sorry, but we don't allow drugs in this bar. They're available in other places – mainly the cafes – but we don't allow them in here.'

My eyes darted over towards the two Americans sat opposite. They looked as equally bewildered.

Bloody hell! I thought. *You can't judge a book by its cover. They both seemed so nice but they were on drugs all along.*

The two airmen glanced over at me and Johnny. No doubt they were thinking, *It just goes to show. These two old dears seemed so nice but they're both on drugs!*

Then I looked at Johnny, who'd been puffing happily on his pipe throughout.

'Wait a minute,' I said, looking back at the owner. 'What makes you think we're smoking drugs over here?'

'It's the smell,' he replied, sniffing the air.

I started to laugh and soon I couldn't stop. Everyone at the table – the pilots, the owner, even Johnny – was looking at me completely baffled.

'It's the pipe,' I snorted in between fits of laughter. 'It's not drugs! It's Johnny's pipe – that's what's making that awful smell.'

The owner blushed a little as it dawned on him that we weren't international drugs barons, just a couple of pensioners from Wales.

'OK,' he replied in a voice that suggested he still harboured doubts, 'but he'll have to put it out, otherwise you'll have to leave.'

After he'd left, the four of us began to giggle – we'd found the whole incident highly amusing.

'Eh,' I said, nudging Johnny as he placed the pipe back inside his pocket. 'We'll have to be careful or we'll end up on the front page of the papers again. I can just see it,' I said, drawing my hand across the air to form an imaginary headline. 'Comedian with wacky-backy pipe caught in major drugs swoop!'

We dissolved into fits of laughter, and the bar owner looked over at us oddly.

Once she'd returned, Rachel offered to give us a guided tour of the red-light district along with a retired policeman, called Harry, and a Dutch lawyer, called Michel. Dozens of ladies were sat in windows, displaying their wares, or stood out in the street. To his delight, as we walked past, a few of them approached Johnny.

'Hello, Johnny,' one cooed.

His head spun around and he looked at the woman with a bemused look on his face.

A few yards down the same street, another hooker draped her arm lazily across his shoulder.

'Hi, Johnny. Want to come inside?' she offered.

Johnny looked over at me, completely flabbergasted. I smiled, but I didn't say a word.

It continued to happen, with different women saying 'hello, Johnny' at almost every building we passed. By the end of the tour, my husband seemed highly delighted.

'Did you see that, Pat? They all knew who I was.' He beamed, puffing out his chest proudly. 'Looks like the old Johnny Stewart lives on, even in Holland!'

Rachel and I shared a secret smile. We didn't have the heart to tell him that, in Holland, they call all the men 'Johnny' as a term of endearment. He'd seemed so happy that we decided not to enlighten him.

'Let's not burst his bubble. Let him enjoy the moment,' I whispered to Rachel.

We continued to visit Rachel. A few years later, she bought her first house. By this time, she'd started a relationship with a man called John and had given birth to their daughter, who they called Eve. With a new granddaughter to fuss over, we decided to go over to see them more often.

One afternoon, we were sat in Rachel's house enjoying a cup of tea when Johnny suddenly piped up, 'I fought at Arnhem, you know. I fought over here.'

We all turned to look at him.

'We were pinned down by enemy fire in some woods,' he continued, lost in his thoughts.

Rachel and John looked at me and I glanced over at Johnny. I was astounded. My husband had never spoken to me about the war before. At first, I thought it might be a figment of his imagination, triggered by the onset of dementia, but Johnny was adamant.

'No, it happened,' he insisted.

I had no idea where Arnhem was in relation to where we were staying, but it transpired that it was only an hour's drive away.

Rachel's partner, John, made a suggestion.

'Why don't we take Johnny to Arnhem on Saturday?'

Johnny nodded eagerly.

'Yes, I'd like that,' he replied.

The following Saturday, we travelled to Arnhem in the car. As we approached, Johnny began to repeat the same thing over and over again. 'We were fighting in the woods – the woods that surround Arnhem. We were held down by enemy fire. It all happened so fast.'

In all our married life, Johnny had never mentioned Arnhem or the woods to me once. In fact, he'd always steadfastly refused to talk about the war. But sure enough, as soon as we approached Arnhem, I spotted the war cemetery – it was surrounded by hundreds of trees.

'I wonder if those are the woods Dad was referring to,' I said to Rachel as we pulled up.

We walked over to the cemetery, which was both still and haunting, and began to wander around it. It had been established in 1945 and was home to 1,759 graves from the Second World War. The soldiers buried there were mostly Allied servicemen who had been killed in the Battle of Arnhem, during an Allied attempt to cross the river Rhine. The failed attempt to break through German lines, in September 1944, had later been made into a film called *A Bridge Too Far*. Other soldiers buried there had been killed during the liberation of the city the following year.

As we walked around in silence, looking at the long uniformed lines of pale headstones, something clicked inside Johnny's brain. It was as though the cemetery had acted like a key, unlocking a small part of his memory that had been closed off years before.

'I lost my mate here,' he said suddenly, his voice faltering to a whisper.

By now, I fully believed everything he'd told us.

'Who was your mate?'

Johnny choked back his emotions.

'Llewellyn. He was only eighteen. He was shot by a sniper in the woods.'

We weren't sure if Llewellyn was a surname or a Christian name, so Rachel's partner walked over to the office to look it up. He reappeared and took Johnny by the arm.

'Come on, Johnny. I know where your mate is buried. Follow me.'

We followed John across the graveyard. After a few minutes, he came to a halt by the gravestone of a young man. His name was Llewellyn, and he'd been killed at eighteen years old, just as Johnny had said. My blood ran cold, as though I'd just seen a ghost.

'Good Lord,' I gasped, putting a hand against my mouth. 'Johnny, you were right all along.'

Johnny nodded solemnly and began to explain.

'We were both with the Fourth Welsh Regiment. I was eighteen years old too, but somehow that bullet missed me, even though I was standing right next to him. I suppose I was the lucky one that day,' he said sadly, shrugging his shoulders.

We stood there in a moment's silence as a mark of respect for all the brave soldiers who'd lost their lives in the bloody battle of Arnhem. Emotion suddenly began to overwhelm me as I thought of Johnny's friend and how the bullet could have quite easily hit my husband instead. My life would've been so different, if only for the hand of fate. I reached for a tissue and dabbed away my tears. On the way back home, the car was silent. We were all lost in our thoughts, thinking of Johnny's friend and what might have been. Suddenly, his voice broke the silence.

'I once hid in a windmill to escape the German soldiers,' he said, unveiling another hidden moment from his past.

For years, Johnny had locked away his wartime experiences in his head, buried along with his friend. But somehow, his dementia had allowed him to reopen the box and bring them out into the open again. It was strange to hear Johnny speaking of life before I'd met him – the time before he'd become a star of both stage and screen. My husband had witnessed such horrors. I wondered if a life in comedy had been his way of helping to erase some of those awful memories.

Once we were back in Wales, Johnny's health began to deteriorate rapidly. His coordination was impeded, his memory fading and his vocabulary failing. It was heartbreaking to hear him stumble and search for even the simplest word, given that he'd once performed to hundreds of people, thinking on his feet and getting by on sharp wit alone. I tried my best to help with his walking. I'd play music from the 1940s, usually 'Roll Out the

Barrel'. Together, we'd march around the house, going through the old dance routines, step by step – anything to stop this awful disease from stealing another part of my husband.

Johnny had been diagnosed with something called 'left-side neglect'. It had been caused by strokes to the right side of his brain. Sometimes he'd falter and, often, he'd fall over. I wasn't strong enough to pick him up, so I'd just sit on the floor beside him and tell him to mirror my movements in an attempt to get him to lift himself back up again. Eventually, he became so weak that he was confined to a wheelchair.

On my seventieth birthday, Stephen and Claire decided to throw a party for me. Rachel and her family had planned to travel over for it, so I was really looking forward to having a get-together. A few days before, I'd decided to take Johnny out for the day, to get him some fresh air. By now, our finances were running low, so I'd sold our house and bought a new mobile home. Unfortunately, it was still being built, so we rented a caravan at Fontgary – the same caravan park where we'd begun our married life.

'Let's get out from these four walls, eh?' I suggested to Johnny. 'We could both do with a bit of fresh air.'

I helped my husband outside and into the car and drove to a nearby shopping centre. Later that evening, after we'd returned home, Johnny suffered a massive stroke. He was rushed to Bridgend hospital, where he remained. Johnny continued to have a series of strokes, so I sat with him from 8am until 9pm every day, leaving only to return home to my bed. This pattern continued right up until Christmas, when the doctors told me

I was allowed to bring him home for the day. I returned him to hospital but, on Boxing Day, he suffered a massive stroke and slipped into a coma.

As I sat by his side, willing him to get better, I noticed lots of things. I felt his care wasn't quite what I thought it should be. After he'd regained consciousness, the staff seemed to be sedating Johnny, rather than encouraging him to get up and move about. I felt as though everyone had given up on him – everyone apart from me and my children. Eventually, I became so frustrated that he was being neglected that I spoke to a doctor. I recognised this particular medic because he'd once transferred my husband to a wonderful respite hospital, specially equipped for people living with dementia.

'Oh, I'm so pleased to see you again,' I began, trying to stop the tears from streaming down my face. 'Please could you take my husband back into your hospital instead?'

'Why?' the doctor asked, concerned.

I explained that I wasn't happy with the level of care Johnny had received.

'I feel as though they're sedating him to keep him quiet.'

'I'm sorry, Mrs Stewart,' the doctor said gently. 'But I can't. He's under another doctor's care, so it's not ethical for me to do it. I just can't intervene and remove him.'

But I was desperate and the doctor knew it. I felt my husband was being allowed to die without the high level of care he deserved.

Later that evening, I was sat at home, unsure what to do or who to turn to, when the telephone rang. It was a colleague of the doctor.

'We are doing some tests into vascular dementia and we'd like your husband to take part. Would you be willing?' he asked.

I knew what it was. The doctor had moved both heaven and earth to bring Johnny back under his care during the last months of my husband's life. The news lifted my heart no end and I readily agreed.

'Thank you,' I gasped, emotion overwhelming me.

To my relief, Johnny was moved the following morning. Within days, because the hospital hadn't sedated him, not only was he moving, but the nurses and I had got him up walking again. I sang and hummed old dance tunes as we stepped through some of the old stage routines – anything to try to keep his brain alive.

Towards the end of his life, Rachel was sat holding her father's hand, as we remembered our visit to Holland.

'Dad,' she whispered, 'would you like to go back to Arnhem?'

Johnny was holding my hand too. As soon as she said the word Arnhem, he squeezed it in reply.

'Well, you're not going back there on your own,' I said, stroking his face gently. 'This time, we'll all be with you.'

I was there with my children and my beloved Johnny when he died just a few weeks later, on 15 February 2000. It was the day before Stephen's fortieth, but he was with us as we registered his father's death on his birthday, and Stephen took care of all of the funeral arrangements on that day. It sounds strange, but we took Stephen a bottle of champagne and a cake because we knew it's what Johnny would have wanted. My husband was, without a doubt, the love of my life and I still miss him with every breath I take.

After his death, we held a simple service at Wick village church, followed by a cremation at Bridgend crematorium. Peter had arranged for a jazz band to accompany us to the church. It must have been the half-term holidays because, as we drove through Wick village, I noticed that children were dancing in the street in time to the music.

'Your dad would have loved this,' I smiled as we passed by in the funeral car. 'Pantomime and entertaining children was what he always loved the most.'

I pulled out a tissue to soak up my tears.

Rachel had chosen one her father's favourite songs to sing in church. It was a pantomime song called 'John Brown's Baby's Got a Pimple on his Nose', although it was more widely known as 'John's Brown's Body'.

At first, I'd been surprised by Rachel's choice but, once she started singing, the whole congregation joined in, clapping along. It was joyful but, at the same time, extremely moving. I knew, without a doubt, that Johnny would have been looking down approvingly. When we reached the crematorium, Johnny's elder brother sang a Welsh song and the British Legion provided us with a bugler, who played 'The Last Post'.

After my husband's funeral, life was a bit of blur. One morning, I searched through some old boxes and pulled out documents with Johnny's regiment and army number written on them. Rachel contacted the Dutch branch of the British Legion, which managed to trace my husband through his documents. An official there spoke to the War Graves Commission in Belgium, which agreed it would be possible to inter Johnny's ashes at Arnhem cemetery. Someone had even asked the Canon of Northern Europe to conduct a service for Johnny, so that his ashes could be formally interred alongside his fellow soldiers.

With all the arrangements in place, we travelled over to Holland with Johnny's ashes in a casket. I'd placed it inside a cool bag because I'd wanted to be discreet. Once we'd cleared customs at Schiphol airport, Rachel met us outside in her Range Rover. Together, we began the final part of Johnny's journey to Arnhem. But as we taxied along the road, the back of the car flew open.

'Rachel, the back hatch has come open!' Stephen called out in a panic.

'Oh, heck!' said Rachel, signalling and pulling to a halt at the side of the road. She turned around in the driver's seat to see the door of the boot swinging open to reveal the open road behind us.

'My God!' she gasped. 'You've not lost Dad out of the back door, have you?'

'No,' Stephen said with a grin, wrapping his hands protectively around his father's wooden ashes casket. 'He's right here, on my lap.'

With that, we all began to laugh and cry with both hilarity and emotion. As usual, Johnny Stewart had had the last laugh. Even though I knew life would never be the same again, it was time for Johnny to take his final bow and bid his audience farewell.

CHAPTER 26

BACK IN THE SPOTLIGHT

Following Johnny's death, I asked myself a question that most widows must find themselves asking: 'What am I supposed to do now?'

I'd spent most of my life caring for my children, and then my husband, so I suddenly felt redundant. I was lost and seemed to have no place in the order of things. One day, something else dawned on me: 'Who will look after me?'

The answer had echoed loud and clear inside my head: 'I will.'

But it still felt odd because it had be the first time in forty-six years that I was responsible for only one person. I'd expected it to feel liberating but, instead, it'd felt lonely. I had lots of acquaintances but no real friends. Johnny's illness had spanned over twenty years and I'd discovered, to my cost, that, if people can't 'see' an illness, they are frightened by it. If something is visible and regular, people accept it. Dementia is not. It's a cruel illness that steals away the person you love until all you are left with is a shell of their former selves. But you refuse to walk away or give up because you still love them.

My family had been supportive throughout, but they had families of their own to care for, so I didn't want to burden them. At the same time, I didn't have a clue what I should do next. One Sunday morning, I was sat wondering where life would take me, when I made a decision. I knew I couldn't stop from growing old, but I didn't want to have to be nursed by my family. I glanced across at the cigarette packet on the side cabinet. In many ways, cigarettes had been my salvation when times had been stressful and challenging. But I knew they'd slowly kill me, just as they'd done to Johnny. I got up from my chair, picked up the packet and crushed it between my fingers. Then I began to search the house until I'd emptied it of all the cigarettes I could find. I picked up the lot in a heap and threw them in the bin. With nothing else to do, I stood up, put on my coat and walked over to the bingo hall. I decided I may as well enjoy Sunday lunch there because I couldn't be bothered to go to too much effort cooking for just one person. After lunch, I sat back to let my food digest. As I did, a telltale wisp of grey cigarette smoke curled around in front of my face. A young woman had lit up a cigarette behind me. As the smoke continued to swirl around in the air, I thought how I would've done exactly the same had I not just binned the lot earlier that morning.

'Excuse me,' I said, turning to tap the woman on the shoulder.

Her head turned defensively, as though I was about to scold her for lighting up a fag directly behind me.

'Yes?' she replied, blowing the smoke out of the side of her mouth.

'My name is Pat Stewart, and I gave up smoking this morning.'

The woman put the cigarette back in her mouth and took a long drag from it as she considered what I'd just said. She blew out a lungful of smoke, looked up at me and smiled.

'Well done, babe,' she said, patting me warmly on the arm.

I'd never been called 'babe' in my life before, so I wasn't sure if it was a derogatory remark. But then the woman did something quite remarkable. She looked at the cigarette in her hand and stubbed it out on the flat metal ashtray in front of her.

'If you can do it, so can I,' she replied.

Her mother, who was sat at the side of her, was also smoking. She looked at her daughter and then over at me. Without a word, she took her half-smoked cigarette and did exactly the same.

'Me too!' she agreed.

We started chatting and the three of us soon became good friends. I began to open up and tell them all about Johnny and his dementia.

'Smoking robbed my brilliant husband of his wit, his memory and his life.' I said as the women listened.

After that day, I never smoked another cigarette. I can't be sure if my new friends stuck to it, but I do know they didn't smoke for a very long time afterwards.

A few months later, my friend Sadie, who was visiting relatives in Wales, called me up.

'Pat, have you seen the *Daily Mail*?' she asked.

'No.'

'Well, you should go out and buy it. There's a woman in there who is claiming to be you. She says she's the girl in the spotty dress!'

Sadie wasn't far from me, so she nipped over with her copy of the newspaper. Sure enough, there was a woman called Norma Edmondson, who had claimed to be me, sitting on the railing at Blackpool prom in 1951.

'Told you!' Sadie said, crossing her arms in annoyance. 'You should ring the paper and tell them they've got it wrong. That woman,' she said, jabbing the paper with her finger, 'is an imposter!'

'But what can I do about it?' I asked.

Johnny's death hadn't just knocked the stuffing out of me; it had robbed away my confidence too.

'You should ring up the reporter and let him know he's made a mistake,' Sadie insisted.

But I was still grieving for Johnny, so I really couldn't be bothered to get involved in a wrangle. However, Sadie had made such an effort in bringing the newspaper over to me that I felt I owed it to her to make the call.

The journalist at the *Daily Mail* was very charming but he suggested that, if I truly was the girl in the spotty dress, I should be able to prove it.

'But how can I do that?' I asked Sadie after I'd put down the phone. 'The photo was taken years ago. How on earth do I prove I'm the girl in the photo and not this Norma whatshername?'

Sadie seemed as stumped as me.

'I don't know, Pat,' she said, shaking her head sadly.

With no energy or clue how to stand and fight my ground, I put the whole thing to the back of my mind. I allowed the lady her moment in the spotlight, while I tried to pick up the pieces of my life. Lonely and bored, I visited Age Concern and offered to become a volunteer. At first, I helped out doing the charity's banking every Wednesday, which helped my confidence return. Slowly, I'd begun to feel like a member of society once more. Desperate to keep busy, I set up a keep-fit class for the ladies who visited the Age Concern café. I ran the class every Wednesday at 9am, charging each person £1, which I donated back to Age Concern. Soon I had more and more ladies attending.

'This is great, Pat! I love coming here,' one of my regulars said after we'd finished the hour-long session. 'It gives me a reason to get out of bed in the morning.'

That's when it had occurred to me: there were lots of other widows, just like me, who needed a hobby – something to look forward to. Our class began visiting other groups of old people in the area, to give a demonstration and to encourage them to get up out of their chairs and move around again. Being the ultimate professional, I used my dance training to choreograph easy-to-follow routines.

'I think we should all wear black with matching neck scarves, so we look more uniformed,' I suggested, recalling my time with the world-famous Tiller Girls.

'That sounds like a great idea!' someone piped up from the back of the room.

With our new uniforms, our 'dance' routines were timed to precision. In fact, we became an OAP version of the Tiller

Girls! I decided to nickname our group The Geriatric Tillers as word spread and the dance class began to flourish. It became so popular that we began to take more and more bookings in old folks' homes.

One of my favourite dances was a cane routine to 'All that Jazz', although most of my ladies used walking sticks instead of canes. After one show, we even received a standing ovation. Recalling my time on the stage, I turned towards our audience.

'Would you like some more?' I cried, cupping a hand against my ear.

The whole room chorused an overwhelming, 'Yes!'

Out of the corner of my eye, I spotted one of my ladies. She was leaning up against her stick, panting for breath.

'No more, Pat!' she begged and we all laughed along with her.

Sadly, the more I danced, the more my hips and knees began to ache. It became so bad that I had to give up teaching. With a more sedate lifestyle, in the years that followed, I became grandmother to nine grandchildren and two great-grandchildren. Inside me there remained an overwhelming sadness that Johnny hadn't lived to witness our ever-growing family. Out of all my grandchildren, only Rebecca had ever seen her grandfather perform, although she was far too young to recall it. I'd have loved the others to have watched him in pantomime or appear alongside him, just as their parents had done.

A few months later, I visited Holland, and I was thinking about Johnny when a crushing loneliness swamped me.

'What's the matter, Granny?' Jacob, my grandson, asked.

I looked down at him, his eight-year-old face crumpled with concern.

'Oh, I don't know, Jacob. I just miss your granddad, that's all. I wish he could be here to watch you all grow but, instead, I'll grow old without him.'

Jacob listened, thought for a moment and then took my hand in his.

'Don't be sad about growing old, Granny,' he said.

'What do you mean?'

'Well, it's like this: the life we are living now isn't our true life.'

I was puzzled. I didn't understand what he meant.

'Go on,' I encouraged.

'No. This isn't our true life. You see, we are all asleep. It's only when we die, like Granddad Johnny, that we wake up. That's when we start to live the life we are meant to.'

I shook my head with bewilderment.

'Who taught you that?'

Jacob looked up at me. Now it was his turn to look puzzled.

'No one.'

'But where did you read it? You must have read that in a book somewhere?'

Jacob shook his head.

'Nope, I just know it.'

I looked down at my grandson as though I was seeing him for the very first time. I couldn't believe a boy so young could say something so profound.

It had been ten years since Johnny's death but, somehow, in just a few words, Jacob had not only managed to comfort me but convinced me not to view death as an ending but as a new beginning. It certainly wouldn't bring Johnny back, but it had made his loss easier to bear.

I was staying over in Holland, looking after Eve and Jacob, because Rachel was away in Belgium, taking part in an art show. I was sat in her lounge, waiting for *EastEnders* to begin, when I heard Jacob's voice shout me.

'Quick! Granny Pat. You're on television!' he gasped, grabbing my hand and dragging me over towards the TV.

I looked at the TV and saw Phil Tufnell, the former cricketer, holding a book up towards the camera. On the front of it was the picture of me and Wendy – the Blackpool Belles – taken on the promenade many years ago. Suddenly, Phil turned towards a woman I vaguely recognised. He started to ask her about the photo. It took me a moment to register but then it clicked – she wasn't an expert, or even a photographer – it was bloody Norma Edmondson, the woman who'd been in the *Daily Mail* – the woman, who, by the looks of it, was saying she was the girl in the photograph!

'The bloody cheek!' I snorted angrily.

I turned up the volume as Phil asked the woman about the photograph taken on that blustery day on Blackpool promenade. But she couldn't remember – in fact, she couldn't really answer any of his questions.

'That's because you weren't there. It's not you!' I shouted at the television.

Jacob looked at me with wide eyes, as though his granny had gone completely mad. But I hadn't gone mad – I *was* mad! I was bloody fizzing!

I was about to ring up BBC's *The One Show* to complain when the phone rang. It was Kay, my friend from Cardiff.

'Pat. Thank goodness! Are you watching *The One Show*? There's a woman on there pretending to be the girl in the photograph!'

'I know!' I exclaimed. 'I've got it on right now! The bloody cheek of it!'

'Pat, you have to tell them it's you. You have to prove you're the girl in the spotty dress, not her!' Kay insisted.

'I know but how on earth can I do that?'

'Well if you won't, I will. Pat, I have known you for over forty years. I know it's you in that photo and not Norma thingymebob. Someone needs to put a stop to this right now!'

'But how?' I said. 'How can we?'

But Kay was adamant.

'I'm going to ring up *The One Show* and tell them they've got it wrong!'

With that, Kay put down the phone to me and spoke to a researcher on *The One Show*. Moments later, she called me back.

'Do you have anything that proves you're the girl in the spotty dress?' she asked.

'I... I... can't think of anything I have.'

Without proof, I knew I was stuck. Who would believe the word of an old lady without proof? Especially when there was someone else so insistent it was her?

Rachel also telephoned the show in protest, but they said, again, that I needed to prove it.

'But how can I prove I was on that promenade fifty years ago?' I said to Rachel.

The producer called my daughter back. He told her that Norma had insisted she was the girl in the spotty dress and not only that, but that her friend Alice had claimed to be Wendy! He explained that Norma had said they'd been in Blackpool in the 1950s when an unknown photographer had asked them to pose for the iconic photo.

'But it's a famous photograph. Bert Hardy isn't an unknown photographer!' I gasped. 'He was one of the greatest photographers of his generation!'

Rachel rang the producer and told him all about Bert. To my delight, he called me straight back.

'We believe there's been a mistake,' he admitted.

He told me Norma had made a genuine mistake and had assumed it had been her and her friend in the photograph.

'What? And she's been making that same mistake for all these years?' I said, my voice incredulous.

The producer didn't know how to answer, so he changed tack.

'We'd like you to appear on the show, if that's possible? We'd like to try and rectify things.'

'I will,' I agreed. 'But only if I can meet Norma whatshername. I'd like to ask her why she's been telling people she's the girl in the photograph for all these years!'

Sensing my anger, the producer promised to ask but said he didn't think Norma would want to meet me.

'I'm not surprised!' I scoffed.

A film crew travelled to the Lamb and Flag pub in Wick, where Phil Tufnell interviewed me for the programme.

'You seem to know a lot more about this than the last

lady knew,' he remarked as the film crew packed away their cameras.

'I'm not surprised. It wasn't her! She wasn't even there!' I laughed.

Phil chuckled.

'Well, it's been a real pleasure meeting you, Pat,' he said, shaking my hand.

Thankfully, my version of events was backed up by Brian Dowling, the reporter, whom we'd met at the stage door all those years before. The interview was screened on *The One Show* in March 2011. They even gave Norma a piece to camera, as she explained that the whole thing had been an honest mistake. To be fair, I think the BBC was extremely embarrassed because it had been the BBC library that had produced the commemorative calendar including Bert, Wendy and me only twenty years earlier. The local newspaper had picked up the story and soon the world's press were knocking at my door. For the first time in years, I was back in the spotlight.

I met up with Brian Dowling, who reminded me that Bert had given me a copy of the photographic contact sheets as a present.

'Of course!' I said.

As soon as I returned home, I dug them out. The photographic contacts pictured Wendy and me in various poses, from sitting on donkeys to building sandcastles on Blackpool beach.

When the journalist from the *Daily Mail* rang to interview me, I reminded him he'd once asked me to prove who I was.

'And now I can,' I said, 'because I have the contact sheets.'

The journalist was extremely charming, but I couldn't help but rib him.

'If only you'd have listened to me all those years ago, this wouldn't be happening,' I teased. 'We wouldn't be having this conversation.'

It made him laugh and me too. Once and for all, I'd proved who I was – I was *the Girl in the Spotty Dress* and no one could, or would, ever take that away from me again.

CHAPTER 27

TAKE A BOW

Today, I feel as though I've led a full and happy life. From that naive, blonde, fresh-faced seventeen-year-old perched on those railings at Blackpool Promenade, to the contented eighty-two-year-old grandmother I am now.

Bert Hardy, the brilliant photographer who shot that iconic image, sadly died in July 1995. It was only eight years after I'd met him for the BBC calendar photo shoot in 1987, but I'm sure he'd be delighted to know that his name and the photograph he took that blustery morning live on. In fact, I've spotted myself on prints, mugs and postcards. I see my seventeen-year-old self staring back at me regularly, which may sound strange, but it's also very comforting.

I actually did finally ring Norma Edmondson. It took a while but, eventually, she came to the phone. When she asked who it was she was speaking to, I told her straight.

'I'm Pat Wilson, the girl in the spotty dress.'

Norma didn't say much, but she made it clear that she didn't want to speak to me. I didn't mind because I'd felt I'd said all I'd needed to say.

Since my appearance on *The One Show*, I've received fan mail. I even received a lovely letter from Lord Lofthouse, Baron of Pontefract, who said he remembered me as a child. It transpired that he'd lived only thirty metres away from my home and he remembered my mother fondly. It's a small world. After my last stint in the spotlight, I was asked to do some filming for the British Legion for its Poppy Appeal, which, given Johnny's time fighting in Arnhem, I was more than happy to do.

Today I can't kick as high I once could because I've had two hip operations. I put them off for years, trying to deny that I needed them. Instead, I took up walking because I convinced myself I could simply 'walk' away the pain, being the stubborn Pat I'd always been. That was until May 2012, when I fell and fractured my femur while visiting Rachel over in Holland. Of course, the Dutch doctor pulled no punches when speaking to Rachel after I'd been patched up.

'Your mother is very foolish,' he said, shaking his head in disbelief. 'She would only be in half as much pain if she'd have had her hip replacement!'

It made me think, so I asked to be referred to a surgeon back home, who agreed with the Dutch doctor.

'You need a hip replacement, Mrs Stewart,' he insisted.

But I still didn't feel quite ready for the op because I was worried it might disable me. My worst nightmare after a life of dance would be to be confined to a wheelchair. Foolishly, I decided I had to 'walk away the pain' and stay active for as long as I possibly could.

A year later, in the summer of 2013, Rachel rang me at home to ask something.

'Mum,' she said, 'do you have any old pantomime scripts?'

I was puzzled and asked her why.

'Because I'm starting up a drama group at the school. It's Jacob, you see. He's started to show some real talent on stage,' Rachel said, explaining there was nowhere in Holland that would benefit him.

I looked, but I couldn't find any scripts, so I leafed through my old contacts book and called a few of the old theatricals to see if they could help. But no one seemed to have anything left. That's when it occurred to me: I'd write the script myself, using all my memories from the thousands of performances I'd enjoyed and witnessed over the years. A few hours later, I began typing away at my computer and, before long, I had Pat Stewart's version of *Cinderella* saved on my screen.

That Christmas, I travelled over to Holland and spent the festive season with Rachel, my grandchildren and my great-grandchildren. I came back to England, before flying back over to Holland for Rachel's first production. Taking my place discreetly behind a pillar at the side of the stage, with the script in my hand, I watched the children perform. There were children of all nationalities and many of them were unfamiliar with the ways of panto. Jacob had taken on his grandfather's old part of Buttons, which he played with comic timing. I was close to tears as I watched him – along with children from different countries – deliver old classic panto lines with brilliant timing.

Finally, the show reached the end. Jacob wandered back onto the stage, front cloth, to introduce the rest of the cast. Suddenly, and quite without warning, he began to ad-lib in the style of his granddad, Johnny Stewart. I looked down at my script but the lines weren't on there – this was coming from Jacob. The theatre was so packed that there were children sat on the floor at the front of the stage. Jacob walked up and began to high-five them, working both sides, with the kids screaming the name 'Buttons' at the top of their voices. It was like watching Johnny all over again.

As he left the stage to rapturous applause, Jacob looked at me and, out of the corner of his mouth, he whispered, 'Now I know just how Justin Bieber feels.'

He grinned cheekily as he passed by.

In that moment, I realised Johnny would never be dead because he and the Stewart 'showbiz gene' lived on in his grandson.

CHAPTER 28

ENCORE

With my hips growing ever worse, I was left in constant pain. Nothing seemed to ease or take it away. Finally, I admitted defeat – I needed medical intervention. The following morning, I rang the doctor I'd seen a few years earlier and enquired about having a hip replacement.

'It's Pat Stewart,' I told him. 'I've changed my mind. Please could you refer me for that hip operation as soon as possible? I've been a complete fool!'

A short time later, I visited a specialist for my consultation and, a fortnight after that, in July 2014, I finally had my left hip replaced. I asked the surgeon if he could squeeze me in before he went away on his holiday because I realised just how silly I'd been to put it off. It felt so amazing to finally be pain-free in my left hip that I asked to be booked in for the right hip just five weeks later. I was worried I'd have to be admitted to an old people's home but I recovered well. Of course, I also had all my friends and family to rally around after me. With my new hips, I felt like a new woman and now there was no stopping me!

During my recuperation, I had Stephen take me shopping.

'What for, Mum?' he said, wondering what on earth an eighty-two-year-old woman could possibly want or need so desperately.

I looked up at him with a steely determination.

'A pair of stilettos. I want a pair of stiletto heels!'

With Stephen's help, I pushed my feet into my new shoes and pulled myself up out of my wheelchair. I refused to back down or give up.

'For God's sake, Mum!' Stephen gasped as my legs began to tremble and wobble beneath me. 'Sit down now! You look like bloody Minnie Mouse!'

A smirk spread across my face because I knew that I wasn't out – not by a long chalk.

I'm convinced all my years training as a professional ballet dancer did my hips no favours. In fact, when the surgeon finally went in, he found that both my hips had completely disintegrated. But bones or plastic, my new hips had given me a new lease of life. I knew I wouldn't be able to do everything I'd done before, but at least I would be able to enjoy a pain-free life and all it had to offer.

One day, following my final hip operation, I was given some literature on how look after my 'new hips'.

'You'll need to call Social Services to see about receiving some occupational therapy. You'll also need some disability aides. Here, this is the number you need to call,' the medical worker said, handing me a leaflet.

Later that afternoon, I picked up the telephone and dialled the number. The gentleman on the other end of the telephone was very helpful indeed.

'I just need to take your name and address,' he asked.

'Yes, of course. My name is Pat Stewart.'

Suddenly, the man interrupted me.

'Sorry, did you say your name is Pat Stewart?' he asked.

'Yes, why? Do you know me?' I asked, wondering if he was related to someone in my village.

'Oh, yes, I know who you are,' he laughed. 'You're the famous Pat Stewart. You're the girl in the spotty dress!'

My life had finally gone full circle.

ACKNOWLEDGEMENTS

Putting this book together has been a wonderful experience for me. It has helped me to relive and revisit many happy times in my life, both on and off stage. Firstly, I'd like to thank my husband, Johnny, who is sadly no longer with us. Johnny was, and will always be, the love of my life, and I miss him every single day. Thank you for being my husband, my confidant and my rock. I shall never forget you.

I'd also like to thank my children for their support and encouragement. To my son, Stephen, who gave me my computer: it has enabled me to recall all my thoughts and memories and put them down on 'paper'. To my daughter, Rachel, who has listened to me endlessly, and to my eldest son, Peter: I love you all dearly. I'd also like to thank my gorgeous grandchildren and great-grandchildren for being such wonderful individuals and for giving me my new role in life as Granny Pat.

To Veronica Clark, my ghostwriter, who has helped guide a fellow Yorkshire lass through her (sometimes) murky and distant past. Thanks, Veronica!

To Andrew Higgs, my computer expert, who taught me how to cut and paste on a computer, and Dai Ellis – my old neighbour – who helped me during the initial stages. Also Cerri Greenslade, for giving even more computer advice to an eighty-two-year-old silver Internet surfer!

Thanks to Kay Davies, who spotted the mistaken identity on BBC's *The One Show*, and to Pauline Thomas of Wick, who realised the potential for a book when my true story first came out.

Finally, thanks to Bert Hardy for taking the iconic photograph on that blustery morning on Blackpool promenade and for making me *The Girl in the Spotty Dress*.